Beyond the Body

Beyond the Body

The Human Double and the Astral Planes

Benjamin Walker

Routledge & Kegan Paul
London

First published in 1974
by Routledge & Kegan Paul Ltd
Broadway House, 68–74 Carter Lane,
London EC4V 5EL
Printed in Great Britain by
Clarke, Doble & Brendon Ltd
Plymouth
© Benjamin Walker 1974

ISBN 0 7100 7808 0

Contents

v

Preface

The wisest maxim of the wisest man of ancient Greece was 'Know thyself'. And we may be sure he meant more than the physical self.

Man has always been anthropocentric. But if he is the centre of things, it is not the physical body that is the centre of man. There exists an elusive element in him that religion, mysticism, metaphysics and psychology have approached, each in its own way. One of the most persistent beliefs of mankind is that every individual comprises not only his physical body, but a Second Self. This entity is the operative factor underlying his physical well-being, mental health and spiritual welfare.

The idea has a venerable ancestry, and this book traces its main lines of descent. It is a brief survey of a vast subject with wide ramifications. In writing this book I have been conscious of my obligation to my many predecessors in the field. The debt to my recent sources needs a more specific acknowledgment, which I gladly make here.

I have derived much information from the work of Sylvan Muldoon, Richard Bucke, Oliver Fox, Lord Geddes, and, more recently, Robert Monroe. Celia Green's and Robert Crookall's studies from material reported at first hand have been invaluable. The bibliography appended to the present work gives further particulars.

I am grateful to the following for permission to use brief quotations from books published by them: W. H. Allen for Dennis Bardens's *Mysterious Worlds*; Doubleday, New York, for John Godwin's *Occult America*; Hamish Hamilton for Celia Green's *Lucid Dreams* and *Out-of-the-Body Experiences*; Hodder & Stoughton for *Man's Concern With Death* edited by Arnold Toynbee, and F. Smythe's *The Spirit of the Hills*; Rider for Ralph Shirley's *The Mystery of the Human Double*; Longman's, for Lord Geddes's article, 'A Voice from the grandstand', published in *Edinburgh*

Medical Journal; and University Books, New York, for Oliver Fox's *Astral Projection*.

A word about the public library service in my area, through whose courtesy I obtained many of the books I required for my work: Gilbert Turner, F.L.A., until recently Borough Librarian at Richmond, Derek Jones, M.A., F.L.A., the present Borough Librarian, and Philip Rayner, District Librarian at Teddington, were most helpful at all times. Penelope Boyland, Assistant Librarian, Teddington, put herself out more than once to obtain the books I needed in a hurry. I am most impressed at the promptness with which available books were found, often from far afield, and for the courtesy of all those connected with this excellent service.

Special thanks are due to Richard Cavendish who first suggested that I write this book. This was only one of a series of opportunities he put before me of presenting my thoughts to the public. I am very grateful indeed for his interest, and the support so generously given during the past five years.

I record my deep obligation to Maureen Abbott for her active assistance, in spite of the pressures of her own busy life, in collecting and checking bibliographical details for this book, and for her help in compiling the index.

Above all, I have to thank my wife, for her constant help, encouragement and faith.

B.W.

Chapter I

The New Animism

The religious and mystical traditions on the one hand, and the magical and occult traditions on the other, although antagonistic in many ways, are in agreement on a number of important points. Both are founded on the belief that there exists another reality beyond the world of phenomena that is presented to our senses; that this reality forms part of another, spiritual, world; that any true understanding of the nature of man must take into account the fact that he comprises more than his physical body; and that he has other, non-material elements through which he is in touch with a totally different sphere of being; that man in fact lives in more than one plane of existence, whether he is consciously aware of it or not.

These ideas are strongly rooted in the teachings of all the great religions, and are widely documented in their scriptures. They are vouched for in the experiences of mystics and saints, and supported by the personal testimony of men of genius in all fields of creative work. Science too has made its contribution, albeit sometimes unwittingly, to the general store of information concerning the non-physical 'otherness' we sometimes discern behind the material dimensions of the world around us. Added to these are the unrehearsed encounters that ordinary people have had in what are called 'out-of-the-body' experiences. Indeed, the literature is so extensive that we must be content to take a random sampling of the evidence, and select a mere handful out of the hundreds of examples to illustrate the subject as we go along.

Nor should we overlook the ideas of the simple tribal societies, which, although primitive and pre-literate, have living traditions of their own, going back in some cases almost unaltered to a time remoter than the earliest civilizations of Egypt, Babylonia and China. No doubt there are dangers in uncritical comparisons between the thought processes of the primitive mind and those of

1

the sophisticated person with a totally different background, but we have moved some distance from the ethnocentrism of the anthropologist who studied the 'savage' in order to prove the superiority of his own way of life. Thus, while it was once held that the savage thinks in a non-rational manner, thereby giving pre-eminence to rationality, it is now conceded that his thinking is pre-rational, marking not an inferior but simply a different, if earlier, stage of development.

Ethnologists working in the field have frequently noted the uncanny rapport that exists between primitives and their immediate environment. They find that there is a natural sympathetic resonance of man with his ancestral hills and caves, with the animals who are joint inheritors with him of the earth's bounty, and with his fellows who participate with him in the dangerous adventure of living. They are taking a second look at the unexamined aspects of the cultures of these peoples, reassessing the abilities of their healing practitioners, witch-doctors and medicine-men, discovering unsuspected wisdom in their folklore, and often extreme subtlety in their philosophy, and they realize that they have perhaps something to learn from them.

A research psychologist named Kilton Stewart, while working as a member of a scientific team studying the small Senoi tribe in the unexplored regions of the central mountain range of Malaysia in 1935, was deeply impressed by some of their beliefs. The Senoi tribesman thinks that it is possible through dreams to utilize the forces of the spiritual universe to help himself and his community. Stewart eventually came to the conclusion that the Senoi system of interpersonal relations was 'in the field of psychology perhaps on a level with our attainments in such areas as television and nuclear physics' (Tart (1969), p. 161).

At the same time, western man has recently been rummaging in his own attic for his own neglected heritage, buried in the beliefs of ancient Greece and Rome, patristic Christianity, medieval Europe, and the Renaissance, to find not merely dry data of scholastic interest, but a great deal that can help him to recover a sense of balance and restore him to a view that takes into account the more-than-physical dimensions of the human being, and the non-material world in which part of his existence is enacted.

Today we see a renewed and ever-growing interest in these

matters, and theories reminiscent of the most primitive thought are being refurbished and presented with much learning by various scholars. Our ideas concerning non-living and non-sentient matter • might well be subjected to drastic revision, and we may yet return full cycle to the standpoint of pre-rational, pre-literate man. His kind of belief, labelled *animism* by the English anthropologist Edward Burnett Tylor (1832–1917), attributed an 'anima' or spirit not only to animals and plants, but even to so-called inanimate creation. Natural objects no matter of what grade, whether trees, rocks, streams, clouds, stars, sun or moon, are thought to be endowed with spirit, are living and sentient, and feel and function each according to its nature.

This concept was by no means confined to the primitive, for the first great philosopher in the history of western thought, Thales of Miletus (d. 550 B.C) expressed the same notion in his own way. 'All things', he said, 'are full of gods.' What is called the Milesian school of early Greek philosophy, taking a lead from him, widely accepted the thesis that life is immanent in everything. In the East, the Jains of India also postulated a vitality ubiquitously diffused, and a degree of life and soul imbuing all things, but differentiated. All things, they said, possessed either one life, like minerals; two lives, like plants; or three lives, like animals.

Among later philosophers, the Portuguese Jew, Baruch Spinoza (1632–77) conceived a theory of varying gradations of life, and said that different kinds of things possessed different qualities of life. Gustav Fechner (1801–87) professor of physics at Leipzig, regarded by some as the father of experimental psychology, held that a kind of soul-life abided in plants and that a consciousness pervaded all creation. The English philosopher F. H. Bradley (1846–1924) said, 'Except in relation to our ignorance, we cannot call the least portion of nature inorganic.'

In a number of philosophical and religious systems, ancient, medieval and modern, animism was carried even further to include the *anima mundi*, or soul of the universe, which was the vitalizing spirit of the cosmos. Plato (427–347 B.C.) in his *Timaeus* (29.30) said, 'We shall probably be safe in affirming that the universe is a living creature endowed with a soul.' The Stoics believed that the whole cosmos was a single organism whose parts were animate and shared in a common experience. The astronomer Johann Kepler (1571–1630) held that the planets were living entities. Dr R. M.

3

Bucke (1837–1902), a Canadian physician whose experiences we shall relate later, 'saw and knew that the cosmos is not dead matter but a living presence.'

A related idea, which held the field even in scientific circles till the middle of the last century, was that there existed a 'fluidic' energy-medium called ether, 'the ghost of matter', which was spread throughout the universe. The theosophists who were its main advocates, taught that all the elements within the universe, from atoms to stars, were varying combinations and concentrations of this subtle and invisible fluid.

The universe in this view is an aggregate of an infinite multitude of life-and-mind nuclei or ents (from the Late Latin *ens*, plural *entia*), an ent being an existent, that is, a distinguishable unit having a separate, valid identity, and possessing an individuality of its own. Every atom of so-called inorganic dust is an ent, and so is every far-flung galactic system, and each ent is a focus of conscious energy, possessing elements of life and mind. In combination with others, larger ents are formed, so that all things, separately and collectively, are ents, each having its own characteristics.

Under the name of *monad* or unit, the ent concept is found in the theories of the Greek philosophers Pythagoras, Democritus and Aristotle, besides other ancient writers. Giordano Bruno (1548–1600) held that every monad was an independent centre containing material substance, form and spirit. Gottfried Wilhelm Leibniz (1646–1716) also graded all things or soul-substances in an ascending scale of such units culminating in God, 'the Monad of monads'.

All ents are related, and the mutual exchange of influence between them is based not on their physical kinship alone but on the links that govern their non-material affinities and the manner in which these alliances operate. The influence of each ent permeates all things. The English mathematician, physicist and philosopher, A. N. Whitehead (1861–1947), held that 'each object is in some sense ingredient throughout nature' (quoted by Fawcett (1939), p. 128). There is an inherent tendency built into the structure of the ent itself that determines how it shall react to the presence of another. The interpenetration of elements is both material and non-material.

To the ancients, and to medieval scholars, analogies, resemb-

4

lances and outward signs often marked the inner connection between things. The world was alive with symbolic relationships. Gestures, shapes, sounds, letters, colours, odours, gems, stones, leaves, flowers, plants, animals, were all specialized concentrations of particular potencies. The whole world was interlinked by these correspondences.

Interrelation could be determined from externals, like similarity of substance or appearance, so that two things that looked alike or had the same colour or were made of the same material were occultly associated. Or again, it could be based on contrast, so that two enemies were linked by their mutual antagonism. Or on relationship, so that cause and effect were linked. But certain cosmic factors were also taken into account, such as synastry, or the relationship between two people born under the same star.

Life and mind being inherent in all ents, it followed that the plant and mineral kingdoms shared, with the animal kingdom, in the possession of conscious awareness in different degrees of intensity. It also followed that if a thing existed as an ent, it also existed as part of a larger ent, and for this reason participated in a life that extended beyond itself. As ents aggregate and merge certain qualities of the individual ent fall into abeyance, and new qualities mysteriously arise. A stone may exist and function in one way by itself on the mountain-side, but when forming part of a cairn or heap of stones over a grave, or when chiselled and carved into a piece of sculpture, or used as a building block in a cathedral, or as a sacrificial stone, it functions in each case with a different emphasis, partaking of the newly created entness that emerges from the new situation. Similarly, the parts and organs of the human body have, as it were, an 'overflow', and reach out in their functions beyond the area demarcated by physiology.

One further concept emerges from these beliefs. There is a 'beyond' in all things, and nothing has the one obvious meaning, not even a clod of earth. According to the Jain philosophers of India, existence both in its totality and in its particulars, is characterized by *anekatva*, 'plurality' or multi-sidedness, so that every existing thing posseses a manifold significance. There can be no absolute unanimity about facts, for facts acquire different meanings when judged from different angles, just as a woman might mean one thing to her child, another to her husband, and yet another to the tiger watching her from the bushes. Statement, judgment, knowledge, they maintain, can be seen from as many as 350 viewpoints.

Perhaps one measure by which the primitive mind can be gauged is that it never fails to find a deeper area of significance in things. As we progress we tend to limit their meaning according to our specialization. A forest which to the tribal man is alive with presences ceases to inspire us with reverence once we start botanizing. Trees become subject to our classification, and subserve only our practical needs. We tame them in our gardens and orchards, interfere with them to produce more, force them to grow differently, and kill them if they are not productive since in our view they then have no right to life.

At one time there was an almost universal belief among all peoples that what really operated when two things came together was not a consequence of their physical proximity, but of the magical environment or aura surrounding them. Everything had its occult atmosphere, or as we might otherwise express it, each ent exists in its own field of force. Everything had this invisible ambience, including rocks, trees, streams, lakes and hills. The mutual interaction between two fields of force was therefore effective even without actual physical contact, and thus constituted a kind of telemagic, a mysterious influence exerted from a distance. Astrology, one of the most ancient beliefs, still widely held, is based on a telemagical principle, that the planets, constellations and other heavenly bodies exercise an unseen power, and influence the lives of people on earth.

Man is an inveterate systematizer and will, if need be, find a pattern in a handful of pebbles thrown casually on the ground. He will make something out of anything, or out of nothing. People look for order and hence discover laws, which put coherence into chaos. Rigid scientific laws such as we formulate do not exist in nature. They are miscellanies culled from natural phenomena and arranged to conform to the pattern of man's thinking, to be used for his convenience, just as we agree to call a handful of matter a kilogram, three paces a yard, and a certain set of days November. The laws of science represent a concensus of opinion based on current information, and are no more than a workable framework into which things can be made to fit. But the outlines of this framework are constantly changing since new discoveries emerge which do not fit into the explanation provided by the earlier formulation. Science can seldom explain without a remainder, and it is this slack that provides material for occult speculation.

The fall of an object to the ground was once explained by the attraction or sympathy that existed between earthly objects and Mother Earth. It was telemagic. When the 'apple falling towards England' raised the momentous query in the mind of Isaac Newton (1642–1726) his mathematics changed telemagic into gravitation, and the doctrine of sympathy into a law of science. The law of falling bodies has now a mathematical basis but still no one knows why things fall, and we are content for all practical purposes to say that the air cannot support them.

Yet the idea that a telemagical sympathy subsisted between things was part of a broader principle relating to *pathemic* or 'feeling' relationships that were to be found everywhere, either of sympathy or attraction, antipathy or repulsion, apathy or indifference. Pathemia may be called a form of telemagic, unaccountably drawing together or dispersing diverse things that may seem unrelated. Sympathy existed between both animate and inanimate things. Thus, roots were said to move downwards because the deeper layers of the earth were sympathetic to them. The branches of trees reached upwards because they were drawn to the sun. Antipathy was found in the repulsion of the like poles of a magnet. The Roman writer Pliny (A.D. 23–79) who collected a great deal of ancient lore said that the antipathy between the wolf and the horse was such that if a horse passed the way a wolf had gone, he would be numbed into immobility. Apathy is found where there is no flow of feeling between two persons, and the existence of either one is a matter of complete indifference to the other.

These three pathemic categories of sympathy, antipathy and apathy served the needs of earlier thinkers, but today's psychologists have added further refinements, thus tacitly giving their endorsement to the underlying idea. We now have such concepts as empathy, which is the imaginative experience of another person's emotions; mimpathy, the emotional state of mind entered into by novelists, historians or dramatists while writing their works; unipathy, the emotional participation of one person in the feelings of another. A wider influx of emotion is implied in the term cosmopathy. All these to a greater or lesser degree work their magic

7

by a subtle process that makes an interchange of feeling possible between two or more entities.

If things have manifold meaning, as the Jains said, then thoughts have an infinitely wider range of significance. Like feelings, ideas too have an overflow. Great spiritual truths with a profound relevance inevitably become restricted in meaning when swathed in grammar, syntax and vocabulary, so that holy writ can become something that a pocket dictionary can interpret quite adequately. The spiritual, allegorical, transcendental, mystical meanings that make up the 'beyond' of words often pass out of reach.

Yet everything has this 'something else' which we often fail to perceive. The activities of the physical body, the ruminations of the mind, our daily round of work, send out pulsations into a secondary world where their reverberations continue out of our ken and beyond our control. It is in this region that the impact is received and remains, no less than in the tangible and perceptible world in which the mechanical operation was initiated.

Communication seems to provide another instance of the subtle exchange that is going on between things. Scientists have long been puzzling over the phenomenon of animal communication. Each species has a limited range of sounds, yet within that narrow range it gets along quite well. Barking, mewing, neighing, roaring, with slight modulations and changes of tone, serve the total purposes of dogs, cats, horses and lions. Crows seem to do nothing but caw in a monotone, whatever they have to say. Other birds communicate by dancing, and species still lower in the evolutionary scale manage their affairs with a language that is confined to touch, smell and movement.

It is becoming clear that outside the audible sounds and visible motions that make up the gamut of animal communication, there is some as yet unknown vibration, a kind of thought transference that probably also takes place and that covers a much wider range of communication. Animals seem to live in a more sensitive psychic field and are mutually in contact through vibrations within this field. We all know animal lovers who insist that their pets have a sixth sense. Stories from earliest times tell of the uncanny awareness of domestic animals. They appear to have a private communications system which is beyond our understanding.

Yet not quite. For the communications system of human beings is equally strange. Without going into the mystique of human language, it might be said that all communication has a pathemic element in it. Indeed, we are constantly communicating with people even without saying a word, and most of what we actually say has unspoken overtones. The poet Walter de la Mare (1873–1956) once said to Sir Russell Brain, 'I believe that telepathy is almost continuous. If you and I were not in telepathic communication we couldn't carry on our conversation' (quoted by Priestley (1972), p. 73). Much more goes into conversation between relatives, lovers, friends and enemies than just words. Professor C. D. Broad said of paranormal cognition in general, that it 'may well be continually operating in the background of our normal lives' (see Crookall (1969), p. 104).

A pathemic relationship established between the participants of a close bond takes no heed of distance or time. Telepathic communication is the transmission of thought-impressions between two persons who are on the same mental wave-length or whose psychic atmospheres are in harmony. They are enveloped in a common aura of sympathetic feeling and share their feelings mutually. Even sensory impressions can be transmitted in certain circumstances. Dr E. Azam, a French physician, found that under hypnosis one of his patients could taste substances that Dr Azam put into his own mouth.

The rapport between hypnotist and subject is only one form of such mutual exchange. There are countless recorded instances of the telepathic transmission of thoughts, feelings and sense-impressions betwen husband and wife, parent and child, lover and sweetheart, friend and friend, master and pet. All this forms part of the wider field of extra-sensory perception, which covers such unexplained phenomena as clairvoyance or seeing things that are happening at a distance, precognition or knowledge of what will happen in the future, retrocognition or knowledge of what has already happened, telepathy or thought reading, clairaudience or hearing the voices of people not present, psychometry or reading the history of an object by touching it.

Some of these clearly telemagical feats have in recent years received the reluctant recognition of scientists, since the methodology of the test procedures, the stringent controls exercised, and the statistical methods used for evaluating the results, have passed the most rigid requirements of statisticians and other specialists. But if telemagical laws exist they have not yet been formulated, because the evidence indicates that ESP 'waves' override the known limitations of distance and time that govern the behaviour of waves in the electro-magnetic spectrum. They are not true members of the scientific family.

The Russians have been interested in telepathy for over fifty years now. They treat it as a branch of what they call paraphysical research, to avoid any implied endorsement of mysticism, and have brought to its study the services of physiologists, doctors, brain specialists, medical hypnotists, psychologists, mathematicians, electronic engineers, physicists and even philosophers. They have recorded their findings in great detail and still hold to their original hypothesis, of some material and so far undiscovered energy generated in the brain.

Some people believe that a pathemic relationship exists not only between men among themselves, or between men and animals, but also between men and plants. Plants can receive our thoughts and feelings and respond with their own. The plant world has exercised a perennial fascination for the human race. The majestic size of forest trees, their great strength, their soaring growth heavenwards, the mighty roots that grip the earth, the strange rustling of their foliage in the wind, all tend to inspire man with feelings of awe, sometimes even of reverence, in their presence. The earliest temples were said to be groves of trees, in which men have felt they could commune with the powers that guided their destinies. It was also believed that every tree was inhabited by a spirit, which was the soul of that tree. The tree was thought to be endowed with consciousness.

People who spend much time with plants have observed time and again that plants respond to love and care. Individuals endowed with a happy faculty in this respect are said to have 'green fingers' and seem able to evoke a response from their plants. In the 1920s a Hindu scientist, Jagdish Chandra Bose, studied the reactions of plants to various stimuli by means of the crescograph, an instrument he invented for the purpose. He proved that plants have a sensitive 'nervous' system and an emotional life, and that they feel pleasure and pain, thus establishing on scientific lines a belief held in India for many centuries.

In 1966 an American researcher, Cleve Backster, tried a simple experiment on a plant, with astonishing results. His speciality was the study of a subject's reaction to questions or situations in order to assess and measure their emotional responses, as in the lie-detector test. An inveterate experimenter, Backster would fix his electrodes to anything that promised to add to his knowledge. One day he fastened them to the leaves of a potted plant in his office. As a stimulant to test the reactions of the cells, he thought he would apply a flame to the stem of the plant. The moment the idea occurred to him, and even before his hand moved to his pocket for the lighter, the needle on his polygraph recorded signs of great agitation and shot upward. It was as though the plant had read his mind and knew that he intended to burn it.

Backster was no amateur. He was a leading expert in his field for more than two decades. He had worked as an investigator in the CIA, and his techniques were the standard methods taught at the military school at Fort Gordon, Georgia. He followed up his discovery with two years of careful work that confirmed his first conclusions, and revealed even more. Plants think and feel; they have extra-sensory perception and react not only to harmful intentions directed at them, but to the hurt that man inflicts on other living beings, plants and animals, in their immediate vicinity.

The extra-sensory perception of animals, which is equally remarkable, is also now well on its way to being established by scientific research. Their sense of direction alone is a miracle still unexplained. Cats carried over a hundred miles from home successfully find their way across country and through the confusion and smell of city traffic to their own back yards. For some unaccountable reason eels from Europe and the east coast of America migrate thousands of miles from their fresh-water homes all the way to the Sargasso Sea and breed there; the parent eels die in the Sargasso and the baby eels make a three-year voyage back to their respective rivers unaided.

The theories put forward to account for these extraordinary homing faculties are in themselves remarkable: an instinctive awareness of such things as the earth's magnetic field, the polarization of light, electrical currents, certain patterns in the night sky. Migratory geese are said to be guided by terrestrial gravity; the tiny robin navigates by picking up vibrations from the Milky Way; the pigeon flies back to its quarters across continents, even if it has never made the trip before, by a comparative reckoning

11

of its astronomical latitude and longitude and that of its home. Salmon return to their home river thousands of miles away aided by a super-acute sense of smell. Bees are guided by the sun. The black-cap bird navigates by means of the stars.

Whatever the explanation, similar miracles occur throughout the animal world, and the seemingly supernormal powers possessed by birds and beasts are taken by men as part of the natural order of things. It is not surprising perhaps that the Egyptians, among other ancient peoples, endowed animals with divine attributes. Equally, sometimes even diabolical powers were ascribed to animals, and in Europe it was believed for centuries that beasts could be possessed by demons and inspired by satanic malice and hatred. Animals, including birds and insects were tried by ecclesiastical courts like witches and heretics, and suffered excommunication, torture and death. The last such trial took place in 1740 in France when a cow was judged, found guilty and executed.

Indeed, animals are almost universally believed to possess certain extraordinary gifts, and each species is said to be entrusted with some occult secret. Folklore is replete with such fancies. In Hindu legend the neigh of the horse conceals the secrets of certain mystic spells, and the swan holds the key to the Upanishads. The Arabs speak of the ninety-nine names of God, and say that only the camel knows the hundredth. In Europe superstitious peasants long believed that the raven, although itself mortal, had the secret of immortality. Bees were supposed to be in communion with the spirit world, and it became the duty of the head of a household to whisper news of important events over the hive so that the bees in turn might keep the deceased members of the clan *au fait* with family developments.

It is for man to unravel these mysteries, and modern research in its own way is doing just that. A comparatively new branch of study, known as bionics, has already proved of service in this field. For example, researchers are gaining an understanding of the remarkable intelligence of the dolphin with whom they are trying to establish communication both in human and dolphin language. They are trying to fathom the astounding physiological miracle of the bat whose heartbeat during hibernation drops from 180 to 3 beats per minute, and breathing from 8 breaths a second to 8 per minute. Master that secret and the Biblical span of human life could be raised from the Psalmist's threescore years and ten to Methuselah's nine hundred sixty and nine.

But when we come to study man himself, we find the magical character of the human being that was first adumbrated by primitive society and the early civilizations, being confirmed by modern research. The ancient Egyptians believed that a great current of divine power flowed from the region of the gods on to the earthly plane. The deities emanated a magical potency called *heka*; their wisdom was a kind of light known as *sia*; their vital force was *sekhem*, symbolized by the reed; their utterances were creative and called *hu*; and all four bestowed their benefactions on mortals.

The separate aspects of man's personality were thus endowed with distinctive power. His *khat* or physical body, corruptible and mortal though it was, possessed the seed of permanence and held some attributes of divinity. His heart, viscera, brains, each made vital contributions to the welfare of his spirit and were given special treatment at the time of embalmment. It was believed that so long as the flesh was preserved the spiritual presence associated with it remained near by.

Every person had a *khaibit* or shadow, which though dependent on the body could lead a separate existence of its own. Then there was the *ka*, a replica of the body, the Egyptian version of what today we call the astral body. This was the element most closely linked with the body, and lived in the tomb with the body, subsisting on the necessities provided for it. Finally there was the *ba*, often represented as a human-headed bird holding in its grasp the *ankh* or ansate cross, a T-shaped implement surmounted by a looped handle. This *ba* became active only after the death of the body, and it was this that travelled to the next world to receive its reward or punishment.

The famous Egyptologist, Gaston Maspero (1846–1916), mentions another belief current in the Nile valley. It was concerned with the *sa*, a mysterious fluid, not like water but rather like air, invisible but sometimes tangible, which carried life, health and power, and could be transmitted by the laying on of hands. The source of this power was the sun-god Ra, whose idol was believed to be imbued with *sa*, when properly constructed of the right materials and under the appropriate astrological signs by priest-sculptors who fashioned it in accordance with the occult canons

13

of proportion. The pharaoh, at his coronation, or at intervals during his reign when his powers were waning, was made to approach the statue of Ra with his back to it and sit at its feet. The god was then believed to make passes with his hand and cause the magic element to flow into and recharge the king.

Belief in the existence of some kind of vitalizing power, which can be drawn down into objects and concentrated there, and from there directed to other recipients, is not an uncommon one. Such a power was once thought to be responsible for the continuance of the universe, for without it the world would fade away and die, like a man whose blood is drained. Some people enjoy a greater share of its benefits, which gives them a natural authority over others. Inanimate things can also possess the same quality.

This concept finds expression in the Polynesian belief in *mana*, a psychic or spiritual force, quite distinct from physical strength, which resides in all things to a greater or lesser degree, and gives each thing its particular character. An extraordinary landscape, a mighty waterfall, a stone of unusual shape or size, an animal of strange appearance, a charismatic leader, all have a share of *mana* larger than the endowment of ordinary persons or things.

Yet another variant of this idea is that each person is surrounded by a tenuous haze, called an *aura*. It is said to be a coruscating border of variegated colours extending about six inches around the body and shaped like an oval, and the individual is encapsulated, as it were, within it. The aura changes its shape, size, contour and density from hour to hour, reflecting the predominating emotions of the persons concerned, whether of fear, love, hatred, envy. The theosophist, C. W. Leadbeater, referred to a health aura, whose colour reflected the state of a person's physical well-being.

Lord Geddes, whose account will be given later, related how while in the astral he could see the auras of people, one person giving the visual impression of blue, one of purple and dark red, one of grey or brown, one of pink or yellow, and so on. People with second sight claim to be able to gauge the physical condition of a person, his moral character, his mental and emotional state, from the appearance of his aura. If so, then popular expressions like being green with envy, purple with rage, red with anger, or pale with fear, may not have a purely physical basis or just be figures of speech.

14

The aura is sometimes said to represent the outer vesture of the astral body. Just as the expression on a person's face often reveals his feelings, so does the colour and configuration of the aura reveal the health of the astral body. Plutarch (d. A.D. 120), the Greek writer, stated that the condition and appearance of the aura arise from the passions and vices of the soul, which react upon the spirit and so mark the aura, producing some extraordinary sights. Some auras, he said, are like the purest full-moon light, emitting a single, smooth, continuous and even colour. Others are marked with faint scratches and discolorations. Others again are quite mottled, dappled with livid spots like adders.

A number of experimenters have attempted to verify the objective existence of the aura and to show that it can be visible to anyone and not to sensitives alone. Among them, Dr Walter Kilner (1847–1920) physician at St Thomas's Hospital, London, using specially tinted glasses was able to examine the vibrations allegedly surrounding the human body and wrote a well-known book on what he called the 'human atmosphere'. Today, adaptations of 'Kilner goggles' are available in occult shops.

Another more recent researcher, the Russian photographer Semyon Davidovich Kirlian, started his work in the middle of the present century. Using highly specialized cameras he succeeded in taking pictures of a bio-luminescent vibration around the human body, and also of strange pencils of light emanating from certain areas around the body. These were later found to correspond with remarkable accuracy to the several hundred points known to a very old system of Chinese occult physiology, and used in their healing by acupuncture. Kirlian's work, it might be added, has since received the approval and support of the Russian government and a number of research centres in the Soviet Union are at present in the process of investigating his photography (Freedland (1972), p. 23).

A still broader base for the human atmosphere is provided by several other theories, popular in the past, regarding a vibratory energy dispersed from all objects. The English mystic, Robert Fludd (1574–1637) wrote, 'All things do emit beams', and went on to speak of the radiation invisible to the naked eye that pours forth from everything. Other scholars have said that just as the stars and planets give out their own characteristic pulsations, so does the earth, whose efflux was given the name of 'telluric force'; minerals and gems emitted their own pulsations in other minor vibratory patterns. Franz Anton Mesmer (1733–1815), the first of the great magnetizers, as the hypnotists of his day were called, spoke of a universal magnetic fluid which manifested in the human body as 'animal magnetism'. Mesmer's flourishing practice and popularity aroused the hostility of his colleagues, and an influential committee, already predisposed to condemn his theories, was convened and came back with the inevitable verdict, that animal magnetism did not exist.

In 1860 the French writer Louis Jacolliot suggested the existence of a force called *vril*, which he defined as a concentration of the cosmic ether radiating from all natural objects. His idea was subsequently developed by Lord Lytton in his novel, *The Coming Race* (1870) where he describes the use made of this force by a people living in a subterranean utopia. A distinguished German chemist and physicist, Baron Carl von Reichenbach (1788–1869) also believed in the existence of a quasi-magnetic energy, which he termed odyle, or od, pervading all nature and visible as an aura or radiation around magnets, crystals and other minerals, and also occasionally around the human body. These are only a few of the dozen or so labels under which this force has been described.

In 1923 Dr A. Gurwitsch discovered his mitogenetic rays, which were supposed to emanate from the living tissues of plants and animals. Some two decades earlier the physicist, Professor Marc Thury (1822–1905) had used the term ectenic force to denote the emanations that move outwards from all things (Fodor (1933), p. 113). The same universal ectenium, coming from a human being, was called anthropoflux by Professor Farny of Zürich, and according to him it was concentrated in the head, hands, epigastrium and genitals. Certain persons were supercharged with this magnetic energy and could use it for healing, blessing, or transmitting power. Therapy by the laying on of hands or by magical passes, which was once widely practised, and still is by faith healers, is based on this belief.

The best-known recent exponent of the subject was the Austrian-born American psychiatrist, Wilhelm Reich (1897–1957), a protégé of Freud's, who discovered a life-energy which he called orgone. This energy, he said, was present everywhere in an uninterrupted continuum and was localized in specific concentrations in material objects. Before his premature death Reich carried out many experiments to trap and augment this force.

The field for this kind of investigation, and the theorizing that follows, seem to be endless, and many branches of research have been drawn into the ambit of such speculations. In 1915 a distinguished French researcher, Dr Paul Joire, professor at the Psycho-Physiological Institute of Paris, made an extended study of bodily sensitivity and found that the sensory perception of a medium or hypnotized subject occasionally extended beyond his body; for example, he felt the prick of a pin even when it was jabbed a few inches away from the skin. Hysterical persons also seem to be able to respond to non-physical contact of this kind.

Among the theories put forward to account for poltergeist phenomena, where objects are flung about, items of furniture moved, raps and other noises made, and fires started, with nothing to account for them, is a kind of long-distance operation of libidinal energy. It has been noted that children of pubertal age are almost invariably occupants of the afflicted house, and they have been suspected of producing the occurences, and sometimes been caught at their pranks. But in many cases they are not to blame.

The hypothesis advanced is that children may be the precipitating cause, but they are not consciously responsible for the phenomena, which are attributed to a psychic discharge generated by the onset of puberty. The repressed aggressions and sex-engendered energy of growing boys and girls can, it is suggested, have enough kinetic impulse to cause curtains to burst spontaneously into flame, furniture to move about, and stones to fly through the air. This libidinal force abates with adulthood, for then the pubertal energies begin to be centred in the sex organs, while the residue is unconsciously tapped for the practical needs of everyday life, or sublimated in art, literature, religion or other vocation.

Invisible radiating forces, it would seem, are everywhere suspected to exist, some in psychological, some in scientific disguise. Besides the new terminology of research, we have our own everyday vocabulary to prove it. The continuing popular emphasis on glamour, charm, personal magnetism, fascination, sex appeal, charisma, shows the persistence of man's conviction that some elusive element underlies the success and attraction of captivat-

17

ing and 'magnetic' personalities, that cannot be explained entirely in terms of physical strength, beauty, intellectual attainments or moral character.

Further reading Abramson (1950); Bagnall (1957); Broad (1953); Eddington (1928); Fodor (1964); Kilner (1911); Leadbeater (1957); Lakhovsky (1939); Mead (1967); Reich (1948); Reichenbach (1926).

Chapter II

Life and Consciousness

The human being is an entity existing and functioning at several levels. He is firstly a physical object, and can be described in purely material terms. The ancient hermetic texts speak of the physical body as a mixture of the four elements of earth, air, fire and water (Mead (1967), p. 38). The European, especially French, philosophers of the eighteenth century declared that man was only a mechanism, somewhat more complex than a clock, and drew ingenious parallels between the human body and a machine. The heart was likened to a pump, the lungs to a pair of bellows, the bony structure to the scaffolding, the intestines to the plumbing; the fuel for this human factory was supplied by the food eaten. This school of thought had considerable influence in the history of philosophy and its adherents can be found today among those who speak of man as an automaton or explain human behaviour entirely in terms of reflexes and reactions to stimuli.

Not many years ago one industrious student tried to estimate the chemical composition of the human body. The flesh and bones, he said, would make a few bars of soap, some lead pencils and match-heads, a tin-tack or two, and 'lime enough to wash a chicken-coop'. Its market value, if a purchaser could be found, would be not more than a few pence. The body, however wonderful when instinct with life and mind, becomes without these intangibles a useless clod of matter. So useless and so different from what it was, that even those who loved it dearly cannot see it buried out of sight or burned to ashes fast enough. Man as body alone, sinks at death—soap, lead pencils, tin-tacks and all—into the bosom of the squashy earth.

But man is more than his appurtenances. He is greater than the sum total of his physical parts and accessories. Analysing the chemical composition of tears or explaining the physiological reflexes that trigger weeping can no more touch on the problem of

19

sorrow or suffering than dismantling Chartres cathedral or the Taj Mahal stone by stone and learning the architectural and engineering secrets that went into their construction, can help in understanding the pious devotion that raised the one and the great love that inspired the other.

Sometimes emphasis has been placed on the animal nature of man and his behaviour explained in biological terms. One ancient Greek thinker referred to man as a 'featherless biped'; Voltaire called him a 'forked animal'; today he is a 'trousered ape'. Others regard him as a political or social creature. But many deplore the exclusive emphasis on one or other of man's many facets; on man as *homo faber*, the maker and user of implements, the technician; or *homo oeconomicus*, the proprietor and possessor of goods; or *homo loquax*, the talking animal, which includes the articulate, literary, philosophical, artistic being, producing clever books and cultural works; or even as *homo sapiens*, if that means that he is gifted with craftiness and cunning. They want to see man as *homo humanus*, endowed with compassion and humanity. The human entity, as Thomas Mann described him, is not only physical, but metaphysical.

From earliest times men have believed that the physical body, 'one fathom high, bounded by the skin', is only an instrument or tool for working with. The real self is not muscle, nerve, viscera or brain, but something altogether different. All these together merely constitute a focal point that the self illumines and through which it acts. Body and spirit are as husk and kernel. The body is the gross, heavy, dense, solid, or earthly container of a very precious entity. To the Greeks the body, or *soma*, was like a tomb or prison, and a non-physical element was trapped within it. In his *Phaedrus* Plato says, 'We are imprisoned in the body like an oyster in its shell.' Plotinus (A.D. 205–70) spoke of the body as a prison-house and said, 'I calmly await the day when the divine nature within me shall be set free from matter.'

In the religious view the body is the training ground for the soul, and an aid to spiritual development. Brain and hand provide the wherewithal for our further progress. The Bible speaks of the body as a temple of the Holy Ghost, and all the great religions emphasize the need for making use of the body as a means of advancement. As Aldous Huxley points out (1946, p. 243), 'There is general agreement, East and West, that life in a body provides

uniquely good opportunities for achieving salvation or deliverance.'
It was the opinion of the Hindu philosopher Shankara (A.D. 788–
838) that birth in a human body was one of the things for which
a person should daily give thanks to God. The agony and yearning
of disembodied spirits and elemental beings for the sanctuary of
a physical body wherein they might participate in the living and
loving of a material world and so achieve maturity and redemption is a recurrent theme in the folklore of many peoples. The
physical world offers an essential environment for the progress of
the human being, for it is through the body that the spirit is provided with some of its most significant experiences.

Whatever pre-eminence might have been given in religious
teachings to the spiritual side of the human personality, the
scientific tendency on the whole has been to deny its existence.
Science is concerned principally, if not exclusively, with the body
of flesh and bone that can be resolved into limbs and organs,
tissues and cells, and subjected to physical examination and laboratory analysis. It does not interest itself in the asomatic or
non-physical components. These asomatic elements include such
immaterial concepts as soul, spirit, psyche, astral body, and even
mind and life, and if they are accepted at all it is only with great
reserve, with varying degrees of conviction, and after they have
been circumscribed by many qualifications.

In religion, of course, life is a divine gift and has an immense
sacrosanctity. According to the kabbalists there are fifty gardens
of knowledge, and no one can ever possess the keys to all. An understanding of plants, birds and natural phenomena provides a
way past some of the gates for the man who can attain it.
Through his own efforts a man of exceptional intelligence can enter
no more than twenty-two gates. By God's grace Solomon passed
through forty-eight, and before him Moses had entered one more
still, but even from him the mystery of the final gate was withheld; that of creating life.

But this myth will not do for the out-and-out sceptic. To start
with, no one has seen life. It cannot be heard, touched, smelled or
tasted, and our knowledge of the varied manifestations of animate
existence around us hardly warrants the veil of almost superstitious
mysticism with which it is invested. The first of the great Greek
philosophers, Thales of Miletus, held that life originated in the
warm mud of the primeval ocean. Democritus (d. 510 B.C.) taught

21

that the earth was the mother of all things, giving birth to plants, animals and men. This is not wide of the modern concept that the phenomenon we call life arose as a result of a fortuitous combination of largely gaseous elements that were present in some remote period of the earth's history, perhaps activated by lightning, without any miraculous factor intervening. The difference between Philip dead and Philip living is explicable entirely in terms of physics and chemistry. Life, it is said, is no more asomatic than the flame of a lighted matchstick, and in a few more years man will no doubt storm that mysterious fiftieth gate.

Like life, mind has been the subject of much learned debate. Mind is the awareness factor in man, and was once believed to be diffused throughout the universe. Everything was mind, and every ent had a basic consciousness. Mind was the man. While life infuses and animates man, mind is his core. In many languages mind is associated not only with the conscious thinking processes but with the deepest levels of the psyche. The universal principle, inasmuch as it is mental, is funnelled through the mind and finds expression in it. Mind in varying contexts is equated with soul, spirit, life, breath, imagination, fancy, belief, opinion, self. Mind is the innermost ego, the identifying element that distinguishes self from others; it includes the intellect that sifts and discriminates, the emotions that colour, the will that acts, and the moral faculty that passes judgment.

This long-held view received its greatest set-back in the eighteenth century, when materialist philosophers came up with the proposition that mind was a product of chemical components and had no existence apart from matter. Pierre Jean Georges Cabanis (1757–1808), a French physician and philosopher, summed up the scepticism prevalent in his day by saying that the brain secreted thought just as the liver secretes bile. This famous maxim has become part of the proverbial lore of certain schools of thought, and mind has joined the other asomatic elements in a kind of scientific limbo. According to one group of psychologists, mind is a needless hypothesis. The operations of the so-called mind are computer-like processes released as a result of electro-chemical activity in the cells that make up the nervous system, and consciousness is 'an epiphenomenal by-product of neural activity'. When the eminent brain specialist Sir John Eccles concluded, after giving years of thought to the subject on which he became so eminently qualified

22

to offer an opinion, that the brain was an apparatus for respond-
ing to the activity of some immaterial agent, the mind, the sceptics
dismissed his 'ghost in the machine' out of hand. Men of intelligence do not hypothesize ghosts to explain phenomena.

Just as the concept of life was said to be an illicit deduction
made from the observation of living things, so the concept of mind
was an unwarranted extrapolation from the fact of consciousness.
We posit a mind, it was argued, because we have a subjective
apprehension of things, but consciousness offers no justification
for this view.

What is consciousness? Within us, seemingly in some area 'in
the middle of our faces', is a kind of lamp that glows and illumin-
ates our immediate environment. Our environment likewise renders
consciousness operative. Kenneth Walker in his *Diagnosis of Man*
(1942, p. 60) relates the case of a boy who suffered from cutane-
ous anaesthesia so that his sense of feeling was absent. He was
also deaf and had only one eye. His waking consciousness was
activated by means of the one remaining eye, and when this eye
was covered he immediately fell asleep. It would appear that our
waking consciousness is contingent on the stimulus received by
our senses. Laboratory experiments in sensory deprivation show
that a certain level of stimulus is necessary for the normal functioning of the brain.

If we reduce for some time the impressions we receive from
outside by shutting our eyes and ears we also reduce the possibility of continuing to be sharply aware of our environment. We
can easily drift into an imaginative state of mind. In a daydream or
flight of fancy our awareness of things around us is diminished.
The waking consciousness is connected with our senses; if no sense
impressions were being received by the brain we, like the boy,
would soon become unconscious.

Actually, consciousness is ever present. We are conscious even
when we are unconscious, a statement that only appears paradoxical because of the paucity of our vocabulary for the varying
grades of our awareness. Thus, we are conscious when we are
asleep, a truth which is established by the fact that we have
dreams. We are conscious, though we may not perceptibly react,
when we are knocked out by a blow, or dead drunk, or even in a
coma. Experienced yogis can remember what has been said while
they were in deep trance. Gay Luce says (1972, p. 109), that 'many

23

surgeons have been chagrined to discover that patients in deep anaesthesia have recalled conversations over their bodies on the operating table'. There is strong evidence to show that the psyche overrides the limitations of matter and that consciousness is independent of the body and brain, and functions outside the somatic environment with a considerable degree of efficiency.

As we shall see in considering xenophrenic states, the norm of what is called full consciousness is arbitrarily taken to be the mental state of the normal waking adult. Full unaltered consciousness thus excludes sleep, drowsiness, abstractions, drug states, insanity, illness, and the mental conditions of pre-natality, infancy and senility, and all other psychological situations when the mind is incapable of dealing efficiently with the practical problems of the workaday world. Bearing this criterion in mind we shall see that conscious awareness, as qualified in this way, is only a small part of the protean psyche. To start with, sleep already accounts for one-third of our lifetime.

At the best of times full consciousness is confined to a narrow linear pathway dimly lit by a flickering light. Even when we are seemingly 'all there', we are simultaneously functioning at other psychological levels. Samuel Butler (1835–1902) once said that a man is only conscious when he performs an act for the first time. The concentration required in learning to tie a shoelace, to play the piano, or to drive a car, is eventually relinquished to the control of the unconscious mind. So rapidly do we surrender our actions to the authority of the instincts and the automatic processes that we might be said to be strictly conscious only a fraction of our lives.

Even a brief examination of his own waking thoughts will convince the most practical person that he spends a considerable time of his conscious moments in brown studies, daydreaming and fantasizing. Reading a novel, for example, involves more than one layer of the mind. We are subconsciously aware of the position of our bodies, and any feelings of discomfort that may arise therefrom. We hear but are not disturbed by sounds outside or within the house. Our eyes read the print as unconsciously as the fingers of a pianist move over the keys of his piano while he carries on a conversation with a friend. As we read we build up spontaneous pictures in the imagination. We approve or disapprove of the characters in the book, or of the novelist's narra-

24

tive style. We think at several levels at once. In our analysis of novel-reading, which could be carried even further, it is not easy to decide precisely where our real 'consciousness' lies. Some persons have suggested that even when we carry out complex intellectual operations we are barely conscious. The Russian-Buriat mystic, G. I. Gurdjieff (1873–1949), was of the opinion that the average person is asleep most of the time he thinks he is awake. He described man as a weather-vane, turned about by every random breeze, or as a sleep-walker striding about in a twilight world, his consciousness a series of trance-thoughts, and most of his actions merely reflex movements. Gurdjieff's remedy for humanity's somnambulism was self-observation in depth.

Putting aside such extreme views, we shall describe consciousness as the awareness we have of ourselves and the things around us, and the means by which we exercise alertness during our waking moments. In the centre of this awareness is the rational self, and its dimension is the solid, tangible and material environment of this world. The conscious mind is that which conducts the utilitarian affairs of the individual's life. For practical purposes it is the most important factor making for his survival, and it is this consciousness with which a man is primarily concerned. But this waking mind, the rational, practical, self-regarding element cannot register information of the individual's total environment. A huge area is closed to this consciousness, which indeed has no pre-eminence over the other facets of the mind.

The fully awake consciousness can in fact be said to be an obstacle to the appreciation of a large segment of possible human experience. It would appear that some degree of obfuscation of our consciousness is a prerequisite to certain forms of knowledge and experience. The obtrusive conscious mind 'interferes' with reality, and its distracting cacophony must be soft-pedalled if the impressions from the other levels are to come through. Paradoxically, we are often greater than ourselves when the waking part of the self is out of commission.

It should be remembered that there are hierarchies of consciousness, and each consciousness is played in a different key, or moves in a different gear. Several layers of consciousness make up the whole psyche, and the waking mind is only one and a thin one at that. The larger part of what is in our mind does not freely emerge into consciousness at all. One of the greatest of American psychologists, William James (1842–1910), concluded that our normal, waking, rational consciousness was a special kind of awareness, and that barely separated from it were other forms of consciousness, entirely different. And he adds (1902, p. 388), 'No account of the universe in its totality can be final which leaves these other forms of consciousness quite disregarded.'

The simplest of these other forms is what is termed *empirical* consciousness, which flows from the personal mind of the individual, growing out of his own encounters and accomplishments. It starts with the pre-natal experiences within the womb, and goes on developing till death. It includes the waking consciousness, and all that can be recalled from memory, with or without effort, as well as all the unconscious data that have been stored and are apparently beyond recall. The empirical mind is largely formed from environmental influences and grows by subjective experience.

The influence of parents, so far as it relates to the inheritance of the individual, forms part of the *ancestral* consciousness. This embraces the history and traditions of the tribe, race or nation to which he belongs. Its patterns are set up by common beliefs, strengthened under the stress of common dangers and established by common rituals. The members of the community pour into the sacramental treasury a part of their personal devotion and enthusiasm and so vivify the racial consciousness, transmitting their experiences, like archetypal legacies, to their descendants. The members of tribal communities and other ethnic groups form a composite whole, sharing in this hypothesized ancestral consciousness. Some part of every individual's mind is thus fed from the common mind of all the members of his tribe or race.

A still larger and remoter pool of inheritance provides the source of the *collective* unconscious, the sum total of all the knowledge and experience acquired by mankind as a whole. It represents the nucleus of memories shared by the members of the entire human race and forms, as it were, a group soul. Just as the biological history of the individual (ontogeny), especially as revealed during the development of the embryo, recapitulates the evolutionary history of all mankind (phylogeny), so does the individual mind summarize all human experience; and just as the rudiments of our earlier physical state of evolution are present in our bodies, so also are our earlier mental states and experiences.

C. G. Jung (1875–1961), who laid great emphasis on the collec-

26

tive unconscious, said, 'The body has an anatomical prehistory of millions of years, so also has the psychic system' (Jaffé (1963), p. 320), and went on to point out that our unconscious symbols have a remarkable uniformity as if they were taken from a common storehouse. He observed that the Negro of the southern states of the USA dreams motifs of Greek mythology, and a Swiss businessman duplicates the vision of an Egyptian gnostic (Goldbrunner (1955), p. 82).

We have evidence of something approaching a collective consciousness among animals too, within their own species. It seems to be a kind of intermeshed ESP, where each individual within a group is psychically in rapport with the others, instinctively participating in their common ventures by patterns set in remote times. Sir Alister Hardy suggested that there is 'a sort of psychic blueprint between members of a species' (quoted in Salter (1970), p. 64). A good example is found in the behaviour of termites, popularly called white ants. Eugène Marais, who studied their extraordinarily co-ordinated activities, was so impressed with the unity of their composite lives within the colony that he postulated the existence of some 'occult power' that integrated their behaviour. He came to regard the termitary, which in some cases might be twenty feet high, as 'a single composite animal', and compared the hard clay shell of the mound to the skin, the corridors to arteries, the workers to blood cells, the royal chamber of the termite queen to the heart, brain and reproductive apparatus.

Over and above the pools of racial and collective consciousness lies the ocean of *cosmic* consciousness, rare glimpses of which suggest that it is outside the range of psychology, and belongs rather to the realm of religion and mysticism. There is thought to be a psychic or mental factor underlying the universe, and, more than that, constituting its very nature. The world is spiritual from top to bottom, and all its constituent elements are enlivened by an all-pervading mind. Each entity represents a variation of the universal awareness in degrees apportioned by its status in the evolutionary scale. Consciousness is conterminous with existence. If a thing is, it has consciousness of a sort, and the kind of consciousness it has depends on its grade in the cadre of creation.

The idea of the basically psychic character of reality has been the common theme of saints and sages of all times. This psychic environment is sometimes spoken of as the 'astral light', which is equated with what an earlier school of occultists called the cosmic ether. It possesses brightness and creative potency, and is pervaded by mind. It was said that before the Fall, Adam 'heard the light speak'.

The cosmic consciousness is a universal mind which broods over the world, and its vibrations set up sympathetic waves in the minds of all beings. The ordinary person is sometimes vouchsafed a savour of this super-consciousness in rare moments of rapture and ecstasy, as when he experiences a religious conversion, or some overwhelming emotion, like great love or great sorrow.

The Islamic philosopher Averroes (d. 1198) wrote that while we have separate bodies, we do not have separate minds, but share in the universal mind, and thus participate in the fundamental experiences of the cosmos. St Thomas Aquinas (d. 1274) after his illumination felt that in comparison with it, all his learning was valueless. St Francis Xavier (d. 1622) said of his mystical experience, 'It seemed to me that a veil was lifted up before the eyes of the spirit, and that all the truths of human science, even those that I had not studied, became manifested to me by an infused knowledge' (Custance (1951), p. 53). Jakob Böhme (d. 1624), the German mystic, after his own moment of supra-consciousness wrote, 'The gate was opened to me so that in one quarter of an hour I saw and knew more than if I had been for many years at a university.' All those who had experience of this consciousness were struck by the fact that it was far beyond the purview of the everyday awareness of things of this world. The experience related to something that was altogether beyond description and seemed to provide an insight into the very core of ultimate reality.

The field of cosmic consciousness was made the subject of a study by Dr Richard Maurice Bucke, a Canadian surgeon, who was also a specialist in mental and nervous diseases. At the age of thirty-five he had a remarkable mystical experience that changed his life and influenced all his subsequent thinking. He describes how he and a couple of friends spent one evening reading Wordsworth, Shelley, Keats, Browning and Whitman. Returning home to his lodgings he suddenly found himself enveloped in what seemed to be a flame-coloured cloud. His first thought was that there was a fire somewhere in the city, but then he suddenly realized that the fire was within himself. He was overcome with a feeling of exaltation and joy and a sense of intellectual illumination. He said that within a few seconds of blazing enlightenment he learned more than in all his previous years of study, and a great deal more which no study could ever have taught him. His brain was momentarily ignited by a lightning-flash of what Bucke calls 'Brahmic bliss', which left him thereafter with a permanent 'after-taste of heaven'. The cosmos, he realized, was not dead matter but a living presence, and the soul of man, being a fragment of transcendent life, was immortal (1972, p. 9).

The psychologist, Professor Abraham Maslow (1908–70), who spent almost twenty years studying the lives of successful and creative people came to the conclusion that nearly all such 'self-actualized people' at one time or another had encountered what he called a 'peak experience', which altered their lives and brought to the surface the best that was in them. Thereafter there was always a 'reverent awe' at the recollection of the experience. This again is akin to a taste of cosmic consciousness or mystic illumination. Freud's 'oceanic feeling' may belong to the same category.

Cosmic consciousness though part of the human experience is also regarded as an emanation of the mind of God. That the divine being has consciousness and is partially knowable by mortals is one of the corollaries of all theistic philosophies, and a knowledge of God is believed to be a prerequisite to knowing what the universe is all about. In this view God thinks and feels, but not as we do. God does not know only by fragments, or by a glimpse here and a glance there. He knows each separate object, gross and subtle, present and future, and all states and conditions, by a single all-pervasive and everlasting glow of the instantaneous knowledge that is also will and power.

According to the Hindu view, one must understand God in order to understand man and the nature of the universe, for the divine being is the well-spring of all knowledge. The Syrian historian Eusèbius of Caesarea (A.D. 263–340) preserves the record of a visit of certain Indian philosophers to Athens, one of whom conversed with Socrates. The Indian asked the Greek sage to explain the purpose of his philosophy, and when Socrates replied that it was an enquiry into human phenomena the Indian laughed, exclaiming, 'How can you understand human phenomena when you are ignorant of divine ones?'

In the Christian view too the divine mind is not entirely beyond our understanding. It is manifest in the universe around us, and is known through the inspiration of prophets and saints and the words of revealed scripture. Every religion implies living in harmony with a manifested divine will. Philosophy in much of its discussion of the Absolute, of Reality and Being, impinges on what borders on divine perception.

However plausible the concepts of the ancestral, racial and collective consciousness might have seemed to some students, they were still highly suspect to many others, while the idea of a cosmic consciousness was anathema to the psychologist of almost every orthodox school. Mind itself was only tardily admitted by a minority vote, and has been subject to drastic revision, yet in a roundabout way this has opened the door to a new mysticism.

Our minds have a basement, where sex and violence hold sway, an attic where a great deal of lumber both personal and ancestral is stored, and also an aerial, sensitive to thoughts coming from other minds. Our thoughts and emotions not only travel along the underground system, or take the fly-over, but use trackways ranging high above the commonplace traffic that ascend to unknown heights.

The greater part of this peripheral consciousness is docketed under the omnibus label *unconscious*. At the time of writing their dictionary of psychological and psychoanalytical terms, Horace and Ava English pointed out that there were no less than thirty-nine distinct meanings for the term 'unconscious'. This lack of precise terminology is only an indication that we do not possess the language for many important concepts, and reflects our ignorance of the vast area still uncharted. But it is a convenient label for an idea with a long antecedent history, for it was familiar to Aristotle among the ancients, and to Aquinas among medieval scholars, and many others. The re-discovery of the unconscious is said to rival in importance the discovery of the New World by Columbus.

Broadly, the unconscious includes the subconscious, the subliminal conscious, the non-conscious, the super-conscious; and also the vast hinterland that is to all intents and purposes unknowable. In varying contexts it embraces the chaotic lumber-room of the mind, the collective experiences of our ancestors, and the all-pervading mental element of the universe, of which a tiny trickle filters into the individual consciousness.

30

With the admission of the unconscious into the ranks of respectability, the occult has entered psychological literature. Through the unconscious all of us are potentially in contact with a great deal besides our immediate surroundings. By a kind of osmosis we flow into things and they into us, and the channel for the interchange of substance and enlightenment lies in the unconscious, which has access to illimitable stores of knowledge.

If the world's prosaic duties are carried on by the conscious mind, the world's religion, art, philosophy and scientific progress are conceived and given form by the unconscious. The waking mind is the civilizing mind, the unconscious is the culturizing mind. The conscious mind is ego-centred, the unconscious is all-embracing. Like Reality and the Absolute it is sometimes dignified with a capital letter, the Unconscious.

The unconscious never forgets, is never fatigued, is unfettered by space and time, is fathomless and immeasurable. Even Freud, who lagged considerably behind Jung as a rhapsodist of the unconscious, spoke of it as 'the part of us that is so much nearer the divine than our own poor consciousness'. Ironically, where mind had once been exorcized as the 'ghost in the machine', the unconscious was now ushered in as the deity superintending the works.

The asomatic or non-physical element that has provoked even greater controversy than the others, is the soul, although the concept of soul or spirit has been accepted in some form or other by all peoples. There is no society, however primitive or advanced, that does not have a substantial body of belief concerning the soul. What exactly is meant by the soul is difficult to say, and what adds to the confusion is that several grades of soul are often distinguished, some equated with spirit, some with mind, some with life, some with a double or astral body, and it is not always possible to differentiate between them.

The ancient Egyptians spoke of the *ba* or soul, and the *ka*, the protecting genius; the Babylonians of the *edim* or spirit, and the *napistu* or life principle; the Zoroastrians of the *daena* or soul, and the *urvan* or mind; the Chinese of the *hun* or spiritual soul, and the *p'o* or inferior, material soul; the Hindus of the *atman*, spirit, and the *jiva*, or life. Often a third element came in, like the Jewish triad of *neshamah*, divine soul, *ruah*, astral soul, and *nefesh*, animal soul, corresponding to the Islamic *sirr*, *ruh* and

31

nafs; the Greek *psyche*, soul, *nous*, mind, and *thymos*, life; and the scholastic *anima divina*, divine spirit, *anima humana*, astral spirit, and *anima bruta*, physical or vital spirit.

Belief in multiple souls is found in a number of pre-literate societies. The early Fijians, for instance, thought that a man had two souls, a dark spirit that went to the underworld, and a light one that stayed in its own home. The Dakotas of North America believed that everyone had four souls: one died with the body, one remained near the body, one went to the spirit realms, and one lingered with the man's hair and was kept by relatives. The Ostiaks of Siberia held that man had no less than seven souls. Other primitive tribes have even greater refinements of the soul concept, shading off into facets of extreme subtlety, accounting for the souls of living persons, of the dead, of animals, trees and stones.

Such fragmentation of the asomatic or non-body principle raises a host of questions, besides violating the elementary 'principle of parsimony' first formulated by the medieval English philosopher, William of Occam (1270–1349), who laid down a useful rule for contingencies that arise in any proliferation of theories. He said, 'Plurality is not to be assumed without necessity, for what can be done with less is vainly done with more.' In other words, in trying to account for something, we should not needlessly multiply hypotheses, and out of several hypotheses that might present themselves, we should select the simple, reasonable and plausible, rather than the complex, miraculous and improbable.

The principle of 'Occam's razor', applied in this case, would suggest a simple convenient premiss—that of a single entity, the astral body, the seat of life and mind, forming a link between the physical element, the body, and the immortal spark, the soul.

The hypothesis of the astral body has seldom gone down well with the orthodox, and it continues to meet with resistance from several quarters. If life, mind and soul were the unmentionable four-letter words to the materialist, the astral body did not enter into his cognizance at all. Though ineligible for scientific status, one could at any rate see a 'living' thing, and experience a 'thought', and the concept of 'soul' at least had the merit of metaphysical and theological backing, for what it was worth, to recommend it. The astral body had no such endorsement and was consequently dismissed out of hand and without discussion.

This attitude was in keeping with the unreasoning bias against any asomatic phenomena that was particularly rife in the late nineteenth and early twentieth centuries. When certain psychic occurrences were brought to the notice of Professor T. H. Huxley (1825–95) he remarked, 'Supposing the phenomena to be genuine, they do not interest me.' Hermann von Helmholtz (1821–94) the German physicist declared, 'Neither the testimony of all the Fellows of the Royal Society nor even the evidence of my own senses would lead me to believe in thought-transmission. It is clearly impossible.' In the opinion of Lord Kelvin (1824–1907) 'nearly everything in hypnotism and clairvoyance is imposture and the rest bad observation.'

Today there is a greater tolerance for belief in the psychic powers of man, which is now passing through the same phase of half-hearted acceptance that beset 'mesmerism' at the end of the eighteenth century and 'thought-reading' at the end of the nineteenth. However reluctantly, both have now received the nod of recognition from men of science, and hypnosis or psycho-somatic sleep, and telepathy or extra-sensory perception have become part of the current vocabulary of psychologists. Today a scientist can approve a telepathic experiment without his colleagues suspecting that he has taken leave of his senses.

To many students who have given thought to the subject, the cumulative tradition concerning the non-physical components that co-exist within the human being crystallizes around the theory of a second or astral body. Standing in the way of its more general acceptance is the fact that experience of the astral body is entirely subjective and private, confined to a few people, is rarely repeatable to order, and hence not amenable to scientific manipulation and scrutiny. For obvious reasons the reality of the astral body is not a simple issue that can be decided by observation and experiment. As scientific evidence for its existence is not forthcoming, it remains a conjecture.

But in spite of the absence of objective proof, the idea of the astral body is indulgently received by many reputable persons and is likely to stay, whatever its official baptismal name might be in the future. So many responsible witnesses have vouched for the reality of the experiences they have had outside their bodies, that

33

the inference that there does indeed exist some experiencing entity, different from that usually associated with the body, is irresistible. The theory is a precipitate of many notions connected with the non-physical elements in man, so that at worst the astral body might be regarded as a term of convenience for a useful hypothesis.

Man, it is suggested, functions not only in his physical body, but in another, second body, a double, which is linked to him through life. There is hardly a field of human experience in which the second body does not play a part. The whole of our contact with the supranormal world takes place through the double. The rationale of mysticism, extra-sensory perception, mediumship, hypnotism, magic and the occult, and all other aspects of arcane belief and practice cannot be fathomed unless one has a clear understanding of this astral medium through which they are made effective.

According to an ancient view man stands at the centre of things. He is an *axis mundi*, a pivot of the world, and a focus of a vast range of forces. Through his body he shares in the material world; through his mind, both conscious and unconscious, he is in touch with the mental principle that is diffused throughout the universe; his astral body and his soul have their own spheres of experience, as we shall see. He is a microcosm, a miniature universe, reflecting the macrocosm or greater universe around him. He is all-inclusive, and contains within himself all the material, psychic and spiritual elements that have gone into the making of the world. The Swiss–German physician and occultist, Paracelsus (1493–1541) summed it up by saying, 'Out of nothing God made everything, and out of everything He made man.'

Further reading   Addison (1958); Bazett (1946); Deutsch (1945); Solomon (1961).

Chapter III

Esoteric Physiology

Having put forward the proposition that a non-physical entity functions behind the scenes of the physical body, the next step is to find out how the two entities, physical and non-physical, belonging to two different spheres, are connected, and how they interact. The suggestion that the two are related as substance and shadow, or that there exists a psycho-physical parallelism co-ordinated by some pre-established harmony, although put forward by some eminent thinkers, is not endorsed by any tradition. One answer to the problem, which receives support from personal experience at many cultural levels, is that there exists an area where the two actually meet, and the study of that area forms the subject matter of esoteric physiology.

Using a stock analogy, the physical body might be compared to an intricate mechanism. It has many facets, but only one is of interest to the physiologist, for he is concerned with no other. But according to the cosmobiologist, who studies the influence of cosmic phenomena on living things, the human mechanism is equipped with clocks and meters of various kinds, which though invisible are of great precision, and we would be underrating the body's many marvellous attributes if we judged it by reading the dial on the single visible face.

Our body is a complex of wonders, and more and more wonders, of which the conscious mind is unaware, are being ascribed to it. Intensive modern research has shown that it registers and responds to a hundred obscure environmental factors such as rhythmic changes in humidity, light and temperature, gravitation, barometric pressure, the passage of time, ionization, magnetic and electric fields, planetary, lunar, solar and stellar influences, cosmic rays, and other phenomena that are beyond the range of our five senses (see Luce (1972), p. 58). More and more refined instruments are being devised to reveal more and more refinements of the body's incredible reception of and reaction to stimuli coming from without. The intricacies of the body's mechanism and its relationship to the environment are still largely obscure, and scientists are hesitant to postulate the existence of a pacemaker controlling the organism, in case they unwittingly conjure up another ghost.

We receive a constant spate of information from our surroundings, most of it channelled through some other system than the senses, for the function of the senses seems to be to reduce the impact of external stimuli. Our senses keep out more than they admit to our cognizance. We live in a welter of incoming impressions and are subjected to a great battering from outside, but are insulated against the onslaught by the narrow specialization of our sense organs. Our ears deafen us to much of the cacophony of outside sounds, and our eyes reduce the blinding glare transmitted in the light waves around us. The brain, according to the philosopher Henri Bergson (1859–1941), is essentially an organ of limitation, its chief function being to filter and canalize the flood of impressions that would otherwise overwhelm us. Our senses allow us only a peep into a limitless panorama.

In their own way, the people of ancient and medieval times were equally aware of the marvels of the human body, and in explanation attributed to it and to its organs and natural by-products a supernatural significance. There is hardly a part of the anatomy that was not assigned to the care of some deity or guardian spirit. Each part was thus cared for, and each had its role in the welfare of the individual. Because head, heart, eye, tongue, foot, hand, hair, bones, spleen, liver, and other organs performed not only physiological but occult functions, they acquired a special sacrosanctity in the scheme of esoteric physiology. This scheme does not belong to the asomatic system proper, but is, rather, an extension of the physical body, for the esoteric organs depend on the physical for their functioning on the material plane.

Nothing so constantly links man with the world around him as breathing. By this means he is ceaselessly taking into his inmost being a part of his immediate environment. Denied the blessing of breath he would die in seconds. The Hebrew word *ruah*, the Greek *pneuma*, the Sanskrit *prana*, the Latin *spiritus*, mean breath as well as soul. From early times breath became the theme of a strange mystique. What was taken in when a man breathed was not just air but a vitalizing aerial substance more important for his survival than food.

The ancient Egyptians, Chinese, Indians, Mayas, the Christians of the Middle East, the Persians and Arabs, all evolved highly elaborate systems of breathing, sometimes combined with the recitation of spells, all with the sole object of increasing spiritual power. There were different kinds of breath; different effects were achieved by inhalation and exhalation; there were differences between breathing through the right and left nostrils; different benefits derived from the hot and the cold air that a man could breathe out in the same single exhalation. Even diseases could be cured by breathing the right way. Among other things, this meant taking in the right kind of air, for the character of the air inhaled was as important as one's diet. Furthermore functions like sneezing, belching, hiccuping, crepitating, yawning, all being connected with the element of air, were also given an occult interpretation.

In ancient belief 'waters' no less than 'airs' had magical qualities. In esoteric physiology the fluids of the body were invested with occult meaning, including sweat, tears, saliva, sputum, semen, and above all blood, which headed the list. A mysterious fluid, intimately linked with the spirit of man and regarded as his life-substance, blood acquired a unique importance in all cultures. 'The life of the flesh', the Bible says, 'is in the blood.' Within it abides a power that is connected with the spiritual realms, and the vapour of shed blood is a direct link with the next world.

Emanuel Swedenborg (1688–1772), the Swedish scientist and mystic, held that the soul of a man was a 'spiritual fluid' diffused throughout the body, and that the medium for its diffusion was the blood, which was thus imbued with power from the divine source. On the other hand the French occultist Eliphas Levi (1810–75) spoke of blood as 'the astral light made manifest in matter', the astral light in this context being the vital principle of the etheric world.

Blood was regarded by all peoples throughout history as a magic substance of tremendous psychic potency and was therefore universally hedged in by taboos. It was the sign of supreme sacrifice; it sealed convenants; it betokened both maidenly virtue and the magic power of virgins. If spilt on the earth blood cried aloud for vengeance. Havelock Ellis (1859–1939) said, 'There is scarcely any natural object with so profoundly emotional an effect as blood.'

When we come down to the actual anatomy of the esoteric body we are confronted with an unusual physiological system, but more surprisingly, we find a general uniformity in the various accounts as given by the different, often widely separated peoples, of their respective systems. The descriptions tally, whatever the source, although the details sometimes vary. They all confirm the existence of a quasi-physical body, so tenuous as to be invisible and intangible, yet functioning parallel to and in harmonious liaison with the physical body. Basic to the system is a molecular meshing consisting of a fine network of 'arteries' which ramify through this body, linking all its parts with the physical organism and interacting with it.

Belief in the existence of the subtle arteries, as they are called, can be traced back to most of the great civilizations of the past. The ancient Egyptians taught that the human body was served by a system of thirty-six radiating channels called *metu*, which circulated the vital energy to all parts of the body. Their physicians cured ailments of deep-seated organs by manipulating the relevant surface area thought to be connected with it by a metu, and so directing the flow of the vital energy towards the afflicted organ.

In Hindu esoteric physiology the subtle artery is called a *nadi*, and the three chief nadis are situated one within and two on either side of the spinal column. These in turn branch out into one hundred and one lesser vessels and these further divide and sub-divide into thousands of tiny tubes forming a network of infinite subtlety. As with the Egyptians, physical disease of an internal organ was treated by manipulating the surface area on the body that was connected to it by a direct nadi. Massaging the back of the ear might, according to this method, relieve a pain in the region of the groin.

Similarly, in the Chinese system there are believed to be twelve major meridians in the body, along which the *ch'i* or vital energy flows, and these connect to about one thousand points on the surface immediately beneath the skin. The precise spot at which each of the twelve major meridians meets the skin is marked out on an anatomical chart, and in case of sickness the

38

appropriate points are located and pricked with a long needle, again diverting the vital flow to where it is needed. This is the principle underlying treatment by acupuncture, which we have already mentioned.

The physical body is believed to be linked to the subtle arteries at certain points known as plexuses. Each plexus is a knot of invisible ganglia which forms a nucleus of vibratory energy, receiving and absorbing radiations from diverse sources and serving as a storage centre for the physical, psychic and cosmic energies concentrated in them. Some occultists maintain that each plexus is the focal point of a separate psychic plane, and can be activated for the distribution of the forces belonging to that plane. Each plexus therefore opens the passage to a different occult zone.

Paracelsus, whose genius touched on many obscure fields of medical doctrine, also spoke of certain centres in the body through which sidereal (stellar) and planetary influences were received, and he named each such centre an *astrum* (Latin, *astrum*, 'star'). According to him, at the moment of a person's birth the heavenly bodies, which are disposed in their particular positions in the sky at the time, engrave their characteristic marks on the astrums, and the pattern thus imprinted determines the future physical appearance, health, character, conduct, and to that degree, the destiny of the person concerned. It is through these centres, said Paracelsus, that 'the heavens work in us'.

The locations of Paracelsan astrums in the body correspond very closely to those enumerated by Chinese, Maya, Middle Eastern and Hindu sources. The Hindus have developed an astonishingly detailed theory of esoteric physiology based on the plexal scheme. In Sanskrit the term for plexus or astrum is *chakra*, a word meaning wheel, and used in this context because the chakras when viewed by trained adepts are found to be shaped like circles or round symmetrical designs. They are described as focuses of swirling astral energy which serve to energize the vital and mental faculties of man. They resemble saucer-like depressions and turn about rapidly like miniature whirlpools.

In most systems several plexuses are mentioned, situated roughly along an axis whose lower end is near the base of the spine. From this tap-root there rises a stem which has its efflorescence in the head. Between the topmost plexus in the cranium and the lowest at the tailbone lie the other major plexuses, from five

39

to fifteen in number, depending on the school, and from these power points the subtle arteries radiate through the body like the distributaries of a river, so that the life-bearing energy pervades the whole physical organism. The chief plexuses have frequently been given an equivalence in the physical body. Thus, modern exponents of the chakras, for instance, equate them with the adrenal, thyroid, pituitary and other endocrine glands.

The spinal column is usually represented as the main trunk of the chakra scheme, and the chakras are described in ascending order along the spine, starting with the basal chakra and working upwards for progressive spiritual enlightenment. This is in accord with a very ancient concept, for we find that the ancient Egyptians too looked upon the spine as the ladder of spiritual ascent and a symbol of resurrection for those destined for the realms of the god Osiris.

The base of the spine is adjacent to several important areas in occultism. The five small bones near the end of the spine, which are fused together to form the back wall of the pelvis, were regarded as a single structure and called by medieval physiologists the *sacrum*, from the Latin word for sacred, since from earliest times it was thought of as a sacred bone. The early Semites believed that the sacrum contained a mysterious fragment, known to the Jews as *luz*, which they conceived of as a tiny particle, so small that it could not be further reduced in size, nor burned nor otherwise destroyed. It was supposed to be the nucleus around which the resurrection body would take shape when Gabriel sounded the last trump.

Just beneath the sacrum lies the *perineum*, sometimes said to be the polar opposite of the bregma, which we shall consider shortly. It is situated between the thighs, in the crotch of dichotomous man, midway between the sex organs and anus. It represents the midpoint of the body, placed between the up and the down, the right and the left, and the front and the back. It is also one of the most important of all the plexuses, known in Hindu esoteric physiology as the *muladhara* chakra, the basal plexus, and is regarded as a platform for the performance of the most secret occult operations.

In this region, according to yoga, there glows the ember of a mystic fire, the seed-spark of a strange force called *kundalini*, metaphorically likened to a tiny serpent, which lies curled up in three and a half coils, fast asleep. As it sleeps it breathes and sends gentle pulsations rippling up the axis along which the other plexuses are situated, and gently activates them.

The kundalini is generally quiescent throughout a man's lifetime, which is as it should be, because it is considered extremely dangerous to tamper with the force. It can, however, be aroused by special methods involving breathing exercises, bodily stances and yogic spells, all of which if undertaken should be done under expert guidance. When it awakens it trembles all over, unwinds its coils, and is poised and ready to move. It can sometimes be inadvertently aroused, in which case the prompt advice of an occultist versed in these matters should be sought. To arouse it properly takes much time and considerable training, and any amateurish attempts to do so will either end in failure or result in a disastrous and uncontrollable upsurge of energy which can disrupt the psyche. The hazards of hurried apprenticeship and misapplied knowledge are very real.

In Hindu esoterics the kundalini is a fire-force. This means that its power when controlled can be helpful, but when uncontrolled, destructive, for it can rampage through the body causing physical, mental and psychic devastation. The serpent-power, as it is called, manifests in lights and flames and intense heat, and also strange sounds (B. Walker (1968), vol. I, p. 574). The Irish poet and mystic, George William Russell (1867–1935), also known as 'AE', speaks of an experience he had when he once awoke the inner fire within himself. He seemed to have 'opened the seals of a cosmic fountain', as a result of which he had the sensation, as he describes it, of 'plumes of fire, jetting from fountains within, feathers of flame or dragon-like crest'. The fire 'ran up like lightning along the spinal column and my body rocked with the power of it', and accompanying it was a sensation of fiery pulsations, cascades of flame and the clashing of cymbals. But recalling the danger of misdirecting the energy, he calmed himself and did not guide the fire.

When properly awakened, on the other hand, the kundalini begins its ascent through the chakras one by one, at each stage causing the chakra it pierces to blossom forth and infuse the adept with fresh awareness. This goes on until it reaches the topmost chakra in the cranium, known as the *sahasrara*, or 'the lotus with the thousand petals'. The union of kundalini and sahasrara is said to provide an experience that is literally out of this world and altogether beyond description.

Alongside the basal chakra lie the sexual chakras, connected with the genitals. The sexual organs have a vast mystique of their own which is found in all parts of the world. In early societies they were believed to be under the control of spirit entities who presided over their activities. Phallus and vagina were linked by invisible bonds to the cosmic process and copulation ritually carried out was converted into a magical act. This was the basis of sexual mysticism as practised in China, India and the Middle East, and in contemporary cults in the West that still perpetuate these traditions. In the Hindu system the male chakra lies at the root of the penis.

The next plexal region in order of ascent is the *epigastrium*, which extends from the sternum or breast bone to a point just above the navel, but is sometimes applied to a larger surface of the abdomen as well. It contains three plexuses of which the most important is the *solar plexus*, a great octopus-like formation of nerves which rules part of the sympathetic nervous system. The epigastrium is an extremely sensitive area and is believed to be associated with the cerebral and cardiac functions as well. Hence it is known as the abdominal brain. In colloquial Arabic it is called the 'mouth of the heart' (Ghalioungui (1963), p. 70).

Many cases of the transposition of the senses, in which the normal functions of the sense organs seem to get mixed up, centre around the epigastrium, as when a blindfolded person will hear, see, taste and smell objects presented to the area of his stomach. This curious phenomenon was noted by the early magnetizers, the eighteenth century pioneers in hypnotism, and still occurs in people of hysterical character. In his book on the human double Ralph Shirley reports (1972, p. 73) the case of a man who said that while he was in the astral body in a strange house, 'a ray of light emitted from my epigastrium which illuminated the objects in the room'.

Somewhat to the left of the epigastric region lies the spleen. This organ, about five inches long, is well supplied with nerves, lymphatic and blood vessels, and like most other organs to which occultists attach special importance, is still something of a mystery. Its exact purpose and function are even now not fully understood. It has some of the qualities of an endocrine gland since it has an internal secretion which it pours direct into the blood stream. But, as far as we know today, the spleen itself can be completely removed without impairing the general health of the physical body. For some reason it gets enlarged in certain diseases like malaria, typhoid, syphilis, turberculosis, rickets and pernicious anaemia.

Occultists state that the spleen is the reception centre for the 'solar breath', and that it stores a kind of radiatory energy which it transmits to all parts of the body. 'There is', says the theosophist Alice Bailey (1944, p. 86), 'a close connection between the spleen and the top of the head in connection with the etheric body'. The radiatory energy is received at the top of the head and from there directed to the rest of the body via the spleen. A French psychical researcher, H. Durville, lists the spleen as one of the points from which the astral body leaves the physical on projection.

Still higher up, in the region of the chest and throat lie a number of other plexuses, each performing separate functions and each, in the occult view, a vortex of specialized energy. One is situated in or near the heart; another in the neck, behind the throat, at the juncture of the spinal column and the medulla oblongata; and a third between the scapulae. Of the last mentioned Alice Bailey says (1944, p. 98), 'The main centre for the reception of prana [vital breath] is a centre between the shoulder-blades.'

The heart chakra is usually dealt with very briefly in occult manuals, as if it were safer left to its function of keeping the physical body alive and not put to other use. Exteriorization methods involving the heart chakra are, however, not unknown. The sixteenth-century Italian mathematician, inventor, naturalist, physician and philosopher, Jérôme Cardan (1500–76), may have hit upon such a method. He claimed that he had the power of leaving the body at will, going into a kind of ecstasy and crossing the boundary of his physical senses. He first detached his other body from the region of his heart, the accompanying sensation being that of his breast splitting open as if his soul were about to withdraw. It was like opening a door to see off a guest. A feeling of painful numbness would spread over his whole body and thereafter he was 'out of himself'.

Finally, the head contains several major plexuses, all located in the brain, which is the control room for the whole bodily apparatus. One is the pineal gland, a small endocrine body the size of a pea and shaped like a miniature pine-cone, whence its name. It is situated near the middle of the skull, not far from the pituitary gland, and is connected with the third ventricle which supposedly governs reason and judgment. The precise function of the pineal gland has not yet been medically established, but it is believed to be connected with the development of early sex feelings. John Bleibtreu says (1968, p. 78) that if ecstasy has any biochemical basis, it is becoming increasingly difficult to avoid the conclusion that 'the substances controlling both its sexual and transcendental manifestations are probably manufactured in the pineal gland'.

The pineal gland was well known to the ancients who referred to its as 'the seat of the soul'. The Greek anatomist Herophilus (*fl.* 300 B.C.) founder of the medical school of Alexandria, described the pineal as 'a sphincter which regulates the flow of thought'. The French philosopher René Descartes (1596–1650) maintained that there was a non-spatial mind infusing the body through the brain, and suggested the pineal gland as the rendezvous of mind and matter. Mme Blavatsky (1831–91) spoke of it as the abode of the sidereal spirits of man.

A number of modern exponents of astral projection have alluded to the 'pineal doorway' through which the incorporeal self comes and goes as it enters and leaves the body, and to the audible click in the head, like that made by a door as it opens and shuts, that accompanies exteriorization. Some people have reported actually being eased out of the body by first relaxing and then mentally focusing on the pineal gland. Even if taken in a figurative sense this association between the pineal gland and the astral body is suggestive.

Oliver Fox, speaking from personal experience, said that with some practice he found he could control his dreams, and participate in them. When having such lucid dreams he was always conscious of a pain at a point in the head which he assumed was the pineal gland. As the pain subsided he would hear a click, after which his consciousness would be wholly transferred to the location of his dream. He could then rise in the air and float through walls.

Certain occultists believe that the pineal gland is in fact the seat of the third eye, even though it is set further back than the point where the third eye is supposed to be. Biologically, the pineal gland is regarded as an evolutionary relic of a third eye, and indeed such a vestigial third eye, even known as the pineal eye, is still found in certain lizards of which one class survives in New Zealand. In man the third eye is invisible and intangible and is said to occupy a position near or within the pineal gland. This invisible organ of perception is situated further back in ordinary people, but when developed by occult training it moves forward to its traditional place in the middle of the forehead, where it becomes visible to other advanced adepts.

Finally, the brain itself is a plexus. No other material substance on earth is so highly complex and organized. Its work includes the control of every single physical and physiological activity. The heart, lungs, digestion, temperature, circulation, metabolism, sexual activity, are all regulated from this central directorate. It is also said to control consciousness, and the processes of thinking, feeling and willing.

An older school of phrenologists tabulated over thirty separate mental functions and faculties, and localized them in various parts of the brain. The possession of a particular faculty caused the development of the related area of the brain, and this moulded the shape of the skull and produced a bump in that region, so that by feeling the bumps on the head the phrenologist could tell which faculties were more highly developed. The lower part of the back of the head was the area of philoprogenitiveness, or love of offspring, and if that had a pronounced bump the expert could confidently affirm that the person was fond of children. James Braid (1795–1850), the Scottish magnetizer who studied phrenology, wrote that once when he magnetized, that is, hypnotized, a patient and pressed the bump or 'organ' of veneration, situated on top of the head, 'an altered expression of countenance took place, a movement of arms and hands, which became clasped; then the patient arose from the seat and knelt as if engaged in prayer'.

A more modest version of brain-mapping is now accepted by most brain surgeons, and areas have been located that are said to control sight, hearing, touch, taste and muscular movement. This is apparently supported by the fact that when a particular area in the brain is damaged the related sense or organ is affected. But here too brain specialists have their reservations. It has been established that substantial portions of the brain may be cut out with

45

no appreciable disturbance to the motor, sensory or intellectual functions.

Patients who have undergone such operations as leucotomy or lobotomy where certain brain fibres are cut, or even hemispherectomy, involving the removal of the entire right or left hemisphere, are still able to talk, walk about and do mental work. In many cases injury to other parts of the brain, including the cerebellum, or the removal of large areas of the cortex or 'thinking' brain, does not prevent a person from living a normal life.

Dr Wilder Penfield, director of the Montreal Neurological Institute of McGill University and one of the world's foremost brain surgeons, after noting that many patients functioned without any loss of their former abilities following surgery in which considerable portions of their brains had been removed, concluded, 'Perhaps we will always be forced to visualize a spiritual element of different essence capable of controlling the mechanism of the brain.'

The centre of bodily consciousness is the brain, we are told, but whole areas of human experience appear to be independent of it. 'The brain', as J. B. Priestley expressed it (1972, p. 122), 'is in the cognitive and not the precognitive business.' As we shall see, there is evidence to show that a kind of thinking and feeling is possible totally outside the physical radius of our brain and body. Perhaps the cerebral system has extensions of which we are not aware.

The construction of the brain has no relationship to its alleged functions. Our prehensile fingers are clearly meant for grasping, the mechanism of the muscles for moving, the translucent eyes for receiving light, the shell-like funnel of the ears for registering sounds. But, if we did not know it, what function would we assign to the 'repulsive matter' we call the brain? It has a decidedly unpleasant appearance, and the very sight of it can give people nausea. But somewhere deep within it lies a great unsolved mystery. It has been called a science-fiction organ, spreading its antennae into dimensions outside our own.

A medical friend of Lord Geddes, after an astral experience when near the point of death, reported, 'Our brains are end-organs projecting, as it were, from the three-dimensional universe into the psychic stream, and flowing from it into the fourth and fifth dimensions'; and he went on to describe how he saw around

46

each brain what seemed to be a cloud-like condensation of the psychic stream.

In occult physiology the most important plexus lies at the crown of the head, at a spot which was believed in many primitive societies to be the point where the soul first enters the body at birth and through which it departs at death. The meeting-place of the three major bones composing the skull, medically known as the bregma or fontanel, is situated approximately in the centre of the cranium. In the foetus and the new-born infant the bregma is open, since the frontal and the right and left parietal bones are not quite joined, so that the spot is still soft to the touch. This, in popular folklore, is said to be because the soul is still in the process of settling into the body and is half in and half out.

In some accounts the soul never wholly enters the body, even in adults. The Greek philosopher Plutarch, who was also a hierophant in a temple and an initiate into the mysteries, wrote that a part of the psyche or soul was half-submerged in the physical and tainted by it, while the incorruptible part, the nous, hangs above the head like a cord, the lower end touching the top of the skull, which was thus the point of contact between the two worlds of matter and spirit.

The natives of the Solomon Islands believed that at death a man's soul ascended to the top of the head preparatory to its departure, and left the body by an exit in the skull after a few days. Post-mortem trepanning, or boring a hole in the skull, such as was practised in antiquity from Scandinavia to southern Africa, and the cracking of the skull as in Hindu cremation rites, fulfilled a similar purpose, that is, to allow the soul to make its exit through the aperture provided. According to Tibetan belief, the soul of a deceased person takes its departure by way of the brain, and the priest attending to the dying person plucks a few hairs from the top of the head to facilitate the release of the soul from the body. Yogic exercises like bending the head forward between the knees or standing on the head, are meant to direct the bodily fluids to the top of the skull.

In Western esoteric physiology too, the cranium was regarded as the seat of a power which was said to be located in the ventricles, the hollow spaces in the brain filled with cerebro-spinal fluid. There are seven such ventricles but Albertus Magnus (1206–80), the great theologian, and other medieval mystics gave pre-eminence to three, which were presumed to govern imagination, reason and memory. From these ventricles there filters down a celestial dew called *ros*, a fluid referred to in occult manuals under various names from China to Peru, often in mystical terms. Kabbalistic texts says that the head of man is filled with 'crystalline dew', and from the downflowing of this dew 'the dead are raised up in the world to come'.

Hindu esoteric physiology speaks of a chakra, already mentioned above, that lies partly within and partly outside the head, called the *sahasrara*, 'the lotus of a thousand petals'. It distils the nectar of immortality which seeps into the brain, but most of it unfortunately expends itself without being used. In Chinese yoga, vitality and spirit produce in the head an ambrosia they call *kan lu*, which seeps via the mouth into the body and nourishes the immortal seed, but here again most of it is dissipated because men are ignorant of its existence and do not know how to retain and use it. Taoist sects in China and followers of tantrik cults in India are almost obsessively concerned about this wasteful expenditure of the precious fluid, and have devised some curious exercises and techniques to arrest the waste and reabsorb the ichor, in order to vitalize the physical frame and thus, in the words of the adepts, 'destroy death'.

Further reading Besant (1911); Hall (1947); Powell (1925, 1927, 1941); Russell (1919); Woodroffe (1953).

Chapter IV

The Astral Body

The idea that there abides within the physical frame of man a non-material entity, more permanent than the physical body, is one of the most persistent beliefs of mankind. This non-physical double conforms in character, thought and feeling to the man himself. Although it coexists with the body it can separate at certain times, as during sleep or trance, and is capable of an independent existence. There are several minor variations of this basic idea. In many societies the second entity has certain features of the 'soul' of religious tradition.

Most primitive peoples believe in the existence of some permanent spirit that survives the death of the physical body. In some cases it dwells within the body throughout life, in others it lodges in a stone, a bush or animal, as an object-soul. One of the treasured possessions of the Arunta tribesman of Australia, for instance, is the *churinga*, a piece of wood or stone incised with geometrical patterns, which is supposed to harbour the spirit of the individual or family. The Tshi-speaking Negro of the west coast of Africa venerates a life-power called *kra*. It existed before his birth as part of the tribal substance and served in the same capacity a long line of his ancestors. As it serves him now so it will serve his descendants. When an individual dies his *kra* merges with the ancestral pool and provides souls for other members of the tribe when they are born. The spirit-stuff is in one sense immortal, like the germ-plasm of the earlier physiologists, for its career continues through the individuals of the community from generation to generation.

The Egyptian hieroglyphic texts speak of the *ka*, a duplicate of a man's body, which represents his 'fluidic spirit', and remains with his body both during life and after death. The Egyptologist Gaston Maspero described the *ka* as a less dense copy of the physical body, exactly reproducing every part of the physical

49

organism (quoted by de Vesme (1931), p. 18). It stayed in the tomb after the death of the individual, and survived as long as the physical body remained intact. Hence the Egyptian custom of embalming bodies to preserve them from decomposition.

According to the taoist teachings of China, the radiant energy of the cosmos is concentrated within the body of man in the form of a spiritual essence. This is normally dim and inert but can be illumined and activated by special exercises devised to develop one's psychic faculties, such as rhythmic breathing, looking mentally inwards, and concentrating on the space between the eyes. The spiritual or vital body energized in this manner can then be exteriorized, leaving by way of the head, while the physical body remains in a trance state. At such times clairvoyance, clairaudience and superconscious enlightenment may be experienced through this second body.

In the Hindu view man consists of three bodies: first the physical, second the subtle, which itself houses the third, the causal body or soul. It is the middle or subtle body that contains most of the non-material elements of the human being, including the five senses of perception, the five faculties of action, the five vital forces, and the lower and higher minds, by means of which a man is able to identify himself as an individual and distinguish the things around him.

The Tibetan belief, again, is that every component thing, living and non-living, has a double which exists in the form of a shadow-reality in another dimension which is interfused with our own. In other words all things share existence in two worlds, which mutually influence each other. The double of a human being is closely linked with his physical body, and the reciprocal interaction between the two continues unbroken during life. The double is invisible to normal sight, but can be seen by lamas trained in second sight, or more rarely, even by ordinary people in certain circumstances. The double moves out of the body during sleep and in some meditative practices, and when freed in this way can operate independently, but with what effectiveness depends on the spiritual or occult development of the individual. The death of the physical body results in the decay and eventual disappearance of the double.

In western occultism the tradition concerning the double, or astral body as it is usually termed, does not differ in essentials from the eastern. The hermetic treatises (from about 150 B.C.) which reflect a late phase of hellenistic thought as evolved in Alexandria, speak of a vapour that arises from the combination of the four elements, earth, air, fire, water, making up the physical body. This vapour which is the astral body, envelopes the soul and circulates both in the physical and astral spheres. It partakes of the nature of both the soul and the gross body, is the means of contact between the two, and gives the creature motion and life. It is separable from the body, but cannot detach itself from the soul. It does not die with the body but persists for a certain time, often near the physical body, and dissipates gradually. Unlike the soul, the astral body is not immortal (Mead (1967), p. 38).

St Paul in his first epistle to the Corinthians also spoke of two bodies. 'There is a natural body', he said, presumably meaning the physical body, and went on, 'and there is a spiritual body', which some think may refer to the astral. On the other hand the natural body could mean the astral, and the spiritual body the soul. The gnostics, whose chief exponents flourished about a century after the death of St Paul, spoke of a 'divine spark which was hid in man', and for this interior deity used the term *augoeides* (from the Greek word *augos*, 'dawn'), which they regarded as the vehicle of the soul.

The neoplatonists followed much the same lines. In his *Physiologia*, Jean Fernel (1497–1558), who made a study of their teachings, said that they assumed the existence of another body on the premiss that two dissimilar natures like body and soul, belonging to two widely dissimilar worlds like earth and heaven, could not be associated without the interposition of some middle agent. The immortal and eternal soul was, according to them, enveloped in a simple shining garment, a kind of star-like vehicle which operated as a mean between the two natures of man. This was the astral body and being stellar in substance was especially subject to astrological influences (D. P. Walker (1958), p. 130).

Medieval and Renaissance scholars did not differ in any important particular from this trend of opinion. Paracelsus is notable for having formulated a rather abstruse scheme of the human constitution, naming seven different elements, one of which was the astral whose activity resulted from the operation of the stars. Alchemists who theorized about their secret art, spoke of an element within the human body very reminiscent of the astral body. This ger-

51

minal seed had to be transmuted into pure aureate matter free from all dross. Gerhard Dorn (*fl.* 1575), an alchemist, expressed the belief that men have in them an invisible substrate unlike anything found in nature, that represented their essential selves. 'Within the human body', he said, 'there is hidden a certain metaphysical substance known only to a very few' (Cavendish (1967), p. 173).

Modern students of the subject have to a substantial degree confirmed these earlier findings, and much data has recently been added about the nature and constitution of the astral body, and especially about the circumstances connected with its dissociation from the physical. It is said that when a normal person, sane and in good health, is awake, his astral body lies within the frame of his physical body, and the two bodies fit perfectly, together forming a single unit. They are then said to be in coincidence, or alignment, terms that have only an illustrative significance, for the natural sphere of the astral body lies beyond the dimensions of the physical world.

But there are occasions when the astral gets loose from its moorings, and the two disengaged bodies then move out of coincidence so that they are separated to a greater or lesser degree, depending on circumstances. The astral bodies of infants are normally in slight discoincidence. The very old, the very weak or sick, are not completely aligned either, and tend to discoincide easily. During sleep or in trance states the two bodies are gently drawn apart, and discoincide. Besides spontaneous and involuntary dissociation of this kind, the astral body can be projected voluntarily outside the body by special projection techniques.

The wealth of names bestowed upon the second body probably best reflects the multiplicity of its attributes, and the ideas that people have had about it. Many of these attributes are taken as the characteristic features of different bodies, so that in some accounts there are as many as seven or nine bodies, hardly distinguishable one from the other, which needlessly adds to the confusion surrounding the subject.

One of the earliest names, used by the neoplatonists, and the one that is still most commonly used today, was the *astral* body (Greek *aster*, 'star') since, according to them, it was a sheath of 'star'-like material enveloping the soul. For the same reason it was called the *sidereal* body (Latin *sidus*, 'star'). Having originated in the heavenly realms it was also called the *celestial* body. Later it became the *etheric* body, because it was thought to be composed of ether, the tenuous substance that was presumed by nineteenth-century physicists to be the medium for the transmission of radiant waves throughout the universe. Sensitives, or those gifted with supernormal perception, who have observed the astral body, reported that it had a luminous glow, and it was accordingly dubbed the *luminous, luciform, shining* or *radiant* body, or the body of *light*. This light was sometimes visible as the *aura* surrounding a person like an aureole.

Its extreme tenuousness and fineness gave it the title of the *subtle* body, or the *fine* body, in contrast to the dense body of flesh. Because it was thought to possess the properties of what earlier scientists called the 'fluidic' substance which lay behind all electric and magnetic phenomena, it came to be described as the *electric, magnetic,* or *fluidic* body. As the factor responsible for the supply of nervous energy to the physical organism it was the *nervengeist* (German, 'nerve-spirit') or the *nerve* body. And again, as the transmitting vehicle of life-bearing energy and 'vital breath', it was the *vital, pneumatic* (Greek, *pneuma,* breath) or *energy* body.

Further, because in appearance it looked like the twin or exact replica of the physical body, it was sometimes referred to as the *double*. So, if the physical body could be spoken of as the first, or alpha body, the astral was the *second* or *beta* body. Being intermediate between the physical and spiritual bodies, it was the *tween* or *between* body, and since it formed a bond between matter and spirit it was also the *unifying* body. Again, since it was neither flesh nor soul, but formed a quasi-material sheath for the soul, it was referred to as the *perispirit*. At times it appeared to envelop the physical frame in a diaphanous vesture and was called the *body-veil*, this latter phenomenon sometimes identified with the ectoplasm of the seance room.

Psychologically, the astral body was believed to be the seat of all the intellectual and emotional faculties in man, and was thus the *mental, rational, feeling* or *desire* body. In a still more refined classification it was sometimes equated with what the Aristoteleans called the 'rational soul', the reasoning part of man, as distinguished from the 'irrational soul' of the five senses that he shared with animals, and with the 'vegetative soul' of growth, nutrition and reproduction that he shared with plants.

53

And finally, if the soul is immortal, it is assumed that the 'self' that goes through the process of dying and the experience of death (Greek, *thanatos*), to emerge on the other side, must be the astral body, which is thus the *thanatic* body. Because it is engraved with the karma or causal process that engenders rebirth, according to the reincarnationists, it is also the *karmic* or *causal* body. In contrast to the immortal soul, the astral body is called the *mortal* soul, which survives the physical body but itself perishes in time, to release the immortal soul. Apparitions that have been recorded throughout history are frequently, though by no means always, glimpses of this mortal soul, which in such cases is known as the *phantom* body or ghost.

Questions concerning the substantiality, tangibility, visibility and weight of the astral body have been the subject of incidental study and investigation for the past hundred years, and pioneers in psychical research have carried out numerous experiments in the hope of establishing some of these attributes on a scientifically demonstrable basis. Man's second body was thought to be composed of a quasi-material substance, of extremely refined consistency, possessing certain physical and ultra-physical properties.

At the beginning of the present century certain researchers thought it might have measurable characteristics, and experiments were carried out in Europe and the USA, as a result of which it was tentatively established that it did have material qualities (Fodor (1933), p. 100). Dr Duncan MacDougall of the Massachusetts General Hospital claimed to have demonstrated that human beings at the moment of death lose from one to three ounces in weight, presumably due to the departure of the astral body.

In 1895 the French psychical researcher Dr Hippolyte Baraduc (d. 1913) addressed a communication to the French Academy of Medicine, stating that photographs taken at the moment of death revealed misty forms emanating from the human body, taking vague shape, and disappearing (Fodor (1933), p. 28). Other investigators photographed similar manifestations over the bodies of animals killed in a chamber specially constructed for the purpose.

Although the search for all such material qualities has since been discontinued, sensitives, mediums, and other witnesses have never ceased to report 'glowing mists', 'cloudy shapes' and 'vapor-

54

ous forms' leaving the body of the dying, and sometimes even assuming the shape and features of the person, and then spiralling up and out of sight, as if it were the departing spirit.

A highly respected clairvoyant, Mrs Eileen J. Garrett, saw at the time of her daughter's death, 'a curly, shadowy grey substance' rising above the girl's body, which curled and floated rhythmically and finally disappeared (see Crookall (1964), p. 72). She also saw 'a grey smoke-like substance' rising in the form of a spiral from the bodies of dying birds. Diane Pike, the wife of Bishop James Pike, had a vision of her husband, as he lay dying in the Israeli desert, leaving his body in a 'filmy cloudlike substance . . . from the base of the neck' (Freedland (1972), p. 217).

Because the astral body is a diffuse medium there have been innumerable conjectures regarding its shape, if it has any. According to the ancient and tribal peoples, the invisible body was variously said to have the shape of a bird, serpent or totemic animal; in the Hebrew and eastern view generally, it was thought of as a tiny or a normal-sized replica of the human being; or else it was believed to assume a cloud-like form or become like a ray of light. At death it rose up from the body and disappeared. For some time thereafter it could manifest itself to people on earth.

Plato who held that the most perfect of all shapes was the sphere, said that the sidereal body, being of divine origin, must be round. In his theory, man as originally created was also spherical in form, but was later split up. Emanuel Swedenborg, the Swedish seer, shared the ancient conviction that man's real self was shaped exactly like his physical body, and this still remains the general view prevalent among students of the subject.

Indeed, if the astral has a shape it is reasonable to believe that it is like the man himself. But the shape of the astral is assumed to be human because it is believed to permeate the living tissues or to fit into the configuration of the human frame in which it is housed. Actually, the astral has no absolute form, but possesses unbelievable plasticity and can take the shape and form of almost anything. Experienced projectionists have averred that the exteriorized astral body normally takes on the shape of the physical body because of the instinctive identification, through long association, of the essential self with the physical shape.

The concept of shape in this context is bound up with the philosophical problem concerning the ultimate nature of form itself. Form is essentially a limiting feature, conditioned by the kind of time and space we inhabit. The astral body, like the soul, is beyond time and space, and has no intrinsic form. The neoplatonists said that when the soul desires to manifest and become visible it assumes a shape to accommodate itself to the situation in which it will appear, and to make itself recognizable. Things on earth have forms appropriate to the earthly environment and apposite to their earthly destinies, so the human astral takes on a human shape. Pure spirit is formless. Our gods are anthropomorphized only because we cannot conceive of them in terms of an abstract metaphysical mist. The shape we associate with the human being is not necessarily that of the astral body or of the soul. There is no essentiality about forms, and if God made man in His own image, it was by endowing him with a soul and not by making him a biped.

One feature of the astral body that recurrently crops up in accounts of exteriorization is the astral cord, which joins the physical body to the astral. Belief in the existence of some such cord is quite common. Anthropologists from Tierra del Fuego to central Australia record aboriginal tales concerning a cord or rod that issues from their bodies and disappears in the twinkling of an eye, and the strange feats they can perform with it (see Eliade (1965), p. 183). The cord, though invisible, is extremely strong and elastic, can move things at a distance, cure disease at a touch, and even kill. This is comparable to the psychic rods mentioned by early psychical researchers to explain the psychokinetic phenomena of physical mediums.

The classical world had its own concept regarding the connecting cord. In his essay *On the Daimon of Socrates* Plutarch, as we have seen, states that a portion of the non-physical body hangs like a cord above the head, the lower end touching the top of the skull. Tibetan lamas believe that a kind of 'strand' links the physical body of the living person and his double, and this link remains for some time after death.

Modern accounts of projection indicate that the cord has frequently been observed during exteriorization, whether spontaneous or willed. The Rev. L. J. Bertrand, who gave the psychologist William James an account of a vivid personal experience, describes how during an Alpine climb when he was numb and frozen and almost dead of cold, he suddenly found himself outside and above his body, attached to it like a captive balloon 'by a kind of elastic cord' (Crookall (1961), p. 5).

Recent exponents have invariably described the cord as silver-grey in colour and having a faint luminous glow. There is also a distinct pulsating movement all along its length. All agree that one end of the cord is attached to the physical and the other end to the astral body, but the point of attachment seems to vary. Sylvan Muldoon says that when the astral and physical are out of coincidence they are connected by a cord which extends from the head of the physical body to the head of the astral body. Robert Monroe (1972, p. 175) found the cord protruding from between his shoulder blades. Other experimenters usually state that the point of attachment is at the front, top or back of the head, or more rarely, the chest or navel.

When the two bodies are only a few inches apart the cord is as thick as the wrist; when they are up to six or seven feet apart, it is as thick as the thumb; and when they are separated by a greater distance, the cord attenuates until it becomes as thin as a thread, although it never gets thinner than that, no matter how far the astral wanders off. It is infinitely ductile and may extend to apparently infinite length without breaking or weakening. The strength of the cord is extraordinary and remains constant in all circumstances.

A small number of experimenters deny the existence of the cord. They state that during projection they have taken the trouble to look for it but have failed to find it. Besides, trailing a length of cord during exteriorization would hamper movement. They contend that the cord is a hallucination, induced by panic. Finding oneself suddenly outside one's body and perhaps in the astral plane can be a most unnerving experience, and the fear of being cut off permanently from intercourse with the familiar world one knows may be overcome by mentally envisaging and objectifying some reassuring lifeline that guarantees a means of retreat in case of need. What better symbol than a cord, reminiscent of the umbilical cord which linked one to the safety of the maternal womb. Seasoned projectionists, it is claimed, do not need to see a cord.

This view is rejected by many occultists. The experience of the astral seldom causes panic in a well-trained experimenter, so there is no question of conjuring up a cord to reassure oneself. It is true

E

that the cord is not always seen, but its existence cannot be negated on that account. The cord does not obtrude itself at any time and whatever turns and circuits the astral body might take, it never gets twisted or interferes with its movement. Besides, during projection one meets with so many novel situations and has so much to observe that the presence of the cord passes unnoticed.

The cord comes into operation only during exteriorization, when it transmits vital impulses to the body it leaves behind. In the waking state, when the physical and its double are in complete alignment, this vital strand rolls itself into a tiny knot whose location is variously given in occult writings. The centre into which the knot contracts is said to be somewhere in the head, usually the crown of the head, the occiput or back of the skull, the middle of the forehead, or the roof of the mouth. According to the neo-platonic philosopher Damascius (*fl.* A.D. 529) the point where the astral cord resides lies within the right shoulder or between the shoulder blades (Mead (1967), p. 60). Other places suggested as the location of the quiescent cord are the heart, the epigastrium, or other major plexus.

At the time of death the cord unwinds out of the physical body altogether and withdraws permanently into the astral, never to regain contact with its counterpart again. Many old legends speak of the snapping of the string by which the spirit is connected with the individual. Greek mythology tells of the three sisters, the Fates, who are responsible for the destinies of men, which they spin on a spindle. One of these sisters is Atropos, who cuts the thread of life with her shears. In the opinion of some scholars the Bible also makes a reference to the astral cord in the verse which reads, 'Remember him before the silver cord is snapped and the golden bowl is broken . . . before the dust returns to the earth as it began and the spirit returns to God who gave it' (Eccles. 12:6).

The manifold concepts relating to the double and its connection with the physical body, as established by general consensus founded upon subjective experience and cultural tradition, might be summarized somewhat as follows. The astral body is a non-material entity, normally invisible but occasionally seen by sensitives. It is the intermediary or connecting link between the physical body and the soul. It operates within the physical body through a superfine physiological system not subject to the known laws that govern the activities of the physical body. It is connected to the physical body through a subtle arterial system which meets the physical organs at focal points.

The astral body of man receives and responds to unseen influences in countless ways, and at many different levels, and all these bring the individual into contact with varying grades of supranormal experience. It is also the medium for such phenomena as clairvoyance, spirit travel, and rising on the planes, and it is through the astral body that magical and occult phenomena take place.

Many diseases result from a pathological condition arising in the astral body, and the best healing operates direct on the etheric system of the patient. Once the existence of the astral is accepted and the impact of the total environment upon it taken into account, such as cosmic rays, stellar and planetary influences, time determinants, electro-magnetic and other physical agencies, then preventive and curative medicine may well shift to a different level.

The astral body is the vitalizing and energizing principle of the individual, by means of which the physical body is enabled to function. Furthermore, it has an influence on the mind and on mental processes, since it is the source of mental activity. It underlies all our experience, and those who have had conscious, out-of-the-body projections confirm that the astral is the seat of consciousness. The powers of the mind are actually powers that inhere in the astral body. Consciousness is dependent on processes taking place in the astral body and not in the brain. Awareness departs from the physical with the displacement of the double. In normal circumstances the brain loses consciousness when the astral is out of coincidence with the body.

Our sensations too are said to have their root in the astral. One of the names given to it is the 'feeling body', because evidence suggests that it comprises that part of the ego that is involved with sensation. John Philoponus (*fl.* A.D. 620), the last of the Alexandrian neoplatonists, laid it down almost as a dogma that it is the non-physical body that feels. What he termed the 'sensing power' resides in the astral, the substrate of the soul. The eyes, nose, ears, skin, are only the means whereby the sensory impulses are referred to the astral, and are the tools devised for operation only on the physical plane. The powers of sensory perception are not localized in any specific areas, but are diffused throughout the whole astral body. The astral is the true sensory agent.

In the occult view the health of the emotions has a special bearing on the destiny of the human being after death. Prompted by conscious and unconscious responses to the stresses and challenges of everyday life, our emotions have a direct impact on the astral, and through the astral, on the soul. It is the teaching of most great religions that the essential factor in the well-being of the ego, and that which ensures the final condition of the immortal spark within, is the balance of our emotions; not the fulfilment of the sensory life, or great intellectual attainments, or high estate in the world's eyes, but the control and maturity of our emotional faculties. The neoplatonist, Porphyry (d. A.D. 304) wrote, 'By the time we approach death, the soul should be exempt from lust and envy, hatred and anger.' Nothing so tarnishes the brightness of the astral body as the unrestrained exercise of the passions.

During the lifetime of the individual the astral operates within the physical body when awake, but the natural sphere of the exteriorized astral is the astral plane, a vast uncharted region and the scene of many experiences recorded by men through the ages. These experiences confirm that it is possible for the individual to exist and be vibrantly alive, without the encumbrance of the physical apparatus that is necessary for survival on the earthly plane.

Although the astral body is sometimes confused with the soul, a distinction between them has been recognized from very early times. Thus the *Odyssey* says (Bk XI), 'When fire has consumed the bones of the dead, and the spiritual substance has flown to the heavens, all that is left of man is an aerial light body.' This perhaps summarizes the general view in its simplest terms. All interaction between astral and physical ceases at death, when the astral withdraws permanently, shed of its masks and postures. It survives the death of the physical body, perhaps lingers for a time near its old haunts, and then continues its existence on its own plane. The astral has no lasting identity. It is merely the temporary vehicle of the higher self, and disintegrates or is diffused when the higher self has worked out its own destiny.

Further reading   D'Assier (1887); Dodds (1963); Eliade (1965); Muldoon (1958); Powell (1927); Spiegelberg (1964).

Chapter V

Exteriorization

The material and astral forms of a man together form a single unit, and, as we have seen, when he is awake his astral body is securely anchored to the physical. Discoincidence only occurs when the body is unconscious or somnolent. During periods of drowsiness, sleep or other xenophrenic states, to be considered later, the astral slips out of its moorings, remaining slightly out of alignment with its physical counterpart, or floats upwards and then away, sometimes a considerable distance. At such times the astral seems to pursue an independent existence and to possess its own consciousness and thoughts, and in some cases will bring back to the brain-consciousness a recollection of its experiences, so that when he wakes up the person can recall quite clearly what he has seen and heard.

In Hindu mysticism the phenomenon of the exteriorized double is known as *videha*, or being without a body, a term used in several other contexts as well; among other things meaning the release of the soul from the bondage of the flesh as a result of spiritual enlightenment. Expert yogis practise a form of trance-consciousness in which they leave the body and in full awareness of their surroundings travel about incorporeally in this world and to other planes at will. In astral form, they claim, they may also enter a body recently vacated at death and reanimate it for a time.

The third-century neoplatonists of Alexandria, who represented the last school of pagan philosophy in the West, held that when a soul was about to occupy a body of flesh at birth, it was first clothed in a shining vehicle (*okhema*), composed of astral matter. This astral vehicle was only tenuously linked with the physical frame, and was periodically freed from its constraints during sleep, unconsciousness, or trance. They said, 'The night-time of the body is the day-time of the soul.' The soul along with its astral vehicle also left the body during certain ecstatic experiences. Plotinus, the most famous of their teachers, records in his *Enneads* (IV, viii, I), 'It happened to me many a time that I have been lifted out of the body, so that I become external to all things and see everywhere a marvellous beauty, and have the certainty of communion with the highest order and identity with the divine.'

People possessing greater than average spiritual endowment are more likely than the ordinary person to have mystic visions, which means that they are naturally prone to project their astral bodies, move into other dimensions, travel to other parts of the earth's surface or perceive clairvoyantly what is taking place elsewhere. Emanuel Swedenborg maintained that he used to have visions of heaven and hell, converse with angelic beings, and was vouchsafed a vision of our future estate. His clairvoyant powers so far as matters pertaining to this world were concerned were well known, and were authenticated by no less a person than the great philosopher Immanuel Kant.

The best-known instance of his paraperceptive faculty took place in 1756. In the month of September of that year he had been invited along with other guests, by a friend living at Gottenberg, to spend a few days with him. At about six o'clock in the evening of Saturday, Swedenborg left the house to go for a walk and returned looking pale and perturbed. On enquiry he told his friends that at that moment a terrible fire was raging on the Südermalm in Stockholm. He was particularly disturbed because it was increasing in violence and had already destroyed the house of a neighbouring friend, and was even now approaching his own home. Uneasy in mind Swedenborg left the house again, returning some two hours later to announce with relief that the fire had been brought under control and extinguished just three doors from his house.

This extraordinary incident naturally caused considerable excitement among the guests. The story was soon bruited about the town and reached the ears of the governor who sent for Swedenborg and heard from his own lips a description of the event that he had clairvoyantly witnessed taking place 300 miles away. On Monday evening official news arrived from Stockholm confirming in every detail the statements made by Swedenborg.

England in the nineteenth century saw a remarkable upsurge of interest in things occult, and particularly in phenomena such as astral clairvoyance, as it was termed, during which a person's spirit was believed to move out of the physical environment and

62

embark on a journey to other places. F. W. H. Myers (1843–1901), classical scholar, psychologist and pioneer in psychical research, preferred to call it a psychic excursion. Today the phenomenon is known by such designations as astral projection, astral travel, out-of-the-body (OOB) experience, ecsomation (Greek *ek*, out, *soma*, body), externalization, exteriorization, discoincidence, dissociation, disengagement, separation, and so on.

Ecsomatic experiences are not as unusual as many people think. There are a great number of records from earlier times of men who have been translated out of their bodies to other places, visited distant scenes, and talked with beings in other dimensions. Besides these there are the accounts brought back by anthropologists, which tell of the baffling trance performances of Siberian shamans, West African medicine-men, West Indian voodoo priests, and primitive sorcerers. Authorities on witchcraft suspect that some proportion of the medieval tales of witches flying off to sabbat meetings may belong to the same category of ecsomatic experience.

If all these are dismissed as appertaining to outlandish times and places, we still have the impressive volume of evidence that can be culled from the personal experiences of our own contemporaries. Dr Robert Crookall, an authority on astral projection, has listed and classified several hundred recent cases which he has exhaustively analysed in his books. The shelves of the various psychical research societies are stacked with similar reports. Dr E. E. Bernard, psychologist at North Carolina State University in Raleigh, estimates that about one person in every hundred has experienced astral projection at least once in his life (Bardens (1970), p. 143). Professor J. H. M. Whiteman, a physicist and mathematician who has had out-of-the-body projections, or separations as he calls them, since boyhood, has recorded over 2,000 such experiences, most of them personal, and he is convinced that the study of such 'inner' phenomena demands a new approach to science, 'substantially different from that of the physical sciences or dogmatic behaviourism' (quoted by Heywood (1968), p. 201). Like others who share his gift he believes that we belong to that inner reality more than we do to the physical world.

Miss Frances Banks, a psychologist, sent a questionnaire to 800 churchgoers in England, one of the questions being about out-of-the-body projections. About 45 per cent of those who replied had

had experiences of this nature. Such experiences are by no means confined to mystics, psychics, or old people, but occur to men in the prime of life with no particular interest in psychic matters. Surveys conducted in the past twenty years show that young people too have their share of astral experiences. In 1952 Professor Hornell Hart asked 155 students at Duke University, Durham, North Carolina, whether they had ever seen themselves from a viewpoint outside that of the physical body, like standing beside the bed and looking at the body lying in bed, or floating in the air near the body. Surprisingly, 30 per cent answered in the affirmative, and of this the great majority had done so more than once (Hart, 1959). In 1966 another well-known researcher, Celia Green, addressed a similar set of questions to a group of 115 undergraduates at Southampton University, of whom 19 per cent answered in the affirmative; and again in 1967 to 350 students at Oxford, of whom 34 per cent affirmed that they had had experiences out of the body (Heywood (1968), p. 200).

Despite this, most psychologists do not set much store by the evidence, and tend to deny the reality of ecsomatic phenomena and the existence of any form of consciousness outside the body. They attribute all so-called astral experiences, where they are not downright fabrication, either to delusion or to some psychotic condition. The apparent viewing of one's own body from outside oneself is known, in psychological parlance, as an autoscopic hallucination, meaning 'imagining that one is seeing oneself', which, supporters maintain, is a convenient way of dismissing a phenomenon by christening it with a Greek name, or palming off a description as if it were an explanation.

To the experient, or person having the experience, astral projections do not have the qualities one associates with a hallucination; to him they are vivid and real, quite unlike a dream or visual fantasy. If it is a dream, then the dream is unlike any other he has ever had. It has clarity and immediacy, and the authentic ring of a real experience. During a dream one's critical faculties are in abeyance, but this is not so in conscious projection. A man who returns to consciousness after a dream knows he has been dreaming; after a projection he is convinced that he has had an actual and not a fanciful experience.

The critic and writer John Addington Symonds (1840–93) records how, while under the influence of chloroform, he fell into a state of utter blankness alternating with flashes of intense light, during which he had a keen vision of what was going on around him in the room at the time, although he lost all sensation of touch. His first thought was that he was going to die; then suddenly he felt a power streaming in like light upon him, and had a feeling of indescribable ecstasy. He became aware that God was dealing with him, handling him in an intensely personal way. Thereafter he was convinced of the reality of the spiritual life. 'My whole consciousness', he wrote, 'seemed brought into one point of absolute conviction; the independence of my mind from my body was proved by the phenomena of this acute sensibility to spiritual facts, this utter deadness of the senses.'

The historian and novelist William Gerhardie who has practised astral projection for many years, relates in *Resurrection* (1934) how one night he woke up and found himself floating in mid-air, enveloped in a kind of opalescent light, although the room was dark. He could clearly see his body lying in bed, and noticed the flushed cheeks and even breathing. He declared that if everyone else insisted that his out-of-the-body experience was a dream he would never be convinced.

Apart from spontaneous projection which occurs involuntarily, astral projection may be induced by various means. The ability to project is sometimes an inherited faculty or a natural endowment. People find quite by chance that they have the knack of projecting at will. Trained occultists can cause their bodies to separate whenever they wish, but such voluntary projections are resorted to for specific purposes, and not indulged in without reason. A woman once told the traveller and writer Alexandra David-Neel that she could move out of her body whenever she wanted, and that when she was outside her physical frame she felt much freer in her movements and could go anywhere instantaneously by just willing to be there. When in her astral body she could also see her physical self lying inert on the couch.

The astral may be precipitated out of the physical as a result of illness, chronic disease, exhaustion or serious injury. Struck by shrapnel in an Italian trench in the First World War, Ernest Hemingway felt something emerging from his body, 'like you'd pull a silk handkerchief out of a pocket by one corner'; it flew around, then came back and re-entered him (S. Smith (1965), p. 22). Hemingway used this experience in *A Farewell to Arms* (1929,

65

ch. IX). A sudden impact can often jolt the astral out of the physical, and victims of accidents have sometimes reported being surprised at finding themselves outside the body, which was lying on the ground, and watching the crowd collecting around their recumbent form. Hughie Green, the television personality, after a car accident, found himself floating above the scene. He saw his body trapped in the damaged vehicle, watched the ambulance arrive, and the men pull his body out of the wreckage (Bardens (1970), p. 144). In a letter to the *Sunday Times* of 25 March 1962, a soldier reported how he was knocked unconscious by a bomb blast during the war in the Western Desert, and found himself viewing his unconscious form lying on the sand, from a point about twenty feet above the ground.

Projections can start without warning, while a man is wide awake, cutting across his activity and transporting his consciousness elsewhere. People have reported taking a casual walk and suddenly finding themselves in mid-air watching their own form continue the perambulation like an automaton. It may have lasted no longer than a few seconds, but has been vividly experienced all the same. There is the case of a man who while conversing with friends suddenly left his body and found himself hovering above the group, which included himself, and heard himself continuing to participate in the conversation. In one instance reported by Celia Green (1968a, p. 18), a boy of seventeen during an examination found himself floating above his desk, while his body was 'writing furiously, trying to beat the clock'.

Asceticism, bodily austerities, starvation, enforced solitude, sexual and sensory deprivation, shock, stress, have frequently been known to result in the exteriorization of the double. Long periods of meditation, autohypnotic suggestion, religious rituals including such methods as the prolonged chanting of spells, and whirling dances, can have the same effect. Psychosis, insanity and 'possession', are believed to result from a pathological loosening of the astral. Drugs of course are a potent source of astral dissociation. Projection can be induced by occult exercises or the use of various techniques deliberately designed to bring about discoincidence, and we shall consider these methods in their place.

There are several kinds of projective states. In one kind of spontaneous projection the subject may be fully conscious as soon as discoincidence commences, so that he is aware of what is happening to him from the very beginning. Such projection usually starts after he has been asleep for two or three hours. He slowly awakens to an awareness that he is somehow different. He may begin to vibrate violently, although this uncontrollable shaking is not apparently connected with the physical body, which remains quite motionless throughout the experience. The sensation can be quite unpleasant. Strange sounds begin to be heard in the interior of the head in the early stages of such projection. The sounds have been described as cracking, snapping, clicking, or chirping, later to merge into a single protracted humming or zinging note.

At first the experient may not be quite clear about the position or direction he is facing, but slowly realizes that he is horizontal, rigid and immobile. After a while the cataleptic state gradually lessens and he assumes a vertical position, with much swaying to and fro and a general trembling of the whole bodily frame. Some people have recorded that they zig-zag uncontrollably or spiral up to a perpendicular stance, upon which the erratic movement ceases. Once upright and stable they get their bearings and realize that they are outside their physical bodies. Others report that they are suddenly precipitated or drawn into the centre of a cyclone, or sucked up by a whirlwind. They are exteriorized with incredible speed, and the sound of a howling tempest assails the ears.

Although accounts of these early projective states in full consciousness do exist, they are very rare, for most experiences begin at the point where this stage ends. If a person is conscious at all, he has a brief black-out and suddenly finds himself outside the body, between six to fifteen feet away. How he got there he cannot tell. He has no recollection of rising out of his body, or of the sounds and tremblings that a small handful of people describe in their accounts. Such amnesic episodes seem to characterize many transitional phases of astral life and experience.

How and in what manner the astral disengages from the physical has been the subject of a great deal of speculation. Ralph Shirley quotes a French researcher, Hector Durville, who carried out a series of experiments on hypnotized subjects and concluded that there was no uniform mode of egress, and that the astral could leave the physical body from the forehead, throat, epigastrium, or even the spleen (Shirley (1972), p. 126), all of which, it may be

67

noted, correspond to the major plexuses of esoteric physiology. Some people think that the astral escapes from the pores of the skin like smoke or vapour, and once outside assumes the shape of the physical body and drifts away. Or alternatively, it emanates from the bregma, the mouth or the genitals, like ectoplasm from a spiritualist medium. Muldoon and several other projectionists have stated that as a rule the two bodies separate at all points simultaneously, so that the astral rises like a duplicate of the physical, as would happen if one levelly raised the upper of two planks placed one upon the other.

A fairly regular concomitant phenomenon in the initial stages of astral dissociation is catalepsy, a deep trance-like condition characterized by total fixity of the muscles and limbs. Medically it is found in certain types of schizophrenia, and in hysteria, epilepsy and narcolepsy. The latter manifests in a sudden seizure that sends the victim into a short burst of instantaneous sleep, even in the middle of some everyday activity like writing a letter or driving a car. On waking from the attack he is unable to move for several minutes.

Catalepsy can be artificially brought on by hypnosis, pressure on the arteries of the neck, and certain other methods. Among these are yogic techniques that wonder-workers in the East use preparatory to their feats of burial alive. Milbourne Christopher (1971, p. 230) tells of certain Coptic cults whose members practise cataleptic trance as part of their regular disciplines.

Catalepsy during projection is believed to be due to the effect of the astral body on the physical. According to some experimenters, Muldoon included, when a person is physically cataleptic, it is because he is astrally cataleptic. When therefore the subject reoccupies his body while his astral body is still cataleptic, his body will be in a state of temporary paralysis. The beginner in projection has no control over his astral states and often finds himself physically immobilized both before and after projection.

During exteriorization the astral is the operative and conscious agent, the physical meanwhile lying inert, passive and unconscious. Those who have projected, and have retained astral consciousness, state that although the astral itself has the power to move, it is unable to pass the movement into the physical body. While outside, the astral body cannot will the physical body to make a movement, like shifting a hand or foot, or turning over in bed, although the astral movements are often mimetically reproduced in barely perceptible bodily reflexes.

Dream researchers record analogous experiences with subjects during certain phases of sleep. At fairly regular intervals during sleep, the sleeper's eyes can be seen moving rapidly under the closed lids, as if he were witnessing something. It is now fairly well established that when such rapid eye movements (abbreviated REMS) are taking place, the subject is having a dream. If during this phase the dreamer is awakened before his muscle tone has had a chance to be restored, then, according to Luce (1972, p. 73), 'he would be unable to move, and might think himself paralysed'. This of course would last for only a few seconds.

Certain physiological phenomena characterize the REM or dream state. The body becomes quite still, and although the skeletal muscles are relaxed, certain superficial tensions are evident. There are very small movements such as twitching and grimacing, and occasionally in males, penile erection. The reason for these movements is not clear, and it is generally thought that the sleeping brain consciousness is witnessing and reacting to a dream. Some researchers on the other hand think that the body is mimetically reproducing by sympathetic repercussion the experiences of the astral double. Dreams, particularly lucid dreams, in which the dreamer knows that he is dreaming, are sometimes regarded as unconscious projections of the astral body, and during such lucid dreams the mimetic movements are often quite marked.

The state of mind during exteriorization, no less than the bodily states, has been the subject of a great deal of study. Normally, when the astral detaches itself from the physical body, the latter remains unconscious. The astral body alone retains a consciousness of events, and it does not normally transmit this awareness to the brain consciousness, either during the experience or on its return to the body. Consciousness during 'unconscious' states such as dreaming, trance and xenophrenia, is generally said to be centred not in the physical but in the second body, and this other body becomes the centre of the dreamer's world, and his interest shifts to that body. In other words, the externalized body carries the lamp of consciousness with it, leaving the physical body in virtual darkness. In the typical OOB (out-of-the-body) experience, the percipient will see the normal world from a different viewpoint to that from where his physical body is situated. If any credibility can be attached to astral experiences as a whole they raise an interesting psychological issue: that consciousness may be independent of the body, and thought independent of the brain.

In certain rare cases the exteriorized person feels that he has dual consciousness and can see, hear and feel simultaneously in both bodies. In other words, he can observe his surroundings from his usual viewpoint as if with his physical eyes, and at the same time see things, including his physical body, from his astral perspective.

Experienced projectionists, however, say that full consciousness can exist in only one body, and that the physical body cannot retain true consciousness so long as the astral is outside. In all ecsomatic experiences, consciousness resides in the other body. To see and think from two places at once is, to say the least, a faculty we associate only with divinity. Simultaneous dual vision is impossible, and in a few instances where it has allegedly been experienced, it is attributed to a crossing of lines, so to speak, or a leak or other fault in the physical-astral 'wiring', as a result of which the physical brain becomes momentarily aglow, giving the impression of consciousness, and producing the effect of concurrent vision. Oliver Fox once sniffed chloroform and was immediately projected, his astral and physical bodies being connected by a shining silver thread. His physical body spoke to his wife and a friend who were present, but as he spoke, he says (1962, p. 68), 'it seemed to me that my words travelled down the thread and were then spoken by my physical self'.

Alternatively, dual consciousness has been explained by the theory that the brain-mind is a system of conditioned reflexes and carries on a partial activity even when the controlling ego has vacated the body, just as the hair and nails continue to grow for a time after death, or as a man continues to feel pain in his phantom leg after his real leg has been amputated.

Many of those who have experienced conscious projections have recorded them in great detail. Some have been frightened at first, but only temporarily. They remain for a time in a state commonly described as that of suspended animation, and become a floating pinpoint of mind. After they have overcome the initial shock they have gone on to face the adventure with pleasurable anticipation. The projected person immediately knows that he is having a special kind of experience. He is quite certain he is not dreaming, nor is he awake in the workaday sense of the word. A kind of higher consciousness supervenes. He is curious and observant, and has a strange sense of detachment.

He is usually conscious of a remarkable augmentation of all his faculties. His powers of perception are enormously increased; the scenery around him seems to glow with a translucent light as if each thing were lit up from within. He has a sense of time-lessness. There is a wonderful feeling of exhilaration and aliveness. His ailments and infirmities are left behind. If he is sick in the flesh, here he is abounding in health; if he is old, here he is in the springtime of life and the prime of manhood. He has a sense of well-being and of boundless joy.

A notable feature of exteriorization is the absence of any distinct shape or recognizable outward appearance of the astral body. Celia Green writes (1968b, p. 36) that experiences of not having a body are more common in OOB states than those of having a body. The majority of those who have projected report, 'I had no body.' Others describe themselves as being 'a pinpoint of presence', or 'a disembodied consciousness', or 'looking at themselves from nothing'.

This is apparently contradicted by the reports of people who state that while in the astral they have seen their own hands and legs, and observed themselves in a mirror and found from their reflection that they did possess a shape, exactly like the physical. In many cases they were also dressed in robe-like garments, made of some light material, or more rarely, in their usual clothes. But the general opinion is that such an image is unconsciously created by the subject himself, because he wants to have a body and clothes, and would feel lost without them.

The astral body is not in itself shaped or dressed like its physical counterpart. Exteriorized subjects instinctively clothe themselves because they are conditioned against nudity by their upbringing. Civilized men and women are so used to clothes that when they move out into the astral they continue to identify themselves with their normal appearance, and without realizing it, shape themselves accordingly, and clothe themselves as well. But unless one thinks about it, one does not have a body in the astral, but remains just a 'conscious presence'. Here again we are involved in the problems arising from the concept of 'form', which we have considered in the previous chapter. Intrinsically, the astral is without shape and its conformation to the body is created by its own unconscious will.

In the astral to think is to become, and exteriorized persons who have acquired the experience can do some remarkable things in the astral world, besides creating bodies for themselves completely equipped with garments. This is regarded as part of the phantasmagoria of the other world, whose reality is of a nature that cannot be fully appreciated until we finally cross the border at death.

Certain experiences seem to suggest that one's thoughts can mould and shape objects as one wishes. Rayner Johnson says (1957, p. 246) that the stuff or substance of the astral world 'is malleable by individual minds to a degree which is far greater than anything we experience here'. Oliver Fox (1962, p. 36) used to experiment in the astral by doing little tricks such as moulding the plastic matter of that world into new forms.

The astral body's creative faculties are supported by its re-markable plasticity, mobility and speed. When a person is first exteriorized he continues to think in terms of the situation that prevailed in the earth-sphere. Just as he gives himself a physically-shaped body, so he continues to imagine that he must use his hands to move things and his feet for locomotion, and that the walls around him have the same solidity they possessed in the physical world. His astral arm can stretch out to incredible lengths, and his legs spread out as if equipped with seven-league boots, although there is no need for this elasticity since the astral in its own sphere can do what it likes and go where it chooses.

In the same way, the exteriorized novice believes that he has to open a door in order to walk from one room to the next, whereas he can pass through walls and doors with ease. Similarly, he imagines that he walks on the floor, when actually the floor is not necessary for him to walk upon. He could if he wished, walk mid-way through the floor of a house, with half his body above and half below it. Astral sight may at first be obstructed by furniture and walls, but this again is only because of the convention so firmly established in the mind by experience of physical objects. In time and with practice the realization of the new conditions dawns on the individual and he then acquires a kind of X-ray vision. Then the solid objects, the furniture, doors and walls appear to him only as if made of a denser kind of air, quite transparent and easily penetrable. He can see through walls and doors, and through houses, and into great distances beyond, as he wishes.

It is the same with movement. One uses one's legs because one cannot imagine oneself moving without them. Movement in the astral is, according to varying accounts, by walking, gliding, levitation, or by thought. In any case a person soon learns that he is freed from the limitations of matter, and that whatever methods he uses for locomotion, he can get where he wants instantaneously. You do not require navigational aids or direction-finding devices, even if you have to traverse large stretches of land and water. To think is to become, so to think is to act. Travel is accomplished simply by thought. Think of a movement and you move. Think of a destination, preferably a person, and you are with that person. If you are conscious of movement at all, the velocity is extraordinary. But frequently there is no feeling of movement. Only space has been displaced and you find yourself where you want to be.

A few experimenters claim that while exteriorized they have been able to shift material objects, open a door, or successfully touch a living person. Reports of such occurrences are comparatively few, and evidence adduced in support of the claims is not conclusive. In general it is believed that because the astral body is non-material it cannot cause movement in the physical plane, and that it is impossible for a person who is out of the body to establish contact with the physical world however much he tries.

A typical instance of the predicament created by attempting to make even simple changes in the physical environment is reported of a lady who once when she was going about the house in her usual manner, or so she believed, tried the light switch in her bedroom but failed to turn on the light, and was quite perturbed when she found she was equally unsuccessful with the other lights in the house. Returning to the bedroom she happened to glance towards the bed and was surprised to find her physical body lying there sound asleep (Bardens (1970), p. 144).

Other accounts tell of persons vainly trying to shift a picture on the wall, remove a book from a shelf, pick up a glass of water, or make their presence otherwise felt by touching or shaking a friend, or shouting aloud to make themselves heard. The impetus does not get through and it is as though they did not exist in the

F

physical world. One of the 'hells' created by those who are obsessed with material things and want to protract the enjoyment of their cherished habits after they have passed over at death, is said to be the frustration at not being able to touch, feel or taste the things they hanker after. The drunkard hangs about the drinking company in bars and public houses, but cannot drink the liquor he craves. The voluptuary likewise cannot satisfy the pleasures in which he indulged on earth, for he no longer has the physical wherewithal to do so.

Where does the double go when it takes off from the physical body during exteriorization? Sometimes it moves out of the physical world altogether and into the astral sphere. This astral world is vast and amorphous, and consists of many planes, as we shall see. Sometimes it journeys to distant parts of the material universe. People have claimed that they have been to different planets, at times bringing back detailed, if not very plausible, accounts of the locale and its people. One such visit was recorded by Théodore Flournoy (d. 1921) professor of psychology at the University of Geneva, who investigated the trance experiences of Hélène Smith (1861–1929), the pseudonym of a Hungarian medium, Catherine Elise Müller. She allegedly paid several visits to Mars and brought back descriptions of its inhabitants, and even learned their language, which she spoke with astonishing ease, speed and consistency. It had a simple grammar, and a vocabulary of its own which on analysis turned out to be a distorted amalgam of European root-words (Flournoy, 1900).

By and large, however, genuine astral experiences are confined to the earth plane, and people when exteriorized usually find themselves in different towns and countries on the earth. Mostly they move about in more familiar surroundings and in their own homes or in the neighbourhood. In spontaneous projection the astral body often remains near the physical body it has just left. People who are seriously ill or under anaesthesia see the doctors, nurses and family members around them.

A curious psychological feature of projection is that the astral double regards the physical environment and even its own physical body with remarkable indifference and lack of involvement. Those who have been ill or met with an accident watch their inert bodies with strange detachment. It is as though it were some alien object unrelated to the self, and hardly of any interest to them. The atten-

74

tion of the hospital staff, the tears and anxious concern of family and friends, the gathering crowd of people, all seem to be viewed as if it were some theatrical scene unconnected with them. The realization that the prostrate and perhaps dying person is himself is not of any concern to him. In some cases the anguish of the people he loves might soften this apathy and make him want to console them, but only to tell them that all is well, and that what lies there is of no consequence, and that the real self is somewhere else, away from it all.

It would seem then that our physical welfare, our material possessions, even our families, are not the obsessive concern of our astral or soul selves. Reports of projection and accounts given by people brought back from death's door, confirm time and again that the mind that is temporarily separated from the body and is observing things from the outside, in most cases remains emotionally unconcerned about earthly events.

In a typical case, quoted by Celia Green, a woman in hospital for an operation found herself looking from a position near the ceiling at the doctors and nurses by her bedside and wondering in a completely detached way whether they would save her and apparently not really concerned, 'which was absurd, for I was young with a husband and two small children'. In another case a mountain climber who tumbled down five hundred feet of ice in the Lake District mountains recalled that he felt neither fear nor panic, but was physically relaxed and mentally detached. 'For all I knew then I might have been speeding to my death or to serious injury but was not even remotely interested' (Green (1968a), pp. 99, 179).

The well-known mountaineer F. S. Smythe, in describing a dangerous fall in which he went over the edge of a precipice, also had a feeling of indifference and detachment as to what was happening or likely to happen to him. His consciousness, he says, was away from his physical body, 'and not in the least concerned with what was befalling it' (quoted in Heywood (1968), p. 197).

Professor F. J. M. Stratton contributed an article to the *Journal of the Society for Psychical Research* for June 1957 in which he relates an experience which occurred to a physician friend of his after an air crash. He found himself removed from his body and found it an 'extraordinarily pleasant' experience. He recalls that he felt no further interest in the physical self and thought, 'Why are these people bothering about my body? I am entirely content where I am.'

Frequently the thought that he will have to return to the body is repugnant to the exteriorized individual. To the freed double the physical body represents the 'bondage of the flesh', or, in the words of the Orphics of Greece, which we find almost literally reproduced in accounts of modern experiments, 'the miserable prison-house of the body'. Many are intensely annoyed at the prospect of having to resume the physical habitation and resent having to continue their existence on the physical plane. Walter de la Mare, surfacing from the effects of an anaesthetic during which he had unusually vivid and impressive astral experiences, had a sense of 'acute regret at being called back'.

But great as the lure of the other dimension might appear, and reluctant as the astral is to return to the body, it would seem that the ego in question has no ultimate control in the matter. Because one's time is not yet up, because one has a duty to perform, or because one feels impelled by the exigencies on earth, the loosened astral decides that it has no choice but to go back to the flesh. Alfred Alvarez cites (1971, p. 17) the case of a girl who, while in a state of coma after she had swallowed fifty barbiturate tablets, had a vision in which she found herself as if on another plane looking down at her husband who seemed to be quite near but inhabiting a different dimension and separated from her by an impassable gulf. She cried aloud to him but he remained unaware of her presence, and with great reluctance she decided to return to him and was soon back in her bodily consciousness.

The interiorization or return of the astral body to coincidence with the physical may occur in a number of ways. After a good night's rest, for instance, the resumption of normal consciousness is easy and unhurried. The astral leisurely settles into the physical, like a bird hovering over and then gently lowering itself into its nest. Interiorization after a normal voluntary projection is equally marked by a sense of ease and placidity. But if for any reason the astral is forced to return suddenly to its physical anchorage there is considerable discomfort to the physical body as it undergoes the shock induced by repercussion. When the entranced or sleeping body is disturbed, or there is an emergency of any kind, a message is communicated by a tug on the cord to the astral, which then snaps back into the body with 'unthinkable speed', however far it may have wandered, and the impact of its sudden resettlement is felt like a jolt that convulses the whole somatic system. Violent palpitations rock the heart, one has a sense of shock and a brief feeling of fear and even panic, which may take some minutes to subside. That is why in popular superstition a sleeping man should always be awakened by first gently calling his name, and only then very cautiously touching or shaking him. It is believed that if a sleeper is awakened too suddenly his soul may not have time enough to return and so may be unable to re-adjust to the body if it has shifted its position, or that it might return with too great a violence and kill him.

Normally, the return to consciousness, like the projection itself, is preceded by a short blackout. One moment one is out there, then there is a blank, and the next moment one is conscious within the physical body, but with a different kind of awareness. The blackout seems to represent a change of gears marking the transition of the focus of mental operations from astral to physical and from physical to astral. Such tunnel periods are common to many xenophrenic states.

In cases of spontaneous unconscious projection, according to Muldoon, the remembrance of what has happened during exteriorization is completely lost, as if the data had not been transmitted to the neural mechanism of the brain. Just as a somnambulist does not recall any of the various activities he has been through in the unconscious state, so the exteriorized double in a state of astral somnambulism may fail to register its experiences.

Other xenophrenic conditions like enforced solitude, when one is in a state of semi-hibernation and the mind seems to wander in a non-material plane, frequently result in similar strange lapses of memory. The French speleologist Michel Siffre who spent sixty days in an underground cave reported that the loss of memory while he was below became so pronounced that it was sometimes difficult for him to recall what he had done only a few minutes earlier. In epileptic seizures the victim retains no memory of what has happened.

Everyone is aware of the fugitive nature of dreams and the way they vanish from the mind without a trace. Only a few dreams are ever recalled, unless the sleeper awakens during or immediately after a dream and sets down the dream in writing at once. Dream researchers therefore make a point of waking their subjects immediately after or during the REM (dream) phase, if they wish to find out what they were dreaming about.

Are our memories so poor, or do we dream with another consciousness? Dreams remembered on awaking often become inaccessible in moments. We can remember exactly what we did three hours or three days ago, but usually if even three minutes elapse since the dream, it goes clean out of the mind. Dreams can evaporate in seconds, between the time of waking and getting out of bed. Mrs Arnold-Forster who studied her own dream-life over a long period said (1921, pp. 78–9). 'A sea-fog rolling in over sea and land and obliterating every outline, is the best image of the mist of forgetfulness that nature often interposes between our dreams and our waking consciousness.'

Further reading Crookall (1961, 1964); Eastman (1962); Green (1968b); King (1971); Muldoon (1936, 1958); Ophiel (1961); S. Smith (1965); 'Yram' (n.d.).

Chapter VI

Strange-Mindedness

The range of our mind's awareness is considerably greater than that revealed by waking consciousness, which represents only a single narrow band in a very wide spectrum. There are varying grades of mental experience outside our usual cognizance, and in determining these other grades and demarcating their extent, the criterion we arbitrarily take as normal is the mental state of the waking adult. His workaday consciousness is normal. Other states of consciousness, as they decline or deviate from this standard, might be termed 'xenophrenic' (Greek *xenos*, strange, *phrēn*, mind) that is, strange-minded, or other-minded.

American researchers in recent years have studied such states of mentation, which they have grouped under one label: 'altered states of consciousness', abbreviated ASCS. In the context of their usage ASCS are somewhat more restricted in their manifestations than xenophrenic states. The unaltered or normal state is defined by Professor Charles Tart as follows (1969, p. 1): 'For any given individual, his normal state of consciousness is the one in which he spends the major part of his waking hours.' The experiences of ASCS or xenophrenia are variable; they may be induced by physiological, psychological or pharmacological agencies, and the borderline between them and unaltered consciousness is not always distinct, but the general pattern is sufficiently clear for most practical purposes.

The indications of xenophrenia vary a great deal. A xenophrenic state is characterized by the displacement of normal awareness and the intrusion of another kind of consciousness. It is as if the unconscious breaks through and temporarily takes over, but operates on a different plane. Electroencephalograms, which register 'brainwaves', indicate that during certain xenophrenic states the brain receives and reacts to external stimuli as usual, but the neural mechanisms do not transmit these events to one's con-

79

scious awareness. In other words, although brain consciousness is not extinguished, the individual's 'presence' seems to have departed. The memory of what has been said or done slips away and is lost.

Although unconsciousness accompanies certain xenophrenic states, as in somnambulism, sleep, trance, fainting, epilepsy and coma, the altered state can occur while a person is awake. This happens in drowsiness, drunkenness, and in serious physical or mental illness, and is the natural concomitant of infancy and senility. In all such cases the physical body is not properly co-ordinated and operates in a kind of blurr, consciousness is confused and vague, objects out of focus, the gait and gestures clumsy, the speech slurred, and full contact with the practical world in abeyance. In terms of the individual's second body, the physical and astral are in slight discoincidence.

Altered states may be natural, as in sleep; or induced by artificial means, like hypnosis; or achieved more drastically, through drugs. A sudden transition to a xenophrenic state such as might result from a road accident, is marked by interior sounds and a blinding flash, often followed by a blackout. Thus, if one receives a blow on the head one 'sees stars' for a moment. Such sensations are said to be produced as a result of the momentary dislocation of the astral body of the victim.

Certain students of astral projection are inclined to believe that each altered state of consciousness represents a different zone of experience and provides a different level of awareness. The content and quality of the experiences are determined by the kind of xenophrenia that is achieved and the method used for attaining it. In its highest form xenophrenic consciousness reaches a kind of mystical enlightenment. The prophet, the sage, the inspired poet, the saint in ecstasy, the visionary in rapture, all seem to be in rapport with another dimension.

Xenophrenia may be induced by physical activity of various kinds, especially repetitive action that leads to fatigue. Sometimes simple exhaustion can cause the astral to drift off and consciousness to switch bodies, and several occult methods of exteriorization involve exhaustion techniques which result in fainting spells, unconsciousness and trance. These techniques require not so much a powerful physique as grim unbeatable determination, and without proper guidance can be injurious and even fatal.

Dancing, especially with rapid whirling movements, is a cardinal feature of certain ecstatic cults. In mechanical terms what happens during such dances is that the centrifugal motion displaces and draws the second body outwards; in physiological terms the fluids in the labyrinth of the middle ear suffer a high tide and the spirit-level governing the sense of balance is upset so that the dancer staggers as if intoxicated.

Whatever the technical or physiological explanation of giddiness might be, it follows gyratory movements. The astral double is unhitched and shifts away from the body, and mental dissociation ensues. The dancing dervish at the height of his ritual is in a state of trance, as if his astral double has escaped from him and is out of space and time.

It is interesting to note that the word *giddy* in its derivation preserves an almost mystical significance. The giddy person is, in Old English, *gidig*, or 'godded', as if possessed by a god. It might almost be an Anglo-Saxon equivalent of *enthusiastic*, from the Greek word signifying 'en-godded'. Giddiness or dizziness are characteristic symptoms of many xenophrenic states. Suddenly awakened from sleep we feel dizzy. A punch on the jaw makes us groggy. Alcohol makes us stagger. After spinning about for some time we totter and fall.

In the course of centuries a number of ritual postures have been developed that are believed to create conditions favourable for dissociation. One that is of great antiquity consists in lowering the head to a position between or below the level of the knees. Numa Pompilius (d. 672 B.C.), one of the early kings of Rome, with whose personality a unique tradition of magic and occultism is associated, was said to have discovered that when the body assumed a rounded position in this way, the mind became more receptive to contemplation. Chinese shamans when calling up the spirits of their ancestors would sit on a low stool and bend forward so that their head rested on their knees. According to the Bible, Elijah on Mount Carmel bent forward and placed his head between his knees, and in this attitude uttered his devotions.

The practice of lowering the head to induce xenophrenia reached its culmination in the headstand, which soon became a regular exercise in occult disciplines East and West. In this, the normal order of the erect stance is reversed and the person stands upside

81

down. The first effect is a feeling of 'chaos', resulting from the unnatural physiological and hence psychological posture, which gradually resolves itself into a certain order, depending on one's preparatory training. The object of the headstand in esoteric terms is to direct the secret rivers and tributaries of the body towards the hidden caverns of the brain. If continued for any length of time a form of trance supervenes.

The health of the physical body often determines the state of the astral double. In general it might be said that when the vital resources of the body are at a low ebb, conditions arise that are conducive to dissociation. Extreme cold and fatigue, an accident especially to the head, injury entailing loss of blood, certain kinds of physical and mental shock, sickness when it reaches a critical stage, all serve to shatter the cohesiveness and integrity of the individual. A physically weak person exteriorizes more easily.

Sir Auckland Geddes (later Lord Geddes), a physician and professor of anatomy, presented a case of an out-of-the-body experience before the Royal Medical Society of Edinburgh on 26 February 1937. At the time Lord Geddes said that it had occurred to a medical friend, whose name he withheld for professional reasons, but it is now generally believed that it was his personal experience.

He described how he was suffering from gastro-enteritis and developed all the symptoms of acute poisoning. Aware that he was seriously ill he was sure that he was going to die, but eventually rallied, to give a full account of what had occurred to him. He went on to describe how during the crisis he gradually became aware that his consciousness, personality or ego, was shifting out of his body and separating from another consciousness which was also him. One consciousness belonged to the body and seemed to be made up of subordinate consciousnesses belonging to the head, viscera and other bodily organs, and this body consciousness was slowly resolving itself into its components. The second consciousness or personality, which was distinct from the other and quite free from pain, was able to track with interest its gradual dissolution as the illness became worse. He saw his own body and the bed it lay in, the nurse who attended him, the doctor, and the other patients. As his vision widened he saw the house, then the garden outside the house, and in fact anywhere he cared to concentrate his attention. He also became aware of seeing things not only in the ordinary three-dimensional world, but in a fourth and more real world. A 'mentor' within him explained that he was 'free in a time dimension of space'.

The whole experience was accompanied by a great clarity of vision, a feeling of exhilaration, the ability to see a coloured condensation or aura around people, the faculty of what is today known as ESP, and of being able to read the thoughts of others. He was intensely annoyed at having to return to the physical body, where he found himself possessed of a glimmer of consciousness, and suffering pain once more. All his experiences, although out of the body, took place on what he calls (1937, p. 367) 'the plane of nature', that is, his astral body remained on the earth plane. Lord Geddes concluded his account, 'What are we to make of this record? Of one thing only can we be quite sure—it was not fake. Without that certainty I should not have brought it to your notice.'

One of the patients of the psychologist C. G. Jung, 'whose reliability and truthfulness', he says, 'I have no reason to doubt', had an experience during a difficult labour, when she suddenly found herself out of her body and, from a location near the ceiling, looking down at herself lying in bed, with the attendant doctor, nurse and relatives around her. At the same time she was aware of a glorious and colourful landscape behind her, sparkling in the sunlight, which she knew instinctively formed the boundary of another dimension. If she turned in the direction of the idyllic scene she could enter in at the gate and thus 'step out of life', but she knew that she would return to her body and continue her earthly existence. In a flash she was back in her body, recovered consciousness and saw the nurse bending over her. Her coma had lasted for half an hour (Jung (1955), p. 128).

Sickness often leads to an altered awareness of things. In his *Timaeus* Plato says that disease favours the emergence of supernatural powers. 'For aught we know to the contrary', said William James, '103° or 104° Fahrenheit might be a much more favourable temperature for truths to germinate and sprout in, than the more ordinary blood-heat of 97 or 98 degrees'. Many writers have noted that there exists an alliance between diseases like tuberculosis, syphilis, rheumatic fever and other chronic or prolonged bodily ailments, and the intellectual faculties.

Altogether, pain is an important agent for actuating other-world experiences. In extremes of pain it seems that consciousness is displaced so that the body might not have to endure too much. Mme Julia de Beausobre records (1948) that during her long incarceration in the Lubianka jail she was able to move out of her physical body when she could bear it no longer. In another instance, an ex-serviceman who had been a prisoner of war in Japan told Rosalind Heywood that when things became too bad in the prison he would move out of his body, and what is more, he was able to teach many of his fellow prisoners to do the same. A scientist friend of the same writer reported that when as a schoolboy he would receive a public reprimand in class, he 'had no difficulty in escaping to a far corner of the ceiling, whence I could look down with amused pity at the poor little boy on the bench below' (Heywood (1968), p. 199). Further, nervous conditions, fright, terror, or just vague anxiety and general foreboding, foster altered states of consciousness. Sylvan Muldoon was of the opinion that nervousness was the inability to hold psychic energy within the bounds of the body, the container being unable to hold the contents. The astral body gets over-active and one becomes responsive to other ranges of existence outside the commonplace. In times of great national or personal stress, financial crisis, or general insecurity, even disbelievers find themselves leafing through old prayer books and family Bibles; during wartime the churches begin filling up, and seasoned air pilots wear talismans, start seeing gremlins and have inexplicable premonitions.

Again, asceticism or the renunciation of the sensual appetites, and the mortification of the body in various ways, are well-tried disciplines with monks and anchorites the world over. Many of those who impose these penances upon themselves do so with the express purpose of achieving ecstatic states. Fasting is one of the commonest methods. The initial hardship of such abstinence is not of long duration, for after the first few days starvation becomes somewhat easier to bear. The pangs of hunger subside in intensity as the body adjusts to the new exigency. But chemical changes begin to take place in the blood and brain. Deficiencies of sugar and mineral content, and the absorption of the products of decomposed adrenalin into the brain result in symptoms ranging from light-headedness or blackouts to hallucinations and visions. But the physiological interpretation of these phenomena are discounted by religious enthusiasts. To them, what happens when the demands of the body are reduced is that the soul, unhampered by the clamour of the flesh, is more freely able to communicate with its own plane.

Sleep deprivation or enforced wakefulness induces somewhat different states of mind. The normal person who has his seven or eight hours' sleep every night, will begin to show symptoms of physiological disturbance if prevented from sleeping for two or three nights at a stretch. He will become irritable, feel a tight constriction round his head; his eyes will burn and twitch, and he will lose his orientation and time sense. If kept awake any longer he will begin to see objects shifting, and haloes and fogs forming around things, and they will start to expand and contract as if they were alive. This will be followed by thinking disorders and auditory and visual hallucinations. Insects will seem to crawl over his skin and even burrow under the flesh. Little men might appear who will menace him with threats and gestures. If his agony is prolonged his mind will crack up altogether.

There is a strong family resemblance between the psychotic fantasies of celibate hermits in the desert, the dreams of desperately bored prisoners in solitary confinement, the mental state of arctic explorers and the hallucinations of those subjected to enforced wakefulness. Under the stress of social and sexual deprivation their normal consciousness shifts or alters for shorter or longer periods, and they see, hear and experience another, unfamiliar dimension.

As we have seen, certain cult rituals are designed to heighten the sensibilities of the mind and render it receptive to dissociation and visionary moods. Many of these are found in initiation rites both ancient and modern. Judging from the evidence we have of the earlier secret societies, it seems that initiation was a profound and almost spiritual experience, and the candidate believed that during the ceremonies his soul ascended and descended through different psychic planes, which brought him face to face with the entities who inhabited them. He returned from the experience a different person, as if he had had a vision of another transcendent sphere and was admitted to the ultimate mysteries concerning the purpose of life on earth and the destiny of the soul after death.

The most famous and probably the oldest of the Grecian initiatory rites were the Eleusinian mysteries, so named from a site near Athens, which had been used for religious rituals from the fifteenth century B.C., by the Pelasgian predecessors of the Greeks. They became very much part of the Greek way of life and most Greeks of any consequence received their initiation at the famous shrine. The poet Pindar (d. 443 B.C.) said, 'Blessed is he who has seen the mysteries before being buried underneath the earth, for he knows the end of life and he knows its beginning'. Sophocles (d. 405 B.C.) echoes this opinion: 'Thrice blest are those mortals who depart to the abode of Hades after having seen the mysteries; they alone will have life there'. Socrates, Plato, Plutarch and a score of other eminent sons of Hellas have added their quota of tribute to the Eleusinian ritual of initiation. Although cynical or sceptical about many things, they regarded Eleusis with due seriousness.

Apuleius (A.D. 125–70), a native of Numidia in North Africa, who wrote in Latin, ends his classic book of tales, *The Metamorphoses* or *Golden Ass*, in a strain of mystical rapture. It contains a description, in part, of his own initiation after due preparation, including fasts and vigils, into the mysteries of Isis, the Great Mother, in which he passes in trance across the borderland of death into the presence of the gods of the underworld and the upper world.

Edward Collinge held that the climax of initiation into the mysteries was 'the exteriorization of the subject in the astral body in full consciousness', so that he might experience what will happen to him after he dies. The methods used to accomplish the projection probably included hypnosis and drugs, and the temptations and ordeals he underwent on the astral plane were deliberately designed as part of his initiation. The classical scholar, F. W. H. Myers, speaking on the subject says, 'These self-projections represent the most extraordinary achievements of the human will, and are perhaps acts which a man might perform equally well before and after death.'

Initiation rites take place in many secret societies even today, although in most cases the whole operation is considerably foreshortened, and consists largely of fabricated versions of earlier degrees with all tests of endurance and vigils eliminated, and the procedures adapted to suit the modern temperament. It is a social occasion and the lodges tend to be established according to professional or other common interest, and this indeed may be said to be the sole justification for their existence, for otherwise the ceremonies are banal and uninspiring. A few occult lodges insist on rather lengthier preparation in esoteric theory and practice, but the overall benefit in terms of intellectual and spiritual enlightenment is negligible.

The kind of initiation received in more serious lodges depends on the degree of the pupil's advancement and on the kind of occult training given in the school. No one should work out of his degree, or use methods appropriate to another school. What are known as the 'right-hand' schools insist on a religious or semi-religious ritual, employ traditional religious symbols, and lay much emphasis on proper moral conduct. The black magicians, or those who follow the left-hand path, resort to drugs and perverse sex, and thus short-circuit the procedure by these very potent measures, which in the long run befog any higher illumination that might be forthcoming for the candidate.

The use of sex rites for the attainment of super-normal experience is as old as occultism itself. According to esoteric, especially the left-hand tradition, sex can be a potent force in ceremonial magic, perhaps the most powerful that exists on the plane of nature. A form of vibratory energy is said to arise from any sexual operation, be it heterosexual, autosexual, homosexual or bestial, each form generating its own specific charge of power. During the tensions of sexual excitement a psychic vortex is created in the etheric planes and the resultant energy is tapped by the sorcerer for his own magical ends. It is an astral phenomenon and one of the most unwholesome features of left-hand occultism, such as is especially prominent in certain tantrik and taoist schools. The subject has already been dealt with in an earlier work and need not be gone into here.

Religious rites are another factor conducive to altered states of consciousness. Their solemnity can exalt the mind and often provide occasion for a change of key from the mundane to the spiritual. The sacrosanctity of places of worship, the austere grandeur of the greater temples and cathedrals, the magnificent decoration and subdued lighting of the interior, the vestments of the priests and acolytes, the chanting of psalms and prayers, all contribute to overawe the participant and attune him to the general atmosphere of spirituality around him. Rudolf Otto (1869–1937) in his classic treatise (1923) on the holy has described the 'numinous' feeling we have when confronted with hallowed situations, and the shuddering impact that contact with objects and places of great sacrosanctity can have on us. Such feelings are beyond reason or explanation.

Prolonged and monotonous repetition of chants, as we find practiced in certain primitive cults, causes the reasoning mind to relinquish control, and a secondary layer of consciousness to take over. Continuous singing, howling and ululation tend to cause physical exhaustion, reduce the oxygen content of the blood and bring on a state of light or heavy trance. Vibrations set up in the chambers of the head as a result of the reverberation of intoned phonemes or brief mantras also induce xenophrenia. Such methods are widely used because they are known to favour the emergence of visionary and mystical conditions.

For these reasons religion is universally accepted as the means for opening the path to another dimension, as nothing else can. In the words of Professor C. D. Broad (1953, p. 172), 'I think it more likely than not that in religious and mystical experience men come into contact with some Reality or aspect of Reality which they do not come in contact with in any other way.' A xenophrenic state usually accompanies religious illumination, mystical enlightenment and sudden conversion, when some spiritual 'meaning' is revealed to men.

Those who devote their lives to God have often first felt the 'call' to serve through some persistent inner prompting. Persons chosen for service are different from the ordinary run of men. Visionaries of a special kind, such as the pythonesses of the Grecian oracles, prophets of ancient renown, seers who advised the tribal chieftains, and others of that category, were chosen because of their natural faculty for tuning in to another channel, so to speak. The shamans of Siberia were recruited from among boys whose emotional and mental stability was easily disturbed. The two strata of the shaman's mind, the bodily and the astral, were loosely layered and it did not take much to separate them. He would go into a trance, travel over sea and skies, hear spirit voices, meet the ancestors, and bring back reports of the other world while in this state of projection.

Some similar quality goes into the making of the spiritualist medium, who must have the gift of displacing her normal consciousness to make room for another. Such a gift often manifests in childhood. It is known that good mediums tend to be highly sensitive, impressionable, and sometimes neurotic and inclined to hysteria. This does not necessarily mean any inferiority as compared with the ordinary stable personality, but only a tenser tuning of the psychic strings, which makes them responsive to the gentlest breezes from the other planes.

Transports of mental and spiritual exaltation, when the soul is caught up in rapture, can take one far beyond the confines of the material world. Religious records are filled with instances of people in a state of ecstasy being taken out of themselves and seeing visions of another dimension. The senses cease to function, mental activity is halted, and the soul seems to leave the body and experience a state of indescribable bliss. 'I knew a man,' said St Paul (2 Cor. 12: 3–4), and he was thought to be speaking of himself, 'whether in the body or out of the body, I cannot tell, God knows, who was caught up into paradise, and heard unspeakable words, which it is not lawful for a man to utter.'

In the power of the right mood, poets have their ecstatic moments, when inspiration grips the soul and guides their work. So strong is the imaginative impulse that it was often thought to be prompted by supernatural agency, or due to possession by a spirit. Plato in his *Ion* makes Socrates say, 'The authors of those great poems which we admire, utter their beautiful verses by a certain natural power, and in a condition of inspiration, possessed as it were by a spirit not their own, and in a state of divine insanity.' Socrates himself referred to his own *daemon*, who inspired and counselled him.

Probably no genius has had full control of his medium, for when he sets about his creative work he is soon taken over by this overmastering urge and becomes its helpless tool. He can do nothing with his apocalypse but in a tranquil moment try to marshal it in orderly fashion as best he can, and put it into words, music, paint, stone, formula or philosophy. Mystics, musicians, writers and others have frequently described the force that seemed to take hold of them and dictate what they should write. During the uncontrollable upsurge there comes to them a veritable cascade of ideas, sometimes even to exact words and phrases, whole poems, lengthy passages of prose, plots of novels. On recovering composure they find themselves unable to account for what they have written. Even scientists, living as they do in a more cold and intellectual world, have not been immune from the influence of outside inspiration. Speaking of his own subject, the astronomer Johann Kepler said, 'The roads by which men arrive at their insights into celestial matters seem to be almost as worthy of wonder as those matters themselves.'

The mystic Jakob Böhme declared, 'Before God, I do not know how the thing arises in me without the participation of my will. I do not even know that which I must write, and how it comes to be written.' The quietist and mystic, Mme Guyon (d. 1717) said, 'Before writing I did not know what I was going to write. While writing I saw I was writing things I had never known.' William Blake (d. 1827) said of certain of his works, 'The authors are in eternity.' George Sand (d. 1876) wrote of 'the other who sings as he likes, for the wind plays my old harp as it lists; I am nothing, nothing at all.' Her compatriot and colleague Alfred de Musset (d. 1857) writing of his poetic creations averred, 'It is not work, it is listening.'

Emily Brontë (d. 1848) said that each creative writer owns something of which he is not always the master, and which at times strangely works for itself. William Makepeace Thackeray (d. 1863) confessed that sometimes it seemed 'as if an occult power was working my pen'. Charles Dickens (d. 1870) said that when he sat down to write, 'some beneficent power showed it all to me.' The Russian composer P. I. Tchaikovsky (d. 1893) asserted that the overpowering force of the inspired mood was such that 'if it lasted any length of time without a break, no artist could survive it.' As the Indian sage and poet, Rabindranath Tagore (d. 1941), referring to one of his works declared, 'I am not the author of the book. I merely held the pen while a disembodied being wrote what he wished, using my pen and mind.'

Xenophrenia is dramatically exhibited in various forms of insanity. Many mental disorders remain a mystery, and psychiatry still has a great deal to learn about them. Schizophrenia might be taken as a typical example of the prevailing uncertainty in this field. Like hysteria and epilepsy, there is so far no absolutely precise definition of schizophrenia. The term covers an amorphous collection of symptoms; treatment, directed at the more obvious ones, is often drastic, and includes brain surgery, electric shock, and the use of drugs of high potency. The well-known psychiatrist Dr Thomas S. Szasz held that 'schizophrenia is a pseudoproblem such as that of ether in yesterday's physics' (Redlich and Freedman (1966), p. 459). The basic questions relating to diagnosis, prognosis, etiology, and therapy, are still largely unanswered.

There are many kinds of schizophrenia, and in most of them there is pronounced introversion and loss of contact with the outside world. The patient may suffer from paranoia and have delusions of grandeur and persecution. In the occult view, schizophrenia, like many other types of insanity, represents a pathological condition of the second body. The astral world starts making inroads into the waking consciousness. The patient hears voices, feels invisible influences and acts in obedience to insistent inner commands. His body assumes strange attitudes which he maintains without moving, for hours on end. Such catatonia is quite inexplicable, but certain of the static postures seem to have an archetypal character, and often resemble the fixed postures of Indian ascetics, or the more extravagant asanas practised by exponents of yoga.

Meditative techniques also help to promote trance and the transference of conscious awareness to the astral spheres. The techniques vary slightly in different places, the differences having a great deal to do with the religious and social environment of the practitioner. As a general principle it is not considered advisable for a student to depart from his traditional background in seeking meditative aids, particularly with regard to the imagery employed, since discordant influences may be contacted as a result.

In most meditative practices a person has first to assume a relaxed position, although people with exceptional stamina can meditate in any position. Socrates, a man not only of great spiritual endowment, but also of heroic physical endurance, could meditate standing up. It is recorded in Plato's *Symposium* that during the expedition to Potidaea the sage became wrapt in meditation and remained dead to the world, forgetting to eat or drink for the space of twenty-four hours. He had started his meditation in the morning and by noon word went around that he had been standing in thought since daybreak, and some men brought out their mats and kept watch to see whether he would stand all night. This he did and it was only with the return of

91

light that he stirred, offered up a prayer to the sun and went his way.

But few men are cast in his mould, and most must be content to assume a comfortable position, either sitting up or lying down, the eastern cross-legged pose being perhaps the most convenient. Yogic manuals recommend closing the eyes to block out distractions; Zen monks prefer to keep the eyes open, since closing the eyes leads to drowsiness and false trance, and not to wakeful contemplation.

Now comes the process of deep breathing, with the object of stabilizing the rhythm of the interior body. Here again methods differ, yoga concentrating the breath in the region of the nose, throat and top of the head, Zen in the belly. Then the mind is emptied of all practical, domestic and business problems, which is usually not as difficult as it sounds. If they insist on obtruding themselves, one should review them with dispassion and without involvement, and they will vanish. Let both body and mind get used to a regular time, place and regime for meditation, and one will soon find that when one enters the meditation room at the appointed time, the problems will automatically take their departure. Perseverance is important, and one must not be discouraged by initial set-backs and failures.

When the mind is emptied and one is physically and mentally relaxed, the next thing is to find something to think about. What one does is select a mental diagram or image of some kind, and here the images chosen are of considerable importance. The image serves as a kind of psychocosmogram, that is, a symbolic picture or map of the cosmos, or as an *axis mundi*, a central point of the universe, and is interlinked by a pattern of correspondences, whose magnificence and symbolism spring from the teachings of the particular schools. Contemplation of the diagram will evoke the appropriate response in the psyche of the student. Just any image will not do, for the old symbolic images used in meditation have their roots going far back into the past, and they are believed to be charged with the original potencies that inspired and sustained them through the centuries. Pick up the vibrations centring around any such symbol and you find yourself in tune with the traditional line of thought associated with it, and if this happens to conflict with your own background, psychic disharmony will result.

92

Hindus and Buddhists use a circular diagram known as a *mandala* to move out of focus with the physical surroundings and establish rapport with the occult spheres. The mandala has many picturesque variations on a basic theme, and its interior is always partitioned off into zones, and the zones dedicated to various deities who are invoked and invited to occupy the places reserved for them. Kabbalists meditate on the tree of the sefiroth, and certain other practitioners on the tarot cards or one of several other devices.

The sefiroth, according to the kabbalists, represent the emanations or outpourings of God, which together make up the created universe in its totality. They are pictured as ten inter-connected circles arranged roughly like a tree, and form the object of meditative disciplines in many schools of western occultism. Each sefira is associated with a particular astral sphere and is allotted its corresponding ruler, angel, image, colour, number, animal and other symbol. The aspirant carries out his exercises, goes into a trance, and 'rises on the planes', carrying full consciousness with him.

Like the mandala, the sefiroth have their obverse sides and can be full of danger. The evolutionary opposite of the sefiroth are the klifoth, which are the shells or husks of the ten original emanations, occupied by malevolent residual forces. In the duality of the kabbalistic concept the sefiroth and klifoth often symbolize two sets of opposing cosmic principles.

In the whole field of spontaneous, pathological and artificially induced xenophrenic states, the commonest and perhaps most extraordinary is sleep, and we shall consider it at slightly greater length. We all experience sleep every night of our lives, but why we sleep no one can tell. The nearest the psychologists have got to an explanation suggests that we sleep in order to dream. Dreaming is the reason for sleep. Yet why we dream, or what a dream is, again, no one can tell. As Dr Gustav Eckstein has said (1971, p. 708), 'Eighty sleep theories have come and gone'.

The first phase in the sleep sequence, known as hypnagogia, is characterized by a gentle drowsiness when the things around us seem to dim and recede from our consciousness. The next phase is often marked by a slight jerking of the body. This is caused by a miniature burst of energy in the brain, lasting only a fraction of a second, and has been likened to a minute epileptic seizure. When this happens the whole body is momentarily convulsed, and sometimes the sleeper lets out a muffled grunt.

In the course of a normal night's sleep a person has several dreams. The first dream starts about an hour after he has fallen asleep. Information based on research conducted in the dream laboratories of several countries, indicates that dreams last for about fifteen minutes, and occur about every ninety minutes. A person is known to be dreaming when REMS (rapid eye movements) are observed beneath the closed lids. If a sleeper is awakened in the middle of an REM period, he can recall the dream without difficulty. If he is awakened during the intervals between REMS, he does not remember having dreamt, so it is assumed that he was not dreaming.

In Hindu philosophy the gradation of man's total awareness ranges over four levels: first wakefulness, during which he is most involved in *maya* or the delusion created by his five senses; second, dreaming sleep when reality is merged with maya and can be viewed, but only symbolically; third, dreamless sleep during which reality can be perceived without images and symbols; fourth, the state of pure transcendent consciousness such as one achieves in samadhi, when the soul is exteriorized.

In this view dreams represent only one level of awareness, but it is possible to attain the deeper awareness of the third and fourth levels. These levels cannot be revealed through laboratory techniques, but only through profound intuitive experience.

We are still short of a proper understanding of the question, but it would be a mistake to dismiss a dream as a curious figment conjured up by the imagination from fragments of our day-to-day life, and presented to us every night for our entertainment. Dreams have significance if one learns to decode their meaning. This was realized by the Egyptian, Greek, Chinese and other civilizations of the past. The Jews took their dreams very seriously as we see from the Biblical stories of the dreams of Jacob, Joseph, Pharaoh and Nebuchadnezzar. In our own day the most eminent psychologists have taken up the ancient study of dream interpretation without losing their reputations.

Men in primitive societies believe that no distinction exists between dream life and waking life, and that both in their own way are equally valid. If a child of the Senoi tribe recalls hitting another child in a dream, his father will give him a present to take to the injured playmate. If a Fuegian sees a sick relative in a dream he will send a messenger next morning to enquire after his health. The Dyak of Borneo will repair to the witch-doctor to have his soul fished out, if he dreamt that he had fallen into a well. The missionary Dr W. B. Grubb, working among the Paraguayan Indians, was accused by one of them of having stolen gourds from his garden because the Indian had seen him do it in a dream.

Children, whose thought processes are said to resemble those of primitive people, often believe their dreams are true. Some children indeed seem to spend a great deal of time in a dream world, and the make-believe situations in which they enact their fantasies are but one remove from dreaming.

Some of the world's greatest thinkers have speculated about the intrinsic reality of dreams. The Greek philosopher Heraclitus (d. 475 B.C.) held that during sleep each dreamer returns to his 'true nature', as if his life in the waking state were unreal, and reality was lived out in dreams. Sir Thomas Browne (1605–82) said, 'We are somewhat more than ourselves in sleep, and the slumber of the body seems to be but the waking of the soul.'

Some have even doubted the possibility of distinguishing between the two. A story frequently quoted tells of the Chinese philosopher Chuang Tzu (369–286 B.C.) who dreamed that he was a butterfly and on awaking wondered whether he was Chuang Tzu who had just dreamed that he was a butterfly, or actually a butterfly now imagining that it was Chuang Tzu. As the first of the modern western philosophers, René Descartes, confessed, 'I am clearly aware that there are no marks by which the waking state can be distinguished from sleep'. His contemporary Blaise Pascal (1623–62), one of the great minds of the age and a mathematician of the highest calibre, gave it as his opinion that apart from faith, no one could be certain whether he was awake or sleeping. 'Who can tell', he says, 'but that when we think we are awake we are perhaps slumbering, from which slumber we awaken when we go to sleep.' The German philosopher Arthur Schopenhauer (1778–1860), like Pascal, could not be sure that there was any definite criterion by which dream and reality could be differentiated.

Most people have experienced at one time or another the immediacy of a vivid dream whose imagery and even message forces itself on their attention. The curtain between reality and dream seems to be lifted and they feel certain that they have dreamed true. 'I have had dreams', says J. B. Priestley (1972, p. 76), that in memory make much of my daytime life seem a mere faint blur.'

Dreaming like other xenophrenic states appears to bring into operation a part of one's self that is different from that interpreted by the cerebral cortex, or the conscious mind. John Locke in his *Essay Concerning Human Understanding* (1690), speculating on the 'sleeping soul', began with the assumption that a man cannot think without being conscious of it (Bk II, ch. I, 10–11). He then went on to suggest that while the body was asleep it would be possible for the soul to have its 'thinking, enjoyments and concerns, its pleasure or pain', apart from the body, of which the man was not conscious. Such a sleeping soul would then constitute an identity distinct from that of the waking man. Socrates asleep would be a different person from Socrates awake. Having presented his hypothesis Locke rejected it as impossible, for it did not fit into the framework of his philosophy.

This rejected hypothesis was none the less accepted by many thinkers, both before and after Locke. It rests on the elementary belief that a dual principle exists within a single entity. Man can have experiences during his so-called 'unconscious' hours while asleep, in trance, or in a drug-state, from which his reasoning mind is excluded by the very nature of waking consciousness. Our totality is multi-faceted and what we call consciousness does not cover the whole range of our experience. The psychologist recognizes that waking consciousness is only the tip of the iceberg and that even at our best we reveal only a fraction of our minds.

It has been said that while waking consciousness is a function of the cerebral cortex, dream consciousness is stimulated by the activity of such organs of the old brain as the thalamus and hypothalamus, that lie near the point where the stem of the spinal cord meets the cerebrum. This old brain has an earlier and different origin from the cerebral system; we share it with creatures lower down in the evolutionary scale, including frogs, and it differs in function from man's central nervous system.

Some students maintain that we dream not with a different part of our brains, but with a different part of our minds. Dreams are not the product of the sleeping cortex, or of the old brain, or the thalamus, or the sympathetic nervous system, but of a non-physical, asomatic system not situated in the brain at all, and it is this transcerebral system that is the vehicle for all psychic functions, and the thoughts and perceptions of xeno-phrenic states.

Dreams thus bring us in contact with an altogether different dimension. In dreams we possess paracognitive faculties, can relive the past, see the future, know what is happening at a distance, although the memory of all such data is garbled when they are passed through the mechanism of the brain on waking. The Greeks believed that prophecy occurred in dreams, and that if the right ritual preparations were made before sleeping, one could always dream true. Among modern researchers, John William Dunne (1875–1949), a mathematician and aeronautical engineer who studied dreams for many years, was a firm believer in the possibility of precognitive dreams.

Others again hold that dreams can serve as a medium of tele-pathic communication. Of the many instances of such telepathic dreams, the one cited by the novelist Rider Haggard (1856–1925) may be taken as a good illustration of a message and a feeling being communicated, in this case not by a man but by a dying animal. He relates how he once had a horrible dream in which he saw his black retriever lying on its side among brushwood or undergrowth of some sort, near a stretch of water. In the vision the dog was trying desperately to speak to him, and conveyed to him in some undefined fashion the fact that it was dying. 'My own personality', Haggard states, 'in some mysterious way seemed to be arising from the body of the dog.' He awoke from his nightmare with a feeling of awful oppression and a sense of making a terrified struggle for life such as would occur if one were in the act of drowning. He related the dream to his wife and it was later found that during the same night the dog had been struck by a passing train on an open-work bridge and the animal had been thrown down into the water below and had drowned.

The whole subject presents fascinating problems that still await solution. The origin of dreams, their causation, content, and significance are all far from clear. The bizarre figments of the dream world and the behaviour of those who take part in it are taken for granted without demur while we sleep, and the sleeping mind is undeterred by the incongruous experiences it undergoes.

Present-day investigators say that a dream lasts for as long as it takes to play itself out, which may be up to thirty minutes. Other theorists believe that the dream is not enacted in time and that the mind has an amazing talent for fitting a dream instantaneously into a situation that is consistent with what is happening to the body at the time. If our feet protrude momentarily outside the blanket on a cold night we build up an elaborate scenario that takes us on a long trek through Antarctica.

At the end of the last century a French researcher, Alfred Maury, recorded a lengthy dream in which he participated in the events of the French Revolution. He witnessed many of the horrors that took place, conversed with the protagonists, was himself implicated in a conspiracy, was tried, condemned, and led to the place of execution. As the blade of the guillotine came hurtling down he awoke to find that the pole of the bed's tester had fallen on his neck. He concluded that the dream had lasted only for a split second, and that the whole panorama of Revolutionary events had been conceived and flashed instantaneously through his mind to provide his consciousness with a reason for the sharp pain he experienced on the nape of his neck (*Man, Myth and Magic*, p. 708).

One could say perhaps that there is something literally out of this world about dreams. Because the material plane is not the natural environment of the astral double, it must periodically seek to be refreshed in its own element, and this it does when it discoincides during sleep and lives in its own apparently irrational universe. There is no time, as we know it, in dreams; there is no logic or consistency. Neither do dreams exist in measurable space. They have a dimension of their own, and as Professor H. H. Price has said (1968, p. 254), there is no sense in asking whether an image seen in a dream was situated 'two and a half inches to the north-west of the dreamer's left ear'. It belongs to a different plane.

St Thomas Aquinas said that the syllogisms of logic go awry in dreams, and Freud remarked that the dreamer cannot do arithmetic, so far is dreaming removed from the practical issues of our world. If dreams open the door to the real world, that world is not rational. Wilhelm Wundt (1832–1920), German psychologist, called dreaming a state of 'normal temporary insanity'. The experiences of xenophrenic states make strange bedfellows of the lunatic, the drug addict, the mystic and the dreamer.

It seems that the rational moulds into which our waking lives are forced need to be shattered at regular short intervals, so that we may be periodically released from the rigid and maddening restraints of reason and common sense. Perhaps in order to preserve our sanity every day, we need to go insane every night.

Further reading   Burney (1952); Clissold (1870); Foulkes (1966); Harding (1948); Heywood (1959); Kleitman (1963); Ritter (1954); Solomon (1961); Tart (1969).

Chapter VII

Methods of Projection

Before we go on to describe some of the methods of conscious projection of the astral body, it would be fitting to summarize the words of caution that have been voiced from time to time by responsible exponents of the subject, about the risks and potential dangers involved in experiments in dissociation.

Spontaneous exteriorization, such as might occur during illness or accident, is one thing, but enforced dissociation is another matter altogether. A prominent psychic once said that those who dabble in these pursuits are likely to become afflicted with pathologies of the astral body, and the auras of such persons have been described as 'ragged, muddy and malodorous'. Even simple methods of projection have their hazards. For one thing, the excitement of the new adventure might result in excessive preoccupation with astral phenomena and occult experiences. It is not unknown for students to become so absorbed in the subject that they lose touch with the everyday world, become alienated from family and friends, and suffer all the domestic, social and material consequences. Again, if one is of a nervous temperament, the experience of finding oneself isolated in the astral plane might create a sense of panic and sudden shock leading to temporary or even permanent insanity, and in extreme cases, death. Likewise, a too sudden return for any reason might, by violent repercussion, cause severe damage to the nervous system.

If the astral body has once or twice been forcibly moved out of alignment by recourse to more drastic methods like psychedelic drugs or some other xenophrenia-inducing agent, the door to the outer dimensions that is normally shut tight during one's waking hours may be loosened, or worse still, remain permanently ajar, creating a 'leak' from outside. Symptoms of such a state may include headaches, dizziness, loss of memory, hypochondria, fainting spells, paralysis, 'voices', hallucinations and nightmares. If

100

persisted in, the exteriorizations may begin to occur spontaneously and projections recur without volition and go beyond control. In extreme cases the hinder side of things, normally
concealed in the unconscious, might turn about and merge with
the events of everyday life. An even more serious possibility is
also to be envisaged. The astral body is intimately connected, no
one knows by what mysterious corridors, to the inner recesses
of the self, perhaps even the soul, and incautious experiments
with astral projection would involve tampering with the delicate
balance of this relationship, resulting in a progressive disintegra-
tion of the psyche.

Another, more concrete hazard of astral travel, is physical
injury to the unconscious body left behind. Before projection
an expert always assumes an easy relaxed posture; if his body
is moved from its position, the 'fit' of the returning astral might
not be in exact alignment, and reintegration can be slightly
delayed. Dizziness and mental obfuscation can ensue, and this can
continue for some time until the two bodies have coincided
perfectly again.

The gravest danger during projection is the possibility of the
death of the unprotected physical body, whether by accident or
murder. For this reason trained occultists are careful to leave
their physical bodies in the care of a trusted disciple or friend,
when they expect to be away for a few hours.

The necessity for this precaution has been noted from very
early days, as we find from the legend of the Asiatic Greek
mystic, Hermotimus of Clazomene, who had the gift of astral
projection and would abandon his body for days on end, and
journey to remote regions of the material and astral planes to
gather prophetic lore. He would leave his body in the keeping
of his wife, cautioning her to be sure that it was not moved in
any way. Returning home he would regale her with his adventures,
unaware of the fact that she was growing more and more resent-
ful of the enforced loneliness she had to endure during his long
absences. Accordingly, she decided to give him a fright and put
a stop to his excursions. She sought the help of two of her husband's friends, not knowing that they were his rivals in sorcery.
She left them to move his body into an adjacent room, but
instead they set fire to it. The wretched man hastily returned
in his astral form but found himself cut off and isolated in the

astral world. For years, it was said, his ghost could be seen in the vicinity of his home, crying pitifully to be restored to his physical self.

To the layman, many of the exercises given below might appear harmless in themselves, but when practised by the wrong type of person, particularly someone who is emotionally unstable, they can lead to nervous and mental illnesses of various kinds. Some of the exercises are definitely dangerous and should never be attempted by anyone in normal circumstances. Into this category fall the various techniques of starvation and exhaustion, and above all, the methods of inducing instantaneous trance, like partial strangulation by pressure on certain nerves in the neck, which can send one out in a few seconds, and if not properly done, can kill. All these methods were known and practised in the ancient world, including Greece, where they formed part of the secret rites of the archaic Dionysia festival. To a lesser extent they are still practised in India, the Middle East, and certain parts of North Africa.

An ever-present danger of most kinds of projection, even when adequate precautions are taken, is the possibility of being mistaken for dead. It has been pointed out that cataleptic conditions often accompany projections and other xenophrenic states, with symptoms closely resembling death. The so-called vegetative concomitants of life may be brought to a standstill, or near enough cessation to deceive an ordinary examination by the family physician. The heart may show no perceptible beat, breathing may be absent and the body cold to the touch. This condition of deep trance might occur at any time during projection, and may be mistaken for death by stroke or heart failure, and the person certified as dead. In cases of severe catalepsy there is, says Oliver Fox (1962, p. 42), 'a very serious risk of premature burial'.

It is medically well established that there is no absolutely certain method of distinguishing death from what is known as suspended animation, and cases of inadvertent premature burial or near-burial have been recorded right down to modern times. These records, which are more numerous than one might think, relate only to those instances that have come to light by accident, and naturally exclude a possibly large number that remain unknown. While theoretically no one is free from this danger unless he dies by being shot through the heart, or is hanged and left hanging for some time, or mutilated and mangled beyond recovery, or until putrefactive decomposition sets in that totally excludes the possibility of the body's return to life, the risk is greatly increased for those who practise astral projection, as the inert body found by relatives or friends might easily be regarded as dead, and this fact even confirmed by the doctor.

Travel in the astral planes, as taught in certain occult schools, should be undertaken, if at all, with considerable caution. The callow neophyte who inadvertently ventures into a dimension for which he is not properly equipped, will fall an easy prey to the non-human entities who are native to those spheres, and who are not slow to attack anyone trespassing on their preserves. Accounts of astral projection even by experienced occultists often describe the encounters with hostile beings in the planes. Those who have been injured in the astral do not necessarily show evidence of their injury in the physical body, but are none the less affected mentally by it. Sometimes the entities take advantage of the person's absence from the body to prevent his complete reoccupation of it on his return, thus causing obsession, and in more serious cases, possession.

Unscrupulous adepts of the left-hand path can take advantage of beginners who venture into the planes to acquire power over their astral body, and thus have an overriding influence on their lives. More commonly they tamper with the cord that links the astral double to the inert body of the practitioner. The cord is susceptible to torsion and black magicians sometimes twist, knot or otherwise injure it. This results in mental disturbance, nightmares, hysteria, and the intrusion of the occult planes into daily life. When the cord is thus injured its hold on the body is tenuous, and this leads to the early death of the victim.

The English hermetic mystic, Anna Kingsford (1846–88), who had a great knowledge of these matters, writing of the dangers of dilettantism said, 'Those who enter into relations with the powers of the astral and elemental, without having made sure of their hold on the celestial, render themselves accessible to the infernal' (Maitland (1896), vol. 1, p. 240).

These then are among the dangers mentioned by occultists. Researchers note that a strong constitution and 'rude' health tend to inhibit all forms of occult activity, whereas a certain constitutional delicacy and nervous sensitivity seem to favour astral projection. For this reason the warnings given are doubly applicable to those who have a weak heart, are highly strung, neurotic or addicted to drugs. It is generally admitted that a certain degree of psychological instability is often found in those who dissociate easily, and such persons can do themselves great harm if they deliberately aggravate their weakness by projective practices.

A small minority of people are endowed with the natural ability of spontaneous dissociation. They retain consciousness and return to recall what they have experienced. In simple societies recruits for the vocation of shaman and witch-doctor were selected from among adolescents who showed a natural tendency to dissociation and trance states. They were quickly spotted, and if their parents were willing, were segregated for training.

By and large most people never reach the condition of conscious projection, however hard they try. The average man, who clings like a limpet to the affairs of the mundane world, is guided by a natural instinct against trifling with the occult, and is protected by his innate scepticism from credulity in such matters. If in addition he is physically robust, he is further rendered immune to the hazards of projection by a constitutional incapacity to experience more than a very slight degree of discoincidence, as during sleep. A few persons have a brief experience just once or twice in their lives, quite inadvertently, as in serious illness. Some acquire the ability to project after a few effortless exercises. A sampling of such exercises is given here.

If anyone is serious about practising projection, he should set aside a certain day and time for the disciplines. It is advisable that the stomach be empty and that no food be taken at least four hours before the exercises. A quiet room is essential, where there is no likelihood of disturbance, and during the exercises the room should preferably be in semi-darkness. The time when discoincidence normally takes place is from approximately one hour before to about three hours after midnight, when one would otherwise be in a state of deep natural sleep. Some experts say that the proper weather conditions are also important, especially during the early stages of the practice. Atmospheric tension or thunderstorms, when the air is humid or muggy, are not conducive to the best results. The weather should be clear and dry, with a high barometer. The best room temperature is between 70° to 80° Fahrenheit.

Relaxation is the first step in dissociation. Muscular tension, mental strain, over-zealousness, are all inhibiting factors and should be avoided. What is often found to be a disturbing element is the thought that one has to complete the exercise within a given time. If any such note of urgency obtrudes it will be sufficient to interfere with the whole procedure. The pressures of time must be lifted, and the schedule for the exercises so arranged that there is no likelihood of any such anxieties being created. There is no time-limit for the routine, and even ten minutes regularly devoted to it are enough. If nothing happens, just go to bed. Besides this, any intense striving after exteriorization, or attempts at super-concentration, or prolonged intellectual exercises, hinder rather than help the process. The mental strings must be slack. A state of mind-wandering, even reverie, helps to 'unfocus' consciousness. As one student put it, 'I never concentrate. I allow silence to enwrap me, and then "sense" the house, room and person I wish to see.'

If concentration is to be directed to a specific objective, it should be confined to the day before the actual experiment is tried. During the experiment itself, as during all the exercises, the mind should be relaxed, and then the objective on which one's attention and expectation have been focused during the preceding day, will spontaneously help to give a fillip to the projective forces.

Achieving the right frame of mind during the exercises can be further assisted by building up the correct psychological groundwork at other times. The power of suggestion is now generally accepted as having a considerable influence on the way we conduct our lives and on the success or failure of what we undertake. We are often unconsciously motivated in our actions by the suggestions implanted in us in the course of our everyday activities. This power can be turned very effectively to one's advantage by making active use of auto-suggestive procedures. A strong desire to project, a frequent reiteration of this desire, and whenever possible holding in the mind an image of oneself projected, will go a long way to promoting the success of the operation when it is undertaken.

Intense desire to be elsewhere can itself in certain circum-

H

stances lead to projection, for the overmastering nature of the wish to be there creates the necessary conditions both for the departure of the astral, and its reception at the other end. In his *Nurslings of Immortality* Raynor Johnson remarks (1957, p. 101) that there are a number of well-attested cases in which deliberately created apparitions have been clearly seen. 'The concentrated efforts of the will-to-appear to another person have led to the latter perceiving an apparition of the agent.' August Strindberg (1849–1912), Swedish author and dramatist, described how once while he was in Paris in 1895 and driven almost insane by the failure of his second marriage, he felt an intense longing to be with his family, and suddenly found himself in a room of his home in which he saw his mother-in-law sitting and playing the piano. She saw him in his astral form and wrote to him enquiring if he were ill.

The key to all astral projection is visualization, which demands the power of sustained imagination, and various exercises have been devised to develop this power. The stages of progress in these exercises are: visualization with eyes closed, or seeing through the closed lids, first without movement and then with movement; then visualization with the eyes open. These are not mutually exclusive and may be practised alternately. A few examples will suffice.

You look at a simple drawing, then shut the eyes and try to fix the picture in the mind. This should be done without concentration. It helps to look at the sketch for a second, then shut the eyes for three seconds and hold the picture in the mind; open the eyes again to check the details and shut them once more, and so on for a dozen or, if need be, a hundred times, until every detail of the picture is vividly clear in the mind's eye. From there one goes on to more complex illustrations and coloured pictures, which should all be given a life-like vitality and realism. Further practice can be had by placing a number of objects on a tray and trying to recall them with the eyes shut, not by mental association or other mnemonic tricks, but simply by visualizing their position on the tray.

Another exercise is to take a simple three-dimensional object like a book, examine the outside carefully, paying attention to the illustrated cover, the title, the spine and the back cover. Shut the eyes and imagine that the book is standing upright on a table at eye level. Visualize walking around the book so that each side slowly comes into view as you walk.

Sit comfortably in a semi-darkened room. Shut your eyes and imagine you are sitting in the other corner. Try the same exercise lying down, your feet pointing to the door; shut your eyes and imagine your head is towards the door and your feet in the opposite direction. These exercises strengthen your powers of imaginative reorientation.

Sit comfortably in a chair, having placed before you another chair facing in the same direction as your own. Close your eyes and imagine that you see the back of yourself seated in the chair in front. Now without rising from your seat try to move forward into that chair and to merge with the form in front. Look through his eyes and see from his position.

Lie on your back and shut your eyes. Imagine that you are rising from your body into the air; not too far, just an inch or so. You must lose all awareness of the pressure of the bed against your back or the pillow against your head, and feel that you are actually floating in the air. From the same prone position on your back and with your eyes closed, think of yourself standing up at the foot of the bed and watching yourself as you lie in it. The thought must be intensified as if your consciousness were actually transferred to the watcher.

Again lie on your back with eyes closed, and concentrate on the loosening form of your astral. While the physical body remains motionless imagine that the astral is turning in bed and lying on its side; then that it is on its stomach, then on its other side, and finally on its back. The process should be gradually speeded up. It is as if the physical body were lying immovable within a loose cylinder which was being rapidly rotated.

All the above exercises are done with the eyes shut, and in many cases their performance can result in exteriorization. Some people find eventually that the simple operation of closing the eyes triggers projection, if the mind is ready. One woman speaking of her method of visiting friends in the astral says, 'My journey is accomplished with the greatest of ease—I am simply there when I shut my eyes.'

The next stage is a series of visualizations in which simple movements are carried out in the second body, while the eyes are open. To begin with, hold the hand up, palm outwards. Try not to think of the physical hand, but through half-open lids imagine the astral hand within or around it. Slowly shift the astral hand out of alignment with the physical. See this second hand distinctly; then move the astral hand some distance off.

More advanced exercises are undertaken on the same pattern as those already given in which the eyes are shut, but these should now be performed with the eyes open, so that when the astral double is visualized as having moved, the actual vision of the practitioner moves with it. In other words, he has to identify with his astral form.

Apart from these methods, which if persisted in long enough often result in exteriorization, there are several specific dissociation techniques, some of which, although quite simple, are regarded as effective. Thus, staring fixedly at a small object placed some distance away and slightly above eye level can lead to dissociative states. The eyes get unfocussed, normal consciousness is relaxed and the unconscious takes over. The best way is to gaze at a small bright point, like a candle flame or a spot on a white wall. Here again there must be no strain or effort; the mind moves lazily and abstractedly over the outer fringes of the object and the imagination is let loose.

This is a very old practice in the East, now widely adopted in the western world. The American occult group known as Eckankar, led by Paul Twitchell, which teaches astral projection, or 'soul travel', by correspondence, recommends lying on one's back and staring without blinking at a coloured disc placed between the eyebrows.

The same group also uses other methods that are reminiscent of the religious exercises of eastern sects. Thus, they chant magical syllables and simultaneously perform cryptic gestures. It is well known that continued monotonous movements and monotonous chanting induce xenophrenia. Even the simple repetition of one's name can be effective when carried on over a length of time. The poet, Lord Tennyson, spoke of a kind of waking trance that he frequently had from boyhood when alone. 'This has come upon me through repeating my own name to myself silently, till all at once, as it were out of the intensity of the consciousness of individuality, individuality itself seemed to dissolve and fade away into boundless being; and this not a confused state, but the clearest of the clearest.'

Long period of medita? , auto hypno. suggs'

Using beads, or a 'fingering piece' like a smooth round stone which is rolled about between finger and thumb, to the accompaniment of some cryptic verse, syllabic sound or phoneme, can lead to trance states. Methods involving prolonged rhythmic breathing, either by special exercises or by chanting mantras, decrease the amount of carbon dioxide in the blood, alter its adrenalin content, and affect the oxygenation of the brain. Dizziness and temporary blackouts ensue, and visual images appear that might be of strange and distant places. Experienced practitioners have their own chosen methods. In his survey of American occultism John Godwin quotes (1972, p. 20) a young American projectionist, Wanda Moore, 'I blank out my mind, slow down my breathing and pulse rate and concentrate on a patch of light somewhere in the back of my brain. It takes me from three to fifteen minutes—then I'm off.'

Another experient, mentioned by Ralph Shirley, uses a different technique. She writes (1972, p. 29), 'I close my eyes and have a feeling of going over backwards.' This is done by lying on the back and imagining that one's legs are rising up and over the head, the rest of the body slowly taking an upside-down position. As the somersault proceeds one becomes dizzy and is suddenly propelled out into the astral. Everyone has a vertigo threshold, which is crossed by some physical situation, and if a person knows his particular weakness he can use it to induce dizziness.

Less difficult is simple visualization that one is ascending or turning around rapidly. This should in all cases be accompanied by the vivid sensations that would normally go with such movements. Useful images are: climbing a ladder, ascending in a lift, flying upwards, swimming upstream or against the tide, rising up in a swing, floating like a bubble in the air, rising straight up, rising horizontally, sitting in a merry-go-round, whirling round and round.

One's particular phobia likewise provides an escape hatch for the astral. Any situation where normal consciousness is benumbed by fear or panic may render the experience xenophrenic. There is a sense of timelessness, the awareness of things around one vanishes and the astral loosens itself and is displaced. Here again a strong imaginative visualization of being in a position of one's phobic weakness can help displacement. Wide open spaces stretching out to the endless distance, walls suddenly shrinking and

109

Very dangerous & stupid because those insects will actually become "real" in the astral plane!

hemming one in, immeasurable heights and precipices, long stretches of water, and, to those who hate them, spiders, cats, furry creatures, hairy insects, or any deeply personal terror and nightmare theme, can send a person out of himself if he thinks about it with sufficient realism.

A simple method of exteriorization is described by George Du Maurier in his novel *Peter Ibbetson* (1891) which portrays with a strange realism the interwoven dream lives of the hero and the girl he loves. Sentenced to life imprisonment for manslaughter, he is visited in his dream by Mary and in turn visits her by project-ing his astral form from his prison cell. This he does by putting his hands behind his head, crossing his feet and then willing him-self to the rendezvous. One of the subjects mentioned by Celia Green in her book on lucid dreams tells how he used the identical method described in Du Maurier's novel. He spent one full day concentrating as far as possible on the idea of projecting himself to a certain place that night. When he went to bed he assumed the position described and immediately found himself in the street out of his body (Green (1968a), p. 168).

Among the recommended methods devised by experimenters today is one in which exteriorization occurs through causing the physical body to tingle. Here the person lies down in a relaxed position and concentrates on the toe of one foot until it starts to feel warm and begins to tingle. He transfers his concentration to the next toe and so on, till the tingling sensation spreads to the other toes, then to the other foot, then up both feet to the calves, knees, hips, stomach, chest, arms, neck and head until the whole body is buzzing. At some stage in this procedure, if properly carried out, the practitioner will find himself out of his body.

Related to this are projections induced by vibrations. These vibrations are engendered in some inner layer of the body that seems to underlie the physical frame, and whose mechanism can be brought into activity by an act of will, to generate psychic im-pulses. The vibrations can start anywhere, the foot, abdomen, arm or head, and are accompanied for a time by strange internal sounds. The physical body usually remains immobile throughout. The vibrations are not dangerous and the sensations of mild electric shocks that sometimes accompany them do not last for more than a few seconds. If one is alarmed at the unusual

110

experience the spell is broken and all is quiet immediately, but if left to work itself out the waves slowly dissipate and the physical body is left with a sensation of warmth and comfort. While in this state the double is suddenly projected. Many projections in the ordinary course too, start and end with vibrations.

A very old method entails concentration on one of the traditional glyphs used for meditation in certain cults. These glyphs are associated with colours, emblems and other tokens, which are thought to be connected by occult correspondences. They have to be mastered, and the subconscious enriched through their study. It involves long sessions of 'brooding' among the symbols, in a kind of relaxed and free reverie, as a result of which the astral body is gently detached and loosened from the physical.

Among these devices are the mandala of the Buddhists and Hindus, and the sefirothic tree of the kabbalists. Another is the tarot pack, of which only the twenty-two trump cards, bearing coloured drawings of allegedly ancient origin, are used. A card is picked at random from the trumps, and the scene meditated on with eyes closed, and enlarged and enlivened by imaginative insight. Then, as the experts have it, one 'enters the scene'. *of a card*

Many experimenters describe how they have assisted projection by imagining that they are crawling through or forcing themselves out of a narrow opening or crevice. In this exercise the person lies on his stomach and not on his back. Describing her own way of embarking on astral journeys, the late Dion Fortune (d. 1946) said (1952, p. 155) that hers always began with a curtain of symbolic colour through whose folds she passed. In his book on the subject, J. H. Brennan speaks (1971, p. 29) of five basic elemental doorways to the astral plane, each associated with one of the alchemical elements, and each with its own distinctive shape and colour: the fire symbol is a red triangle, air a blue circle, water a silver crescent, earth a yellow square, ether a black oval. The practitioner meditates on the chosen symbol, visualizing it as large as a door, seeing its shape and colour vividly, and then walking through it. Constant perseverance in this method will in time build up a strong suggestion of going through the door, and a sudden vivid realization of a new dimension will confirm that one has indeed crossed the threshold. *DooR INTER - DimenSioNAL*

The magician Aleister Crowley (1875–1947) devised for his pupils a method that is now well known in occult circles. The student imagines a shut door set against a blank wall. On the door is a glyph or symbol that has previously been the subject of his meditation. The idea is to visualize the door slowly opening, and then to pass through it. Kenneth Grant who tried this method reports (1972, p. 93) that after he had projected his consciousness through the door, 'I found myself suddenly bereft of my body; a sensation of extreme lightness and freedom characterized my movements.' The landscape that lay before him had a glow and reality beyond earthly scenes, and it was peopled by figures resembling human beings, with whom he was able to communicate.

An occult organization known as the Stella Matutina, a splinter group of the once-famous Order of the Golden Dawn, issued a manual of instructions for its initiates under the name of Flying Rolls. Among them was a kind of magical operation designed to promote projection of the double, called 'Travelling in the Spirit Vision'. In this exercise consciousness is detached from the body and transferred to a phantom figure especially conjured up out of the astral sphere. The progressive steps include visualizing the figure walking before one, then imagining that the figure is oneself, looking through the eyes of the figure, feeling its sensations, and finally, actually directing its operations.

A Japanese method of astral travel known as 'counting the steps' was employed by Shinto magicians to deliver messages to distant pupils, and by the lovelorn to visit their sweethearts. Here again a strong power of visualization is essential. The person concerned lies down, preferably at a time when the other party, that is, the prospective recipient, is likely to be asleep. He assumes a relaxed position and concentrates on the trip, and then imagines himself carrying out his mission from start to finish. He steps out of his house and sets out in the general direction of the other person's residence. Now it does not matter how far that other person's house is, and whether he has to cross the seas to get there. What is important is that he should step out in imagination a given number of paces, about sixty are enough. He should count sixty paces, and visualize himself standing at the door of the house. He must then knock at the door, be invited in and meet the other person. Visualization must be particularly strong here. Delivering his message distinctly he must then depart. Outside the house he should take the same number of steps back till he returns home.

Celia Green reports (1968a, p. 178) an almost identical method employed in the course of an experiment in parapsychology, in which a woman living in Stockholm paid an astral visit to a person living near London, whom she had never met. She relaxed in bed and tried to think of herself performing the journey: 'Now I am travelling by train to Gothenberg . . . now with the steamer across the North Sea . . . arriving at Tilbury . . . travelling to London . . . then taking the train. . . .' She found herself in an English street and was soon in the house concerned. Later an actual visit to the place confirmed the details of what she had seen during her vision.

The hypnagogic state of drowsiness that precedes sleep is sometimes used as a starting point for projection. This borderland condition between somnolence and slumber is a difficult one to maintain because of the overwhelming desire to let go and fall asleep. The method has been described as 'sending the body to sleep while the mind is kept awake'. Pre-Buddhist Bon magicians of Tibet were said to be past-masters in astral projection, and by means of a rite known as *mi-lam* could enter at will into their own dreams, and also those of others, in full consciousness and without loss of memory afterwards.

The Russian mystic P. D. Ouspensky (1878–1947), a disciple of Gurdjieff, used to practise entering into his dreams while he was in a 'half-dreaming state just before falling asleep', and learned to retain consciousness in sleep, so that he was able to observe and later study his own dreams. One way to achieve this is to build up a dream picture during hypnagogia and then 'step into it' and participate in the dream consciously. If the subject falls asleep that is the end of the night's experiment, so special methods are used to hold the hypnagogic state as long as possible. For example, the subject lies on his back, with the body relaxed and arms by his side. When he feels he is getting drowsy he raises the lower half of one arm to a vertical position on the bed so that it stands upright resting on the elbow. Each time he falls asleep the arm drops and he is awakened. This will prevent sleep, protract hypnagogia, and assist projection.

Conscious projection is also possible and apparently not infrequent from the state of sleep. Experimenters have found that it helps to have as a last meal a supper of highly salted food, without drinking water. Intense thirst, if it does not awaken the subject, will cause him to project. In Sylvan Muldoon's opinion

113

suppressed desire is the greatest single factor in inciting spontaneous projection, but this applies particularly to hunger and thirst. In general it is felt that if a purer type of experience is desired, it helps to reduce the demands and discomforts of the body.

Like sleep, unconsciousness produced by anaesthetics has occasionally initiated spontaneous exteriorization. The subject has not so far been explored in depth, but a number of eminent persons have vouched for the efficacy of anaesthesia in inducing visionary experiences. Sir Humphry Davy (1778–1829) experimented with nitrous oxide gas, and on inhaling it 'lost all connection with physical things', and on return from his experience declared, 'Nothing exists but thoughts. The universe is composed of impressions, ideas, pleasures and pains.' Sir James Crichton-Browne said that when one is under the influence of nitrous oxide it seems as if the profoundest secrets of the universe are being revealed to one. The psychologist William James took nitrous oxide and was profoundly stirred by what he felt was its extraordinary power to stimulate the 'mystical consciousness'. He said, 'Depth beyond depth of truth seems revealed to the inhaler.'

Similar qualities are ascribed to chloroform. Dr George Wylde, suffering great pain, inhaled chloroform to obtain relief, and 'suddenly found my soul, clothed and in the form of my body standing two yards outside my body which lay motionless on the bed'. He later called on three professional 'chloroformists' to enquire whether any of their patients had ever had such experiences and was informed that several had expressed such ideas and had experienced similar sensations. One patient after an anaesthetic said, 'I thought I had got at the bottom of the secrets of nature.'

Drugs, especially the hallucinogens, are among the most drastic of all methods used for achieving discoincidence. As the drug takes effect it seems to the experient as if another dimension, layered between the physical and astral worlds, slides into his awareness and he is conscious of both worlds from an inter-land. The senses become confused and the ordinary world around him takes on a dream-like quality. Familiar objects become distorted and his perception of light, colour, movement, size and sound is dramatically altered. There are strange distortions of space, material objects, and especially time. Days slip by like minutes and minutes like days. Drugs like hashish, psilocybin, and mescaline produce dis-

114

sociation, fantasies and symptoms akin to insanity. The effects of LSD often resemble schizophrenia.

From the point of view of exteriorization these chemically induced altered states of mind have many disadvantages. For one thing the subject not only does not see clearly, he cannot bring back a proper report of what he has seen. The experience of drug-induced projection is therefore regarded as 'impure' by most practitioners. Drugs more than any other method put into abeyance the higher faculties of the psyche and permit the more illusory perceptions to take over. The ill effects of drugs are a fact to be taken seriously into account before trying this method. According to occultists the psychic 'atmosphere' of the drug addict is exceedingly unhealthy, as compared even with the common criminal, whose atmosphere, says Dion Fortune (1952, p. 67), 'however bad is not nearly so noxious'.

Further reading   Crookall (1964); King (1971); Muldoon (1936, 1958); Ophiel (1961); S. Smith (1965).

Chapter VIII

The Planes and their Inhabitants

The natural habitat of the exteriorized double is the astral plane, a region of many zones, having ranges of manifestation within those zones, and grades of being within the ranges, each with its own features of bewildering variety. A paradoxical situation prevails in the planes, revealing a lack of rationality, coherence and common sense, and the absence of causality, materiality, time and space as we understand them. Yet this location is not cloud-cuckoo-land but, to those who have experienced it, vastly more real than the world about us.

Maurice Nicoll, a well-known specialist in psychological medicine, who wrote analytical commentaries on the teachings of Gurdjieff, spoke of the fascinating territory that lay within each of us, an inner world which we should try to explore if we wished to make the best use of our lives. Within us we can find, according to him, all the landscape we find without; forests and mountains, snowy pinnacles and burning deserts. And cities and towns as well, with their palaces and slums, and he bade his readers explore their inner psyche and decide for themselves where they wished to live.

Where the astral planes are, is not easy to define, but in the view of occult exponents they are not places as we understand place. They are not different countries in a geographical sense, nor different levels like the floors of a skyscraper. The astral world is sometimes said to be in a fifth dimension, again a term of convenience that is not related to the dimensions of the physicists. The planes are not at 'right angles' to our world or anything of that nature, but belong to a totally different order of experience, that needs 'second sight' or a 'sixth sense' to apprehend. But although Elsewhere the planes are also Here, and all their dimensions are present in ours. They intersect with our physical plane and we are separated from them by a razor's edge.

Scientists today do not deny the possibility of other spheres of which we are unaware, interfused with the material sphere and functioning, as it were, on a different frequency. These spheres are open to a specialized mode of perception and offer a particular range of experience not found in our own. The physicist Denys Wilkinson says (1960, p. 96), 'Perhaps there do indeed exist universes interpenetrating with ours; perhaps of a high complexity; perhaps containing their own forms of awareness; constructed out of other particles and other interactions than those we know now. . . .'

All the planes together form a single continuum of a vast world, presenting a rich and multiform landscape, populated by denizens much more varied in character and activity than those of our earth. The planes comprise the habitations of all supernatural entities, the locale of gods and demons, the void where the thought-forms dwell, the region inhabited by spirits of the air and other elementals, and the various heavens and hells with their angelic and demonic hosts. The zones interpenetrate and there appears to be a curious overlapping in parts, but it would seem that the inhabitants of one zone cannot freely enter into contact with other zones when they please, and the exact nature of their mutual relationship is not clear.

Anything approaching an exhaustive description of the planes and their populations is obviously not feasible, nor can their extent be more than guesswork, for we have no clear knowledge what they hold, or how we can get there. We are not sure whether they move into our range, wave-length or rate of vibration, where they can be perceived by us, or whether we are translated to their level.

Certain areas fall occasionally within the range of sensitives, but even the ordinary person may become a percipient in exceptional circumstances. Then the solid objects around him shimmer and melt away, or seem to become semi-transparent, and the plane that is being presented to him rolls forward and comes into focus, or in some other manner is brought to the borders of vision. He may become aware of presences, hear or rather overhear voices, not with the senses but with some interior organ, for it is his astral consciousness that presumably experiences the planes. Aleister Crowley, an expert in the matter, describing the objects and inhabitants of that world from personal observation said, 'They are not like material things; they are not like mental pictures. They seem to be between the two' (quoted by Cavendish (1967), p. 96).

The most easily accessible plane, and one to which most of the journeys are made by the exteriorized body, is the earth-astral, or what Lord Geddes called the plane of nature. It is a spectral or mirage-like replica of our earth, some say slightly out of focus with it, and distinguished from the material world only by a greater vividness of the scenery, and the sometimes vibratory and translucent character of the surroundings. This may be due to the heightened perceptive faculties of the observer.

Very rarely, through some quirk of natural law, it may be possible in full daylight to walk into the astral plane as if, in the language of science fiction, we entered a warp in the time-space continuum, and then stepped out again. This was the case with two English women in August 1901. They were Miss Anne Moberly, the principal of a girls' college at Oxford, and daughter of the Bishop of Salisbury, and her companion Miss Eleanour Jourdain, the headmistress of a girls' school at Watford. Miss Moberly, it might be added as a point of interest, was the seventh child of a seventh child. While on a sightseeing tour of the palace and grounds of Versailles they got detached from the other group of tourists and found themselves walking through a woodland glade towards the Petit Trianon. Both suddenly became conscious of a feeling of depression and unreality that they could not shake off; it was as if they were walking in a dream. For a space of several minutes they saw people dressed in costumes outdated by more than a century who spoke in stilted French which had a slightly archaic flavour. Their experience, related in their work, published pseudonymously, although discounted by sceptics is accepted by many as a genuine astral vision.

As we have seen, it is sometimes claimed that the planes can be entered by a deliberate act of conscious astral projection. With the help of ritual procedures, trained persons believe that they can 'rise on the planes', and experience these regions in full awareness. Knowledge of the occult planes through ceremonial magic is part of a very ancient inheritance, handed down from remote antiquity. Perhaps the earliest text we have of initiatory procedure is to be found in the Egyptian *Book of the Dead*, whose origins

118

go back to about 3000 B.C. Although commonly regarded by scholars as a kind of *ars moriendi* for helping the recently dead to overcome the perils they encounter in the next world, some occultists prefer to think of this document as a manual for initiates as they proceed along the planes. Here we find exact formulas for greeting spirits, the correct responses to be given to placate menacing entities and, significantly, spells to help the soul to return safely to earth. 'I entered in as a man of no understanding', says the text, 'and shall come forth as a strong Spirit.'

The descriptions of the planes as found in the writings of other countries do not differ substantially from one another. The use of ritual magic for ascending the planes seems to follow a standard pattern, as if the methods for reaching certain levels of awareness are specialized for those levels, and the adoption of a different technique would take one to a different plane.

Obviously many areas of this vast continent are unknown even to the best practitioners of these rites, but within the limits fixed by their experience they have to some degree mapped out the regions they do know, and each esoteric school teaches its initiates the topography of the planes of its specialization, together with a description of the denizens, the variegated symbols and sigils belonging to each grade, and the intricate but rigid protocol that must be observed in each situation.

Just as no one would venture into a dangerous jungle unarmed, or climb a difficult mountain without a guide, so no one should try rising on the planes without qualified direction. The pupil is warned about the watchers on the threshold of the planes who will menace him when he attempts to enter; he is taught the evocations that summon demon entities and the spells and procedures that banish them; and he learns by heart the protective formulas that bring to his aid guardian angels and spirit helpers in case of need.

Certain long-established disciplines like alchemy, requiring many years of devoted attention to arcane processes, also seem to open the way to a vast undiscovered dimension. The Swiss psychologist C. G. Jung, who was only the most notable of a score of students who have seriously investigated the implications of alchemy, concluded that the alchemist attributed to matter what really belonged to his unconscious, and that alchemical symbols were projections of the unconscious contents of the mind.

119

Alchemy is thus elevated to a different level from the tedious operations with alembics and crucibles described in medieval texts. The ancient hermetic art emerges as a fundamentally mental process involving work on different levels depending on the intended purpose of the operation. Each stage in the process represents a new experience and a new awareness along the path. Wherever it was practised, whether in Egypt, India, China, the Middle East, or Europe, alchemy had its mystical exponents who believed that the paraphernalia of the alchemical laboratory, the furnaces, vessels and implements, were contained within the alchemist himself and who saw in it an ultra-physical discipline for tempering and transmuting the essence within.

Taoist alchemy through the evocation of the immortals, the illustrious dead and other supernatural beings, sought the creation of the seed-pearl of immortality inside the heart. Arab masters of the art disdained those dabblers who sought the gold of the market-place, and insisted on the personal transmutation of the operator himself. Hindus made of alchemy a mystical doctrine and a way of salvation. Christian scholars of the middle ages who practised the art said that in the final process the alchemist purged of his dross in the furnace of tribulation would be worthy to enter the golden city of the New Jerusalem.

To this amalgam of theory the rosicrucians added their own ingredients and so did the other occult groups including the black magicians, so that the alchemical furnace, for instance, might symbolize the purifying flames, the heat of mystical enlightenment, or the fire of sexual power. To many indeed it was a form of phallic magic, the vessels, implements and so on being interpreted in the light of sexual allegory. One critic spoke of alchemy as 'a vast sexual reverie' (Lilar (1965), p. 129).

A wide and miscellaneous class of mental experiences is produced by drugs. Some of them are so vivid and striking that they have been classed as astral. If drugs do constitute genuine plane-transcending media, they are unique in presenting a many-storied tenement in some special area of the astral world. Each drug has its characteristic effects, and seems to carry one to a different floor of this tenement, or to special chambers on those floors. No one knows how it happens that this group of chemical substances gives such a wide panorama of hallucinations, each within its own class providing an almost exclusive kind of inner vision.

Spirit forms and ancestral beings may appear before the sight of the South American native drinking yage, a concoction brewed from the stem of a Brazilian liana. Epena, the snuff of the Indians of the upper Amazon, evokes gigantic monsters like the reptiles of the mesozoic swamps. The Greek geographer Strabo (55 B.C.–A.D. 25) records that the priests of the Getae tribes of Thrace would get into an ecstatic state, see visions and utter prophecies after inhaling the smoke from burning hemp. When the starving Roman legions, retreating from their defeat by the Parthians, ate the poisonous thorn-apple, they saw strange designs on the stones along the way, and could not resist picking them up and staring intently into them as if seeing visions in a crystal glass.

Henbane was a favourite herb with medieval witches who used to inhale its fumes, go into a trance and have sensations of flying. They would also apply a salve containing belladonna, hemlock and aconite, and other strong excitants to their bodies, which sent them off on imaginary trips, from which they would return with tales of wild sabbat frolics.

An excessive intake of alcohol brings on delirium tremens, where the sufferer sees spiders, rats and snakes that no one else can see except another alcoholic in the same state. This again differs from the 'horrors' resulting from amphetamine excess. Little gnome-like people dart furtively about from corner to corner when one is under the influence of cocaine, and crawling and loathsome insects infest the scenery of the ergot victim.

Not that all drug-induced hallucinations are unpleasant. The French poet Charles Baudelaire (d. 1867) once said, 'The hashish smoker beholds the Infinite.' Mescaline brings inanimate things to vibrant and technicoloured life. LSD, a synthetic drug, stands in a class by itself, in that it seems to produce effects that mimic any xenophrenic condition. Another recently developed synthetic compound, DMT, which is smoked like marihuana, is even more potent. One user stated, 'I took a puff—and my arms and legs fell off. And then the garden of God opened up' (Stafford and Golightly (1967), p. 244). These and similar drugs have been called psychedelic, which means 'mind-revealing', or more popularly, 'mind-expanding', and they all produce weird and wonderful fantasies of sight and sound. But whether in fact the experience can be accounted for as a flight to another reality, higher or lower as the case may be, or merely as a 'pharmacologically-induced'

I

altered state of consciousness without any mystical overtones, remains a matter of opinion.

Man in his unconscious is always aware of a landscape beyond the horizons of his everyday world. Conscious experience of the astral planes and subplanes could be interpreted variously: as the sudden burst of cosmic consciousness into everyday life; as detached wisps of the collective or ancestral memory drifting through to the conscious mind; as projections of repressed mental contents; or as the symbolical fulfilment of wishes and fears. Or again, it could be the simple physiological reaction of the neurones or nerve cells to the stimuli of stress, fatigue or toxins brought on by such things as hunger, over-exertion, solitude, sickness, sleep-deprivation or drugs. In this broad view a plane may be described as the scenario created by the individual himself when a particular facet of his conscious mind becomes operative, whether in trance, sleep, meditation, insanity or ecstasy.

If we admit drugs as a legitimate aid in helping the transit to the planes, and add drug-taking to the other valid techniques that have been listed in previous chapters, we are on very uncertain ground as we approach the lower reaches of those xenophrenic states that border on unaltered or normal consciousness. If the condition of being drugged transports one to the planes, does the condition of being madly in love or going berserk do the same?

The sudden emergence of unruly or dark moods is a common enough phenomenon in our lives, and both popular sentiment and the legal system accept it as a major motivating factor in our conduct. The fact that a man has killed another in the heat of the moment can be a mitigating circumstance at his trial. In some countries the unpremeditated crime of passion is judged in a special category and often considered not even tantamount to manslaughter. A person is 'beside himself', or 'not in possession of his senses', or 'out of his mind', because a xenophrenic state supervenes and another dimension leaks in, and his usual set of values and mode of reasoning are displaced. The man who commits suicide does so 'because the balance of his mind is disturbed'. But does every climactic moment of our lives send us out of this dimension? Is a person who is in a transport of hate, actually transported to another sphere?

It is not possible to say whether the hypothesis of the planes is necessary to account for all areas of human dissociation. If we regard every xenophrenic state as an astral experience we approach the borders of mysticism. Heraclitus said, 'Those who are awake have one world in common; those who are asleep retire every one to a private world of his own.' Perhaps every plane is a similar private world, and every altered state of consciousness with its particular mode of perception opens the gate to a different reality. In this view, we are then almost always on the planes and the reality of our practical world is a very tenuous layer in a series of infinite stratifications, or at best a very limited order of reality. Otherwise, as the mystics say, we are in almost constant touch with other dimensions, and the simplest alteration of consciousness shifts our perception.

There is thus the plane in which dreams are enacted, and the planes to which we migrate when under the influence of drugs. The sensitive, the diviner or psychometrist when functioning at his best shifts slightly out of alignment on to a new plane. The divine afflatus that suffuses the soul of a prophet, the inspired mood of an artist, the creative intuitions of a great scientist, might be derived not only from a different layer of his own consciousness, but from a different level of existence. There are the planes of the beatific vision, or angelic visitations, and ecstatic experiences. There is the region to which profound meditation transports the mystic. The delirium of high fever, the whirling of the dervish, the murderous passion of a jealous man, create a common state of dissociation which deprives an individual of his rational faculties and plunges him into another range of awareness. The lunatic, the lover and the poet are perhaps as much in contact with the planes as the medium in trance or the saint in rapture.

Any speculation about the planes naturally leads to the question concerning the inhabitants of these planes, and this again to the problem of whether any kind of existence is possible in a form other than life as we know it on earth. The question has been answered in a number of ways.

The existence of other forms of life outside the earth but in our own physical universe is generally regarded as being well within the bounds of possibility. Today's scientists readily admit that conditions needed for the emergence of life are not confined to the terrestrial sphere, and do not deny the likelihood of sentient beings existing in other parts of the cosmos. The appearance, physiological apparatus, functions and life-span of these forms might differ considerably from ours, depending on circumstances. Science-fiction writers, some of whom are scientists themselves, venture further into the realms of speculation by describing these extra-terrestrial beings. Some are like earthlings, some do not resemble us at all, depending again on the physical conditions that determine the evolution and survival of species in their particular environment. Yet these imaginative accounts might very well be the actual visual characteristics of life-forms in other planets of the universe.

But we are not really concerned with the inhabitants of the planetary regions, however intriguing the subject might be. Our interest lies with beings who belong outside the physical sphere altogether whether in our solar system or in the farthest galaxy. The astral planes are non-physical, and their inhabitants do not properly belong to our world at all, although, as we have suggested, this is not incompatible with the idea that some of their inhabitants might be in our midst. According to esoteric Buddhist belief, the earth plane alone has six orders of being, of which men and animals make up two orders, and invisible beings make up the other four.

The famous naturalist Alfred Russel Wallace (1823–1913), co-discoverer with Charles Darwin of the principles underlying evolution, wrote in his voluminous work, *The World of Life* (1910), of the multiplicity of life-forms in this world, and declared that infinite variety was a basic law of the universe. Wallace found it reasonable to believe not only in a single, solitary and eternal Being responsible for the manifold operations of the cosmos, but in a whole hierarchy of beings with varying capabilities and spheres of influence, and possessed of the requisite power, knowledge, wisdom and authority to make their operations effective.

The interacting influence of these agencies was to be seen everywhere, the higher acting upon the lower, and raising the lower to enlightenment. This hierarchy included both superhuman and subhuman agencies, and just as the former acted upon and influenced man, so it was needful for man to realize his place in the scheme of things and by his faith and conduct assist in the evolution of those under him. Wallace affirmed that 'the universe requires the continuous co-ordinated agency of myriads of intelligences', and that 'man is destined to a permanent, progressive existence in a world of spirit'.

124

No metaphysical system based on belief in God can conceive of a vast world where there are only two orders, namely, a Supreme Being and the living species in the material world. 'Isn't this brave universe,' asked William James, 'made on a richer pattern, with room in it for a long hierarchy of beings?' Once a creative God is posited, a whole gradation of other entities intermediate between God and man also comes into existence to make sense of the system, and such a gradation is recognized in all religions. In other words, all theistic systems assume several orders of created entities. Zoroastrianism, from which much of our angelology and demonology derives, speaks of many classes of celestial and infernal beings: rulers, ministering spirits, messengers, mediators; and adversaries, evil spirits, tempters and others.

The inhabitants of the planes may therefore be said to include many classes of beings which have formed part of the human tradition from the very beginning, and which are found in the religious beliefs, mythology, folklore and superstitions of every nation in the world. Some have been so vividly described that, for those who believe in them, they might have been portrayed from life. These entities are in varying stages of evolution and possess varying degrees of consciousness, and the elements of good and evil in them are found in varying proportions, depending on their spiritual enlightenment and allegiance. Sometimes they communicate with human beings.

There are the lesser divinities who preside over the government of the world, the celestial hierarchies of archangels, angels, powers and principalities, the aeons and logoi of the occultists, the chohans of the theosophists. There are vast gradations of the infernal hosts, led by Satan, Ahriman, Beelzebub, and what the neoplatonists called the *antitheoi*, 'anti-gods' or opposing spirits. Also inhabiting the planes are those orders whose pedigrees go back to the ancient mythologies, notably the pagan gods of the Greeks, such as were worshipped by the rational Athenians, and below them, in more malevolent aspect, the heathen deities of the Egyptians, Babylonians, Canaanites and Hindus. There are also certain apocalyptic figures armed with the vials of wrath and destruction, demonic beings who seem as if conjured up out of medieval grimoires, guardian spirits who help mankind, all the lesser entities known to the gnostics and kabbalists, and heraldic animals whose descriptions are preserved in medieval bestiaries.

125

There are also the ghosts or spirits of the dead, the errant wraiths or phantoms of the living, the debris or shells of astral entities, and elemental or nature spirits. If we accept the fantasies of the morbid psyche we shall have to include the nightmare creations of drug addiction, the imps who tempt the anchorites living in solitude, the animal and demon familiars of witches and sorcerers, and all the thought-forms created by passion and violence.

An essential link between the astral spheres and the human plane are the great adepts no longer of this world, who guide chosen disciples to teach mankind. The belief in hidden masters has an ancient lineage in the magical tradition, but it became particularly widespread in recent times after the Theosophical Society gained momentum from the end of the last century. The need to give an ultramundane boost to her mysteries was strongly felt by the founder, Mme Blavatsky, who guessed that a straightforward mission without supernatural sanction was not likely to get a hearing or inspire a following. Hidden masters and mahatmas were introduced, with whom privileged theosophists were in constant communion. Although they were popularly given a local habitation somewhere in the Gobi desert or Himalayan solitudes, they were known to be in the astral planes.

At the age of fifteen, Rudolf Steiner (1861–1925), who later became both a rosicrucian and a theosophist and went on to found anthroposophy, made the acquaintance of a learned botanist, and subsequently came to believe that this strange person was the envoy of a master who was directing his affairs from afar. The most important of the *fin de siècle* magical societies, the Hermetic Order of the Golden Dawn, and the several other independent orders into which it split up in little more than a decade, all claimed direct access to certain occult teachers in the astral plane. Thereafter, Hidden Chiefs, Purple Adepts, Sun Masters and sundry Egyptian and Arab adepts inhabiting the astral were claimed as inspiring and controlling these groups. The trend reached its climax in the life and work of Aleister Crowley, one of the most unusual personalities of this century, whose inspirator was a being named Aiwass (rechristened 'Eyewash' by his detractors), who declared that the annals of Christianity were now a closed chapter in the spiritual history of mankind, and that another chapter had opened marking the beginning of a new dispensation which Crowley named after himself, Crowleyanity.

A friend, and later rival and enemy of Crowley's, Samuel Liddell ('MacGregor') Mathers (1854–1918), also claimed to have established personal contact with certain Secret Chiefs at a midnight rendezvous in the Bois de Boulogne in Paris. He stated that it was almost impossible to support their presence when they manifested even their non-physical bodies. The effect of their proximity was such, that it made him feel as if his own body were completely drained of its energy. Communication with them resulted in an almost unbearable shock whose physical symptoms were nervous prostration, cold sweats, breathlessness, a feeling of strangulation, and bleeding from the nose, mouth and occasionally the ears, that left him in a state of near-fatal exhaustion.

One need not always go out of one's way to contact the beings of the planes or to sense their presence. There are many accounts of such experiences where invisible beings, not necessarily inimical, are felt to be near by, often as if to provide help and companionship. Crowds and noise seem to be unfavourable to any manifestations of this nature, and solitude and silence conducive to them. Lonely wayfarers or those travelling in small groups in deserted places, have frequently mentioned being overcome by a strong sense of a presence in their midst, an Alius or Other, which has occasionally even been seen as an apparition or heard as a voice.

Sir Ernest Shackleton (1874–1922) records that during his long trek over the glaciers of Antarctica he often saw four persons instead of the three with him, and could not explain the presence of 'the one more than could be counted'. Frank Smythe, the distinguished English mountaineer, climbing alone at 28,000 feet said that he sometimes had a strange feeling that he was accompanied by another, who was friendly. The presence was so near and so strong that he instinctively divided what food he had into two halves and turned to offer it to his companion (Martin (1955), p. 243).

Superstition and folklore are crowded with creatures of the earth-astral, inhabiting a plane on a slightly different alignment from ours, who may at times be seen by human eyes. A large proportion of these creatures belong to the class known as elementals, who like the inhabitants of the natural world are

127

mortal, and die and disintegrate in their own sphere. Elementals depend for their existence on the substance provided by the exhalations of material elements, hence their name. For the same reason they are spoken of as nature spirits. In the course of evolution they have mutated and proliferated, so that there are said to be as many classes of elemental beings as there are phyla, genera and species in the animal kingdom.

It would not be difficult to compile a descriptive classification of the denizens of the elemental kingdom as preserved in the mythology and folklore of people through the ages, but there would be no purpose in doing so for they would be largely repetitive descriptions of the kind with which we are all familiar. The lesser-known ones, however, have a science-fiction flavour. The spirits which are seen by the Australian blackfellows include the kokolura, a string-shaped demon who wanders about the camps at night and strangles men as they sleep; the jimbarkna, a snake-like vampire who imprisons a man's soul in a net; the rubaruba, a demon with a downward-hanging head, with long hair trailing in the dust and spindly legs dragging behind him. From Malaysia come descriptions of the owl-faced pontianak whose viscera hang down from his open belly; the penanggalan with a trunkless head having his stomach attached to the neck; the bajang, a ghoul which when pursued dissolves into a messy puddle or evaporates into a poisonous vapour.

A less malignant class of beings inhabiting the earth-plane are the dryads, brownies, elves, gnomes and fairies who fill the childhood imagination. Belief in this type of elemental is not confined to simple or rustic societies, or to children and cranks. William Blake witnessed a fairy funeral, but then it might be said that he had many strange hallucinations, since he once claimed that he saw the Devil, and what is more drew a portrait of him. The creator of Sherlock Holmes, Sir Arthur Conan Doyle (1859–1930), who was also a pioneer in psychical research, published photographs of fairies allegedly taken by two girls, and declared that the incidents connected with them were epoch-making. Dr Walter Yeeling Evans-Wentz produced over a hundred first-hand accounts by contemporary witnesses who had seen or had conversations with fairies and other elementals.

Some of the entities that infest the astral planes are the creations of sorcerers, and have their genesis in the imaginings of men and women. W. B. Yeats (1865–1939), under guidance from an occult organization to which he belonged, was convinced that as a result of concentration, certain images could well up before the mind's eye that emerged from another source than conscious or subconscious memory. Such mentally-evoked images, if powerfully sustained, can become thought-forms, astral creations which take up habitation on the lower planes and can become the most persistent and tenacious of its denizens. This perhaps needs further elaboration.

Thought is a highly personalized product yielded by the mind. As we know, these whisperings of the ego can be passed through the mesh of syntax and expressed in language, or poured into the moulds of variegated art forms, or directed into active pursuits. Literature, philosophy, painting, architecture, music, science, are all captive by-products of thought. According to the old notion, 'Thoughts are things'. In the occult formulation, thought is a refracted image cast on the ether, and thought-impulses can in the right circumstances be made visible, and even material enough to affect physical objects. *Move or create . . .*

For over a century now, experimenters have carried out tests to see whether it is possible for thought-engendered energy to be projected on to a photographic plate. Anyone attempting to hoodwink the trained investigator today would have to be a man of quite extraordinary talent, and fraudulent claimants have been exposed by the score. Yet genuine instances of such thought projection have been established beyond dispute. The most notable recent case is that of Ted Serios, who was examined by Dr Jule Eisenbud, professor of psychiatry at the University of Colorado, and subsequently investigated by several professional photographers and physicists. Serios whose gifts, like those of most psychics, are not always consistent, usually works by looking into a camera, belonging to, brought by and loaded by others, and through intense concentration projecting on to the plate or film, pictures of historical and other scenes.

In his book John Godwin, a somewhat sceptical Australian journalist and foreign correspondent, reports on an experiment in which Ted Serios in this manner impressed an image on the film of a polaroid camera brought along by a magazine photographer. About a dozen pictures, peeled off seconds after being taken, revealed nothing but the photograph of Serios looking into the camera. And then came the blurred, badly focused, but distinctly recognizable picture of a building. Godwin was unable to explain how it happened, and concluded (1972, p. 142), 'All I know is that, while staring straight at the camera, he somehow eliminated his own face and substituted a building, and that this single feat will haunt me for the rest of my life.'

Controlled experiments in scientifically-equipped laboratories suggest the possibility of thought energy being able to move material objects. In this phenomenon, known as psychokinesis, abbreviated PK, a person controls the throw of dice so that they fall with the desired face uppermost, or makes a matchstick shift its position by thought alone. Psychologists and scientists have recently been according this thought energy an almost objective existence, and believe that it might account for certain paranormal phenomena.

Among them, C. G. Jung posited the existence of psychophysical entities called psychoids, which were probably responsible for certain phenomena like ghosts and synchronicity. The Cambridge mathematician and physicist Adrian Dobbs also spoke of psychic elements, named psitrons because they were presumably the medium through which psi-phenomena like foreknowledge were communicated. Valdemar Axel Firsoff put forward the theory of elementary mind-stuff particles, like the elementary particles of physics, which he proposed to call mindons. The English psychologist Sir Cyril Burt used the term psychon for units of mental energy, having configurational rather than particle character (Koestler (1972), pp. 59ff).

Besides the physical energy it is believed to direct outwards, thought has a potency that can affect and change the individual himself. Doctors and psychologists have put into their own idiom a truth known to mankind for generations. Thought can cause bodily changes in the thinker, and strong passion can affect the chemical composition of his blood. Many diseases, we are told, are psychogenic, 'mind-originated', and modern psychosomatic medicine is devoted to the study of the influence of mind over body. Today everyone knows that peptic ulcers may be due to tension, migraine to frustration, asthma to insecurity, heart conditions to the competitive urge in business, politics and social life.

According to theosophists thoughts not only affect the thinker

130

but give rise to definite changes in the etheric environment he lives in. Negative thoughts, sustained by selfishness, sordid motives, evil impulses, and above all, fear, have been growing in strength ever since the mind factor began to take ascendancy in the development of the human race. Through the millennia this has produced a dark cloud over human affairs. 'A gigantic thought-form', says Alice Bailey (1944, p. 948) 'hovers over the entire human family', and it is the life work of every dedicated adept to help in dissipating this oppressive swirling fog to permit the creation of a healthier psychic environment for mankind.

Not all occultists share this dismal and melodramatic view, but most of them do believe that each individual is responsible for the creation of his own thought atmosphere, which if harmful can charge the ether around him with poisonous exhalations. Every evil thought, even when not expressed in speech or manifested in action, darkens the atmosphere. Conversely, a kind thought creates a kind and sympathetic vibration around the thinker. Cumulative group-thoughts are believed to combine into larger masses of thought-forms in the ether. Thoughts are what give atmosphere to rooms where great passions have been engendered or scenes of violence enacted.

Great novelists sometimes have to contend with the characters that spring from their thoughts. They talk to them, get to know them intimately, may become fond or even frightened of them. They discover that their creations tend to go off on their own, refuse to behave, dress, talk and respond according to plan, and seem to take on the semblance of an independent life. When Charles Dickens was engrossed in the writing of *Martin Chuzzlewit* (1843–4), one of his fictional characters, Mrs Gamp, would accompany him to church and whisper into his ear so that he was unable to control himself and would burst out laughing. This became so embarrassing that he threatened to have nothing to do with her if she did not behave herself. If not true thought-forms, such obsessive brain-children are near approximations to them.

Artists, who are naturally endowed with vivid visual imaginations, may be open to similar influences, especially if they bring to their work a passionate absorption and strong faith. In eastern occultism the artist responsible for painting or sculpturing an image to be used in conjurations has the status of a priest, and

131

magical powers are attributed to him. The portrait that steps out of the frame is a fictionalized version of what is believed to happen to such magical creations on the thought plane. From Tibet comes the story of a scroll painter who became deeply involved in the portrayal of one of the figures in his painting. It was the figure of a demon, which so obsessed his thoughts that it became animated, and for long followed him about like a shadow which was seen by his companions.

True thought-forms can become separate entities. They are created by the energy currents that emanate from the concerted operation of thought, will and emotion. They are conations of the self that are believed to emerge like bubbles, take on form and drift away. Mostly they are evanescent and short-lived, and burst and vanish almost as soon as they appear, like a feeble glimmer that comes momentarily into being and then fades away without a trace. But a thought clearly conceived, charged with emotion and directed by the will can be built up into a more enduring form and become instinct with energy. The vibrations of the mental plane, that spring into activity with such wisps of thought, coalesce into a kind of substantiality and independent existence. It becomes a conceptualized shadow-self that lives and moves and, if sufficiently condensed, can sometimes be seen as densified air.

A number of eastern sects have developed the art of creating thought-forms by intensive meditation. In tantrism the plastic substance of the astral planes is moulded by the imagination and becomes detached as a separate entity. This tradition is especially deep rooted in the pre-Buddhist Bon religion of Tibet. Here the simulacrum formed by thought is known as a *tulpa*, and can be created either by purposeful solitary meditation, or inadvertently by the collective phantasies of a group. Thus, a pilgrim's hat blows off and settles on a bush where it has the appearance of a tall masked figure. Passing travellers think it is a spirit and the spot takes on a sinister reputation. As the months go by the phantom figure is repeatedly infused with the combined beliefs of hundreds of itinerants who project upon it their own fears of its actual presence. Then one day a slight wind rustles the bush and a group of fearful travellers take to their heels and the spirit actually gives chase. It has become animated.

Alexandra David-Neel whose work on the subject of Tibetan

magic records the tradition, tells of her own attempt to create a tulpa. To achieve her purpose she went into retirement and concentrated on the type of tulpa she wanted, a rotund and jovial Tibetan monk. At last after several months of meditation he began to take form, and was at first a welcome companion on her long journeys, whose figure when seen by others was accepted as that of a genuine monk. At first he appeared only when summoned, and vanished when dismissed, but in time began to come when not called and persisted in staying. His fat form began to get leaner, his jocund face took on a menacing look and the lady realized that the tulpa was getting beyond her control and would soon make her life a nightmare. Resolutely she set about trying to extricate herself from her predicament. But this proved to be more difficult than expected, and it was only after six months of the most rigorous concentration that she was able to disintegrate her unruly creation. (See Mme David-Neel (1936) for an account of this and related phenomena.)

Further reading   Bozzano (1938); Burt (1967, 1968); Carrington (1938); Dobbs (1965); Eisenbud (1967); Evans-Wentz (1912); Firsoff (1967); Jeans (1930); Leadbeater (1968); Nicoll (1964).

Chapter IX

Magic in the Planes

A great deal of activity takes place on the planes, and some of it has its earth-based, human participants. Certain authorities suggest that everyone during sleep takes innocuous short-range trips into the astral world by discoincidence, giving the astral body a breather in its native habitat. Consciousness may or may not be brought back, sifted and garbled in the form of dreams, but the journeys are said to take place all the same. On the other hand, the practised adept who rises on the planes knows what is happening to him, and remembers every detail on his return.

A feeling of levitation frequently marks the first stage of projection, and dreams of flying, especially common in adolescence, could be interpreted as the unwinding of the astral from the tortions of the physical body. Indeed, some of the astral adventures of earlier times are thought to be preserved in legends of heroes who flew through the air by means of artificial wings, winged sandals, or magic power.

An old Chinese legend tells of the two wise daughters of the patriarchal emperor Yao, who were powerful in magic. They taught the emperor's protégé Shun (c. 2230 B.C.) the art of flying like a bird, and he in due time married his two instructresses and ascended the throne. Shun became a model king, noted for his piety and good works, and among the peculiarities recorded about him was the fact that he had double pupils to his eyes, which was another way of saying that he could see into both worlds. The perceptive girls had recognized his gift and helped him to develop it.

Greek mythology abounds in flying men. The best known were Daedalus and his son Icarus, but there were others. Abaris, a semi-legendary Scythian high priest of Apollo, could be in two places at one time, and would ride on a golden arrow performing miracles wherever he went. Aristaeus, the first of the 'everlasting men' such as the Wandering Jew and the Count Saint-Germain, could leave his physical frame and journey in spirit form to distant lands. Epimenides, who is believed to be the Cretan mentioned by St Paul (Titus 1:12), subsisted on a sparse vegetable diet of his own concoction which he would store in the hoof of an ox. His prolonged fasts enabled him to leave his body at will to undertake various missions on behalf of his beloved Crete.

All these ancient legends, where they are amenable to reinterpretation in the light of occult knowledge, are taken to represent astral journeys. Many other traditions can also bear a similar significance. Primitive tribal peoples living close to nature, whose minds have not been subjected to the perturbations of civilized life, often have highly developed psychic gifts, and their witch-doctors and shamans, as we have seen, are chosen for their natural faculty for dissociation. Their feats of astral travel have been recorded time and again by independent observers in South America, Africa, Siberia, Australia and elsewhere. A distinguished French researcher, Professor Paul Joire of the Psycho-Physiological Institute of Paris, in his book on supernormal phenomena (1916) relates an incident of such a journey by a chieftain of the Jabikou tribe.

A Roman Catholic missionary, Father Trilles working in Gabon, equatorial Africa, gives a first-hand account of a trip he witnessed in 1913, which may be taken as a good example of this class of phenomena. A native once told Father Trilles that he was going to attend a meeting of sorcerers on the following day at a certain prearranged place. Since the place was four days' walking distance away, the missionary asked him how he expected to get there, to which the man replied enigmatically that he had his means. Father Trilles then asked the native to deliver a message to a merchant who lived in a village on the way and to bring back a box with him. The man replied that he would deliver the message but could not carry anything as his was a special kind of journey. He invited Father Trilles to be present at his departure for the strange trip and the missionary saw what took place. The sorcerer smeared his body with an ointment, walked several times around a fire he had lit, and chanted prayers to the spirits of the air and the guarding spirits of his secret brotherhood. He staggered, showed the whites of his eyes and fell to the ground in a cata-

135

leptic trance. He returned to consciousness some twelve hours later and throughout the period Father Trilles had not left his side. The sorcerer declared that he had been to the meeting and delivered the message. This was confirmed by the merchant who arrived with the box after three days and reported that a message had been called out to him outside his hut three nights earlier, to the effect that Father Trilles wanted such and such a box which had been left in his charge (De Martino (1972), p. 149).

Those who are familiar with the history and literature of witch-craft have often been struck by the similarity of detail in the confessions made by men and women, and even children, of jour-neys to secret rendezvous, where sabbat meetings were held, followed by dancing, feasting and sensual delights till cock crow. Although many of these confessions, which carried the risk of death to those who made them, were extracted under torture, quite a number were freely given, and the sincerity of their belief in their experiences cannot be doubted. W. E. H. Lecky (1838–1903), historian, agnostic and rationalist, who studied the matter impartially, said that instances of witchcraft had been examined in tens of thousands of cases throughout Europe by tribunals which included some of the acutest lawyers and ecclesiastics of the age, and many of them, including men of great and distinguished talent, were defenders of the belief. These eminent men maintained that 'there was no fact in history more fully attested, and that to reject it would be to strike at the root of all historical evidence of the miraculous'.

Witchcraft has been examined as a study in human super-stition, prejudice, credulity and folly, but there are some who feel that it may be something even more extraordinary. They regard witchcraft not just as a matter of historical interest or as a psychological problem, but as a psychical fact and worth a more searching look from this angle.

Be that as it may, the persistence of this belief through six centuries in Europe, and a short but equally impressive term in America, has to be accounted for. In addition, we have the evidence of witchcraft cults in other countries. The genesis of these ideas is long anterior to the time of the European witch craze, and tales of witches in their traditional form, accoutred in tall pointed hat, riding on stick or animal, and flying through the air accompanied by hordes of night demons, are found in local folklore from China to Peru. All these tales, including those of Europe, are remarkable for their consistency, especially in one particular—the flight through the air.

The commonest method used by witches to induce this aerial experience was to rub an ointment containing strong hallucinogenic ingredients on the pulse areas at the wrists, on the neck, temples, groin and ankles, and on the nostrils, anus and sex organs, that is, the vaginal membranes and the male glans. This helped to bring on a trance-like condition, with the accompanying feeling that one was being transported through the air. Chinese, Indian, Arab, Mexican, African or European sorcerers all ring the changes on this basic procedure. European witches said figuratively that they usually first 'flew up the chimney', a variant of the levitation that preceded transvection.

An alternative explanation for this illusion could be that many such experiences were the result of astral projection, which helped to perpetuate the myth. By these or other methods people may have actually achieved projection, and 'flown off' in the astral, retaining the memory of what happened to them. Some went to join members of their persuasion, like the Gabon witch-doctor mentioned above, some like the medieval witches to attend the sabbat, others to ascend one of the planes to work out some magical operation.

In the Tibetan ceremony of *chod*, 'cutting', an occult sacrifice is performed in which the Bon priest offers up his astral body for ghouls to feed upon. It is performed at midnight and in solitude and usually takes place in a cemetery or cremation ground. The magician starts a weird hopping and gyrating dance to the accompaniment of a small drum, while he intones a mantra inviting the demons to come and feast on his body. He continues this until he falls to the ground exhausted. The rest of the gruesome drama is enacted on the astral planes. The spirits led by a female ghoul approach him, rend him limb from limb and feast on him. Throughout the ceremony the adept himself experiences in the astral double the full agony of what is happening to him. When the fiends depart he reassembles his astral form and returns to physical consciousness.

An early record of a somewhat similar experience is contained in a text embodying the 'visions' of a Greek gnostic, Zosimos of Panoplis, who lived in Upper Egypt in the fourth century A.D.

K

These visions relate to the adventures of an aged priest, apparently the 'double' of Zosimos himself. He has encounters with demons and dragons and suffers torments at the hands of various spirit entities. He is run through with a sword and dismembered, and the fragments of his body thrown into the fire. In his dream Zosimos tries to grapple with the old man but only succeeds in turning into a dwarf-like homunculus which disappears into himself.

The text has usually been given an alchemical interpretation, but Zosimos, besides being an alchemist, was proficient in the occult sciences, and according to modern occultists it seems more than likely that he was describing an astral ascent on the planes and not the stages of an alchemical experiment. Certain scholars believe that the visions were a symbolical reconstruction of some ancient mysteries or mystical initiation rites. C. G. Jung was of the opinion that Zosimos had a very significant psychic experience that he wished to communicate.

The literature of hermeticism and the occult is replete with narrations of this nature, recounting astral experiences set off by drugs, rituals or disciplines, as a result of which the subject wanders off into another plane. There are occult organizations that admit promising recruits to their ranks by first testing their eligibility on the planes, unknown to the prospective candidates themselves. Sir Arthur Conan Doyle described how he met two members of the Order of the Golden Dawn who told him about an astral journey they made together to central Africa. Doyle showed an interest in the society and one of the two persons apparently paid him an astral visit to ascertain his suitability as a candidate for initiation. As it happened, Doyle decided not to join after all. He goes on to say, 'From what I learnt I should judge that the powers of this society included those of loosening their own etheric bodies, in summoning the etheric bodies of others (mine for example) and in making thought images' (Howe (1972), p. 200).

Occult organizations like the Golden Dawn teach the art of astral projection, and their members are expected to keep diaries in which they record their experiments on the planes. These often have a bizarre character, as may be seen from the first-hand account we find in the *Magical Diary* of Victor Neuburg (1883–1950), an English occultist of Jewish parentage who was educated at Trinity College, Cambridge (Fuller, 1965). While still a student he fell under the spell of magic and occultism and became the protégé of Aleister Crowley, a formidable guru whom he often courageously opposed. Later in life, after he had abandoned magic, Neuburg assumed the role of literary guardian of Dylan Thomas, whose talents he discovered and whose poems he helped to launch.

Neuburg achieved his projections through ritual magic, in which he burned incense, recited formulas to invoke the Bornless One and other gnostic creations, and went into a trance. As he rose he had nightmarish encounters with demonic beings who attacked and injured him. He describes how he was wrenched from himself, drawn into whirlpools, sent hurtling through space and flung into swirling abysses. Thereafter his astral nightmare is reminiscent of the Tibetan *chod*. He saw sundry entities of strange shape and character, distorted versions of his parents and ancestors, ancient gods and hideous spirits. He met his own guardian angel and slew him; was crucified by celestial beings who cut off his hands and feet and sacrificed him on an altar. He was hacked to pieces by a giant and finally forced back into his body. He writes, 'I had great difficulty in arranging myself in my body after my return.'

The planes often provide the cockpit where rival magicians meet and do battle. The biographical accounts of black magicians record many such hostilities. One case relates to the French occultist, the Abbé Joseph-Antoine Boullan (1824–93), a defrocked Roman Catholic priest, who fell foul of certain rival diabolists, and a veritable battle of the sorcerers ensued on the astral planes. Both sides brought into vengeful operation the full panoply of their magical knowledge, with ritual curses, spells and black-magical rites designed to damage the astral body and incapacitate the physical. They celebrated the death mass over miniature coffins in which lay wax figures representing their rivals. Boullan seems to have got the worst of the encounter. He began to hear strange thuds and noises about the house; felt invisible blows on his body; and watched curious bruises slowly appear on his face, neck and chest. He began to feel ill at ease in body and mind and went into a rapid decline. Then he seemed to rally for a day, but the following evening suddenly collapsed and died in an agonizing seizure.

Another battle took place early this century between two of the best-known magicians of modern times, Aleister Crowley and S. L. Mathers, leader of the Order of the Golden Dawn. According to the legends current at the time, at one stage Mathers dispatched a female vampire to assault Crowley, and the latter retaliated by summoning fifty demons to chastise Mathers. It seems that Mathers was worsted in the long run. He started to suffer inexplicable reverses of fortune and failure in health, his career being finally terminated by a fatal bout of influenza. Many people were convinced that his end had been hastened by Crowley's magic.

Later still, in January 1946 another strange magical duel took place, this time between master and pupil. The guru concerned was Wilfred T. Smith, of Crowleyan affiliation, who tried to make an astral attack on his recalcitrant pupil, John W. Parsons, while the latter was preparing a magical ceremony. Parsons' scryer and scribe, who was an expert knife-thrower, pinioned the manifested astral form of the intruder to the door with his magically-charged knives and left him suspended there. That same night Parsons was awakened by a shrill voice crying to be freed. Parsons recalled the events of the evening, and although he could not see the victim realized that Smith was still spread-eagled to the door, extracted the knives from the woodwork and gave him formal licence to depart, thus freeing the astral body from its predicament.

If such accounts as these strain the credulity of the reader, we are reminded by occultists that skirmishes on the astral must necessarily lack the verisimilitude we are accustomed to expect in incidents occuring on the material plane. The planes belong to a different dimension and the activities that take place there need not be in accord with the concepts and conditions that prevail in our environment here.

Besides having to contend with their rivals and enemies, magicians working the planes are also exposed to the hazards of attack from various non-human entities who inhabit the astral regions. Such dangers are not confined to magicians, for innocent persons venturing into the planes are just as likely to be beset by these entities. Oliver Fox describes how during a projection in February 1916 he felt powerful forces straining the atmosphere, and noticed bluish-green lights coming in flashes from all sides of the room where he lay. He then caught sight of a being which he describes as a 'hideous monster', a white, filmy amorphous mass which spread out in green patches, with bulbous protuberances and snake-like tentacles. He goes on (1962, p. 93): 'It had two enormous round eyes, like globes filled with pale blue fire, each about six or seven inches in diameter.'

These creatures can be exceedingly ferocious and sometimes threaten and attack the exteriorized double without provocation. An American businessman, Robert Monroe, president and chief executive of a television and electronics corporation, giving his personal experiences in the astral, describes how late one night in July 1960 just as he was on the point of falling asleep, he was attacked by an entity like a large dog about four feet long, which tried to bite and scratch him. Monroe struggled with it for some time and was finally able to push it towards the window and hurl it out. It was only after the fight was over that he saw that his physical body was still lying in bed, and realized that he had had the fight in his astral form, and presumably with an astral entity. He had another encounter with a similar entity which he could not see and which seemed to possess no personality, but he was convinced that it was 'incredibly vicious' and was trying to get rid of his independent ego in order to take something that was his (Monroe (1972), p. 142).

Magic in the planes covers all forms of activity involving the manipulation of astral powers, whether for good or evil. Commonly all such magic is regarded as 'unlawful', for even if it is not performed for the personal advancement of the magician, it makes use of hidden psychic powers in a manner not approved by orthodox religions. Perhaps the most unwholesome form of magic is that practised by adepts of the left-hand path. The term 'left-hand' has a wide diffusion and many shades of meaning. Right-hand is equated with correct or good, and the left with wrong, evil and, literally, the sinister. In occult parlance left-hand occultism connotes black magic with a sexual emphasis.

When sexually aroused, a man is believed to release certain psychic energies, and in left-hand practices these are dedicated to the powers of evil and used in sexual magic. The extension of this energy into the astral plane can be aided by meditation on phallic symbols, by recourse to stimulants and drugs, or by secret exercises that create conditions of prolonged spasmic erethism akin to orgasm without emission, sometimes lasting for several hours. Used in conjunction with ritual copulation, perverse sexuality, and imaginative concentration, the energy can be made destructive, or even creative in its own right, on the astral level.

But apart from the physical partners, one of the participants in sexual magic might very well be an astral figure not physically present. This can be achieved in various ways, and replete as the eastern beliefs are concerning such *congressus subtilis* or intercourse in the astral, the European tradition is also remarkably full in its treatment of the subject. We shall consider them both very briefly.

The chief vehicle for intercourse in the tantrik belief is a female elemental known as the dakini, called in Tibet the khadoma or 'ether-going-woman', or the female who travels in the void. These beings are hostile to men but are prepared to teach psychically endowed persons the secrets of 'death-sexuality'. Dakinis symbolize the vulva and are described as ugly, wrinkled and ill-smelling, with bloodshot eyes and streaming nostrils. They feed on emanations from human entrails and blood. Like the chod ghouls they are conjured up in burial places, and there exist ritual techniques for intercourse with them. They inhabit a lower plane of the astral world which is intermeshed with the physical, and if they so choose they can appear to mortals in ravishing forms of seductive beauty. Union with such creatures is one of the stages of the adept's progress towards an understanding of the mysteries of power over spirits. The practitioners who have commerce with dakinis are greatly dreaded, for they are thought to be dabbling with the worst forms of black magic.

According to Hebrew legend the first wife of Adam was a demoness of wondrous beauty, with twenty secret names, one of which is Lilith. The prophet Elijah succeeded in extracting seventeen of her names but she finally eluded him and the names are lost for ever. But each name was a word of power capable of revealing one secret of sexual mysticism, which she learned from her partner, the archfiend Samael, the name assumed by Satan when he deceived Eve. The sin of Eve, according to this tradition, was perverse intercourse with Samael. Lilith was the mother of a host of elementals known as incubi who can assume either sex and have intercourse with mortals to pervert them.

The idea that it is possible for men to have sexual relations with quasi-material, elemental and astral beings has a long tradition in all parts of the world. Sexual intercourse in this belief is not so much a physical as a supra-physical activity involving the second body of one or both participants. The whole subject is intimately connected with the esoteric physiological system and the exchange of subtle fluids that is believed to take place during such intercourse if performed in the right way.

Taoist and tantrik teachings speak of the invisible or non-physical constituents of the human organism. The erectile powers, according to them, do not lie in the physical organism, but depend on a blood supply which is ultimately triggered by a sex force latent in the double. A woman has twenty muscles more than man; five each in her two breasts and the other ten in her vagina, and of the vaginal muscles four are in the astral. All are activated by the double. The woman gives off over a dozen secretions from the vagina, in addition to which there is one that is not physical. The whole physiological apparatus only becomes relevant when properly geared to the astral body.

The sexual act in the astral involves the utilization of all these invisible appurtenances. Chinese taoists believed that during intercourse the woman gave off a vitalizing energy known as *khuai* which the man had to absorb by special techniques taught in their schools. In the animal kingdom this energy manifests as oestrum and is more powerful than the human khuai. Indian tantrik adepts have in turn devised special 'oli' techniques such as vajroli, sahajoli and amaroli for utilizing this same force. During intercourse the male with his penis 'sips' the female's energy-bearing nectar and draws it in by upward peristalsis and makes its essence ascend to the brain. The companion who participates with the magician in these practices does not have to be a magician herself, but the astral vampirism to which she is subjected is utterly disastrous for her, for after a few such sessions with a practised tantrik she withers and dries up under the impact of the violent reflexes to which her astral body is subjected. The whole operation is one in which the astral body plays a paramount role.

In kabbalistic lore the psychic energy and procreative power of man's seed are never lost. Astral sex imps are engendered from the emissions of men during sleep, onanism, bestiality or other unproductive occasions. They abide in their legions in the astral

143

world, ever hovering around men and women waiting for a chance to tempt them, so that they might produce more bodiless progeny. In a medieval gnostic text Elijah before his ascent to heaven is delayed by a succubus who accuses him of being the father of her children. To the chaste prophet's objection that he has lived a blameless life she retorts that during his sleep he has often been emptied of the flow of his body, and that at those times she received the seed and bore his children.

From the beginning these succubi have disturbed the meditation of Christian saints. Their seductive advances and salacious gestures worsened the plight of many a desert hermit, including St Anthony of Thebes (d. 356). Elemental male creatures haunted convents and created hysteria among the inmates. The church's testimony on the subject, as recorded in the middle ages, was collected by the Franciscan monk, Ludovico Sinistrari (d. 1710), whose work on demonolatry presents the evidence and adds many interesting and curious observations. He relates how such an asexual creature assumes female shape as a succubus, and receives the sperm of a man, which it then hurries to store in a central repository maintained by Satan. From this store it, or another like it, simulating the shape of a male, now known as an incubus, takes a quantity of seed to impregnate a human female. The object is to corrupt mortals by teaching them perverse ways of sexual intercourse, and by means of the stolen sperm to breed progeny who will be subject to Satan's influence.

The pursuit of *congressus subtilis* was taken up with great earnestness by a number of French occultists during the last century. Joris Karl Huysmans (1848–1907), whose novel *Là-Bas* (1891) collates the floating traditions of his time, describes the practices of the black-magical cults of nineteenth-century France. One of the characters in Huysman's novel, Dr Johannes, was taken from real life, the original being the Abbé Boullan, the defrocked Roman Catholic priest mentioned above. With headquarters first in Paris, later transferred to Lyons, Boullan established a flourishing cult devoted to satanism, scatology, perverse erotic rites, and secret ceremonies involving incubism and succubism and every variety of sexual aberration, both carnal and astral.

Bestiality was practised not only with animals, but with beast-androids known in French as *humanimaux*, half-human and half-animal elemental monsters that were engendered in the astral as

144

a result of the cult members uniting with animals. Besides sex magic in the physical plane, Boullan's methods included the utilization of 'celestified organs' created on the astral plane, like the winged phalli and vulvae of the gnostics. A select group of disciples of both sexes were taught to put themselves in a trance and take astral excursions for the purpose of enjoying sexual congress with entities at all levels of evolution, starting with lower elemental orders like satyrs, fauns, nymphs and fairies, with demonic creations like succubi and incubi, and progressing to angelic and celestial beings. They were further instructed in methods of having union with their own astral double and other astral bodies, including the recently dead and historical figures like Cleopatra and Alexander the Great.

Here again, the idea that the souls or spirits of the dead can be called up to serve the sorcerer sexually is very ancient. The body manifested for the purpose is presumably a reassembly of the disintegrated astral shell. The medieval magician Dr Johann Faust (1480–1540), around whom a cluster of colourful legends has grown up, was said to have evoked the shades of Greek and Trojan heroes, and once even succeeded in summoning the beautiful Helen of Troy, an incident dramatized in Christopher Marlowe's version (1589) of the Faust legend.

Before leaving the subject, we might consider whether any other tradition besides the magical has anything to add about the character of love and sexual activity in the non-physical world. What kind of sexuality can exist in the astral plane becomes an interesting point when it is realized that the physical body is excluded from participation in the activities of the next planes, and that conditions of strong affection may arise where there are no physical means to satisfy or express them. The question that first comes to mind is whether in fact there exists any differentiation between the sexes in the astral; and if so, in what manner the two sexes unite.

From the available evidence it would appear that the possession of sex organs renders a person obtuse to the infinite possibilities of spiritual union hereafter. Many people have spoken of the intensity of bliss that is experienced when two compatible souls come together, and the fusion of their spirits into a great mystical harmony takes place. Love seems to be intensified with the shedding of the physical body. The physical sex organs are essentially

145

the means of propagation, and sexuality only remotely reflects what will be experienced when two discarnate lovers embrace in the next world. *each atom*

Swedenborg states that two souls who are true counterparts of each other fuse together when they meet on the astral plane. As they touch their united bodies become a light and there is a single conflagration which from a distance appears as an incandescence. As W. B. Yeats wrote, 'The intercourse of angels is a light.'

The French exponent of astral projection who wrote under the pseudonym 'Yram', said that love on the other planes is more real, and more spiritual, than any earthly affection. In his out-of-the-body experiments with his fiancée, he found that when they united in the astral plane he felt a kind of general warmth which permeated his whole being and filled his spirit. In turn his aura penetrated hers and he had the sensation of melting into her. So intense were the vibrations that he felt giddy from their effects.

In the course of his sojourns in what he calls the Second State (out-of-the-body), Robert Monroe, whom we have previously mentioned, found that sex played a prominent part when the body was exteriorized, and that the sex drive could be surprisingly strong in the Second State. The act itself was a kind of exchange of electric current, and was seemingly consummated by two persons just coming together, their contact being accompanied by 'a quick momentary flash of the sex charge', which felt like a mild shock (Monroe (1972), p. 197).

Further reading   Baldick (1955); Fortune (1952); Fuller (1965); Grant (1972); Summers (1927); B. Walker (1970).

Chapter X

The Folklore of the Double

There is a widespread tradition concerning the various manifestations of the double that forms part of the folklore of peoples throughout the world. It is based on the belief that an essential part of an individual, be it his psyche, soul, astral, spectral form or other asomatic or etheric element, may become dissociated, wholly or in part, from his body, and lead an independent temporary existence.

There are countless variations on this theme. The double may appear in the shape of a ghost, wraith or other apparition; it may be captured in a reflection, or live on as a shadow; it may possess the body of another living person, take on animal form as a werewolf, reanimate a corpse as a zombie, continue its existence after death as a vampire. Sometimes the conflicting elements within the same person may rise to the surface in rotation and manifest themselves as different personalities.

This duality or even multiplicity of the individual is a recurrent theme of many stories ancient and modern. Robert Louis Stevenson's masterpiece about Dr Jekyll and Mr Hyde (1886) is perhaps the best example of its class. But the idea has more than a literary, legendary or didactic significance, for the existence of a twosome within each individual is a psychological fact substantiated by common personal experience. The French novelist Alphonse Daudet (1840–97) describes how at the age of fourteen he was struck by the fact that man was *homo duplex*, a duality within himself. When his brother died his first self wept in genuine sorrow, and the second dispassionately observed the scene, commenting cynically on the dramatic attitudes of his mourning father. 'This frightful duality has often given me cause for reflection', he says. 'Oh, this horrible second me, always still and watchful, while the other is actively living and suffering. I have never been able to make the second shed tears or go to sleep or get intoxicated. How it sees into things and how it mocks.' Oliver Fox relates that he once saw his other self in the form of what he calls his 'Twin of Darkness'; it looked old and incredibly evil, but though he was shocked he was not afraid of it.

Psychological literature draws some classic examples of multiple personality from real life, showing the astonishing contrasts of character alternating in the same individual. In the past these contrasts have seemed so striking that it was believed that an evil entity had invaded and taken over the individual. Today it is regarded as an attempt on the part of the self to pass off the shady side of the personality as an intrusive entity. Whatever the explanation, the theory of demon possession held the field for centuries, and still finds a surprising number of adherents.

Some people feel that a man is sustained by the opposition between the two elements within, and regard it as an expression of the universal polarity that is found in all nature. To attempt to oust the alternate self would be to risk the removal of certain abrasive elements whose friction provides the warmth and vitality that make existence possible and even purposeful. Deprived of indignation, impatience, intolerance, passion, even the saint would be ineffective in his mission. When the German poet Rainer Maria Rilke (1875–1926) was undergoing psychotherapy, he withdrew after a few sessions saying, 'If my devils leave me, I am afraid my angels will take flight as well.'

The double of a man may appear in the form of a misty and transparent replica of the person, but may sometimes be as solid and substantial as if he were in the flesh. The apparition is called a ghost if the person himself is dead, and a wraith if he is still alive. Equally mystifying is the comparatively rare phenomenon of autophany, or seeing one's own wraith, usually taken to be a warning of death. Queen Elizabeth I saw herself as a wraith, which warned her of her approaching end. Catherine the Great of Russia saw her double seated upon the imperial throne and her indignation at this affront was so great that she ordered the imperial guard to fire at it. When Shelley saw his wraith it made a motion pointing towards the sea where the poet was soon to meet his end.

The German poet Johann Wolfgang von Goethe (1749–1823) relates the circumstances in which he once saw his own wraith. He had just parted from Friederika Brion, daughter of Pastor Brion at Sesenheim and was returning home in an uneasy state of mind when he saw, 'not with the eyes of the body but with those of the spirit', another man on horseback coming towards him. This person was none other than himself, dressed in a suit of pale grey with some gold, unlike anything that Goethe himself owned. 'As soon as I had shaken myself out of this reverie,' he continues, 'the form vanished.' Eight years later as he rode towards Sesenheim intending to visit Friederika once more it suddenly struck him that he was riding along the same path as before and he recalled his previous vision and realized that he was dressed exactly as he had earlier seen himself (Tymms (1949), p. 26).

The wraith, which is also known by its German name of doppelgänger, 'double-goer', more commonly appears to others. It seems that when a person is very ill, or at the point of death, or else in great mental distress, the hold which the waking physical self has on the astral double is loosened so that it easily drifts away. It can be seen by others although the person himself may be quite unaware that his astral has travelled and visited someone else. In his book on telepathic hallucinations (1909), Frank Podmore (1856–1910) showed that there were three times as many 'realistic apparitions of living persons' as of dead people. There were, in other words, more wraiths than ghosts.

Like the ghost, the wraith often appears with striking realism, and gives the impression that it is the individual in person. Men of saintly character are said to be able to project themselves to distant places and appear visibly and with apparent materiality to others. This phenomenon, called bilocation, or being in two places at one time, is recorded of holy men and mystics the world over. A well-known example concerns St Anthony of Padua (d. 1231), a Franciscan friar noted as much for his extraordinary gift of preaching as for his piety. On Holy Thursday in 1227 he was conducting a service at the church of St Pierre du Queyrrix at Limoges when he suddenly recalled that he was due at that hour to assist at a service in chapel at the other end of the town. He bowed down and drew his hood over his head, while the congregation waited. It was later reported that he had appeared before the monks in the other monastery, read the lesson and the appointed passage in the office and then vanished. A second case, also frequently quoted, is that of St Alphonsus Liguori (d. 1787) founder of a priestly order known as the Redemptionists. He suffered from chronic ill-health, and one day in the autumn of 1774 he fell into a trance and remained in his cell in the monastery of Arezzo immobile and without taking nourishment, for five days. When he regained consciousness he told the friars that he had been present at the death-bed of Pope Clement XIV, four days' journey away. His statement was later confirmed by those who had been in attendance at the bedside of the dying pope.

Mostly, wraiths are not operative in the physical world, but merely appear to others and then without saying a word, disappear. It is recorded that the dramatist Ben Jonson (d. 1637) saw his son's wraith a short time before he, Ben Jonson, died. The poet John Donne (d. 1631) while on a visit to Paris saw the wraith of his wife bearing in her arms the body of her dead infant at the very moment that she was delivered of a still-born child in England. Goethe saw the wraith of a friend named Friedrich. This person came to visit the poet while the latter was away, but was caught in a rainstorm and arrived at Goethe's house soaking wet. He changed his clothes and dressed himself in Goethe's dressing-gown, nightcap and slippers, sat on a chair and dozed off. He dreamed that he had gone to meet his friend, and at the same time Goethe, who was returning home, met Friedrich on the way, dressed, he noticed with astonishment, in his own dressing-gown, nightcap and slippers. When he reached home the two friends met in reality and exchanged accounts about the extraordinary event.

There are hundreds of more recent cases of wraiths, of which one, quoted by Ralph Shirley (1972, p. 59), involving three members of parliament, may be cited as typical. The chief character in the incident was Sir Carne Rasch, who lay ill in bed at the time, but was seen in the House of Commons on the same occasion by two other persons, both friends of his. One of the witnesses was Sir Arthur Hayter, who was positive that he saw Rasch that morning and noted that he looked extremely pale and that he occupied a place some distance from his usual seat. The other was Sir Gilbert Parker whose friendly nod and enquiry after his health were met by a silent glare from Rasch who then suddenly vanished. The bewildered Parker who knew of his friend's illness, interpreted the phenomenon as a sign that Rasch had actually died.

A wraith bears the identifying outward features of the individual, yet it does not constitute his essence or self. A man's identity is a composite of many factors that make him what he is and distinguish him from others. Ultimately, the main component in

150

his make-up is the spirit within, and it is this spirit that shines through and constitutes his individuality. Aleister Crowley claimed that he could render himself 'invisible' by so altering his visage by an act of will that those about him would fail to recognize and to see him. Gurdjieff allegedly had the same power of changing his appearance by some internal alchemy that transmuted the spirit and caused his features to undergo a striking alteration so that he virtually became unrecognizable. Like Crowley he claimed that he could make himself invisible.

A Jewish legend tells how King Solomon was once punished by God and deprived of his identity. He owned a magical brass-and-iron ring engraved with the Holy Name, signifying his dedication to Jehovah, and it was his habit during his ablutions to hand it over to his chief wife to preserve it from pollution. In time Solomon turned away from Jehovah and paid homage to the lascivious *elilim* and worshipped the idols that his foreign wives had brought into Jerusalem. The demon Sakhr was therefore prompted to steal the ring. One day while Solomon was performing his ablutions as usual, Sakhr assumed the outward royal form and took the ring from the king's wife. God made the light of Solomon's soul grow dim, and when he emerged from the private chamber and asked for his ring his wife failed to recognize him and raised a hue and cry. The royal guards turned him out of the palace as an impostor, and he became a wandering beggar. When he had learned his lesson from his exile he was restored to his rightful place.

A medieval anthology, known as the *Gesta Romanorum*, relates a similar story about the arrogant and headstrong emperor, Jovinian, who was punished by being replaced by a substitute, who assumed the role of emperor and had him driven from the palace by his own courtiers. Although he produced every proof to establish his identity he was not believed, again because 'the light of his soul had been dimmed'. It was only after he had drunk to the dregs his share of humiliation that he was finally reinstated.

In other legends like these the man's self is depicted as slipping away from him like a shadow, leaving only a robot-like shell behind, devoid of the vital spark. Popular superstition once had it that the shadow of a man was as much a part of him as his body; it was his spiritual *alter ego*, often identified with the soul. It was in fact the visible soul, and it was believed that a man could be subjected to interference by tampering with his shadow. It could

151

be made to fade and attenuate and, through ritual magic, even separated from his body. This was the prelude to his death, for the living were always accompanied by their shadows, and a man without a shadow was as good as dead. Spirits were shades without bodies. The dead in purgatory recognized Dante as an inhabitant from the land of the living because his figure, unlike theirs, cast a shadow.

In many earlier societies the vulnerability of this visible double is recognized in their beliefs concerning it. Hurt the shadow and you injure the substance. Separate a man from his shadow and you kill him. The Zulu would not walk near a dark pool at night in case his shadow was caught and dragged under by the malignant spirits who inhabited it. The brahmin felt his food was contaminated if the shadow of a low caste man fell upon it. The Algonquin word *otachuk* means both soul and shadow, and similarly some common word covers both concepts in several other languages. We still poetically speak of the 'shades' of the dead.

In ancient Egypt the hieroglyph for *khaibit* or shadow, was a sunshade, which also signified one's personality and generative power. Here the shadow resembles the astral body rather than the soul. It has a vitality of its own and is intimately connected with the physical body.

From early times the foundations of new buildings were 'established' with the blood of an animal and, in the case of important structures like temples, bridges and forts, with the blood of human victims. When this became no longer feasible substitutes had to be devised, so the shadow of some unwary bystander or passer-by would be secretly measured and the string used for the purpose surreptitiously buried under the foundation stone. When the man died, his spirit thus secretly commandeered for service, would take up its station in the building and guard it from attack by hostile entities.

Men are sometimes tempted to sell their shadows to the devil because such a transaction, while providing some of the material benefits that come from selling the soul, does not carry the penalty in perpetuity. The shadow thus sold may represent the astral body, which the devil bears off into the astral world for his own nefarious purposes, whatever they may be. But the absence of a shadow, like the absence of a soul, renders life's pleasures like Dead Sea fruit and no real benefit accrues to the unfortunate man.

The tale by Adelbert von Chamisso entitled *Peter Schlemihl* (1814) illustrates this point. The story tells how Peter surrenders his shadow to the Devil in exchange for wealth, but is soon ostracized by his fellow men because of his shadowless appearance, and leads a wretched existence for which his wealth is no compensation. The Devil then offers to restore his shadow in exchange for his soul, but Peter has the strength to refuse, preferring to continue his solitary punishment rather than jeopardize his immortal self.

One of the commonest surrogates for the double is the mirror-image or reflection. Because the mirror so faithfully depicted the features, it was believed that it could capture the soul of the person who looked into it. The mirror was regarded as an *axis mundi*, a cosmic crosspoint which gave access to another world, and it was possible for a person's soul to disappear into the depths of a mirror, or for a spirit to emerge from it and carry him off into the strange world of the looking-glass. In some parts of the East a special kind of magic is performed in which a mirror is secretly held up to reflect an enemy and immediately washed so that a part of the victim's soul is in the water. This water is mixed with earth, and a clay image or poppet made, which is then tortured, stabbed or burnt.

Because clear pools, like mirrors, reflected the features, they were also regarded as a source of danger to the soul. Often, tribal people will not look into a pool for fear that the water spirits will carry off the soul. Greek myth relates how the youth Hylas, who accompanied the Argonauts on their famous expedition, was sent to fetch water when the ship touched the Mysian coast, and was dragged down into the pool by the water nymphs, never to be seen again. There is also the story of Narcissus, a youth handsome as a god, whose mother was informed by an oracle that he would live only 'if he never knew himself'. Beloved of all the woodland nymphs, he remained unmoved by love's passion until he looked into a pool one day, saw his own reflection and became desperately enamoured of it. Unable to touch it without making it tremble and disappear, he sat by the water's edge gazing at his face, and pined away until he died. Narcissus' self-enslavement has been the subject of much philosophical and psychological excogitation concerning the futility and destructiveness of self-love.

The mirror-image is in a way the self, because it reflects the out-

L

ward features of an individual, but what reflects his inmost self is something that might bear no perceptible resemblance to him at all. In a broad sense every human creation is the image of its creator, because it reflects his ego and bears his spirit, much as the robot reflects the efficiency, ruthlessness, pure 'intellection', and lack of feeling that we suspect in the science that invented it. A piece of sculpture portrays the thing it is meant to portray, as well as the sculptor himself. On one occasion when Sir Joshua Reynolds (d. 1792) was asked how long he had taken to paint a certain portrait which he had completed in a few weeks, he truthfully replied, 'All my life'. Each great work creatively accomplished is the distilled essence of a great self. Oscar Wilde (d. 1900) called criticism a mode of autobiography, but that goes for all writing, and indeed all art.

'He who would paint a figure,' said Dante, 'if he cannot become that figure, cannot portray it.' Hence every image is also the image-maker, and the medieval occultist sometimes chose to interpret this quite literally. What was needed for the manufacture of the homunculus or artificial manikin, which was allegedly made by great magicians like Simon Magus (fl. A.D. 37), Arnold of Villanova (d. 1312) and Paracelsus, was the blood and semen of its fabricator. Some vital part of himself had to be contributed to the new creation. The sorcerer making a poppet to torture and stab, embeds in it the saliva, hair, or nail-parings of his victim in order to enliven the image with that person's vitality. Then he baptizes his creation with the victim's name, for names are important too. Man is divine because although all creation was made by God's fiat, man alone was made by God's breath. Man gave the names to all created things, but God Himself named man.

Medieval Jewry conceived the idea of the golem, an artificial humanoid creature shaped out of clay by masters of the kabbalah. The word golem means a lump of earth, and the clay they used was taken to represent a sampling of the *massa confusa*, the primordial stuff from which the universe was made. The clay was shaped like a body, with limbs and a head, and was thus provided with a semblance to the original Adam, who had also been moulded out of the original dust that emerged from the chaos of *tohu-bohu*, the formless first substance.

The kabbalist applied all the methods deemed requisite for a magical ceremony. He utilized the energy of sound; he intoned a name of power; he performed a circumambulation. Then he engraved upon the forehead of the inert android the Hebrew letters AMTh, which means 'firmness'. If the golem for any reason became recalcitrant the magician had only to erase the first letter and reduce the word to the talismanic root MTh, which means 'death', thus bringing its career to an end.

But after the magic letters were engraved, one procedure had still to be observed before the creature could begin to receive the pulsations of power that would imbue it with life. When the golem had been fully fashioned and all the accessories fixed in position, the all-important vitalizing ritual had to be performed, without which the image would remain what it was, an inert and lifeless clod. By ritual means involving the chanting of secret words and certain trance-inducing gestures, the creator would enter into a state of ecstasy and then transmit a part of his own vital spark to his model. Without the xenophrenic state there could be no golem, for the creator must bestow upon his creation some part of himself that was awakened in trance.

In the Jewish tradition the golem symbolized the guardian spirit of the Jews under Christian persecution. It was sometimes depicted in legend as a kind of Frankenstein's monster, parading the entrance to the ghetto to ward off the attacks of marauding youths. Although a few greatly respected rabbis were credited with the making of these heathenish idols, the art was generally assigned to sorcerers who worked contrary to the will of God.

A curious novel entitled *Der Golem* (1915) deals in great detail with the legend. Its author, Gustav Meyrink, an occultist deeply versed in traditional Jewish lore, was a member of a masonic-inspired secret society in Prague whose members allegedly prac-tised the rites he described in his work, in their search to estab-lish contact with the astral forces. In the novel the wife of one of the practitioners, seeing the golem, is struck with the thought that her soul has escaped from her body and that she now beholds standing before her, within a stranger's form, her own projected spirit.

We have already touched upon the belief in demon possession, where an evil entity is thought to invade the mind of a victim and take over his physical body. Akin to this is the belief in ex-personation, which is the displacement of the ego from the body and the occupation of the vacated place by another human or

155

animal entity. It is human or brute possession, as distinguished from demon or spirit possession.

Certain kinds of direct involvement with the mental activities of another person are often near approximations to genuine expersonation. The intrusion of outside thoughts into the mind of a man who is under the influence of a hallucinogen at the time, has been mentioned in accounts of experimental sessions with psychedelic drugs. The guide, who is the one controlling and directing an LSD or other psychedelic trip, has been known to project himself inadvertently into the mind of his subject by a process of thought transference. According to Stafford and Golightly (1967, p, 167) this can sometimes be done with sufficient clarity to produce the phenomenon where the guide's 'mind' is inside the subject's head. Again, persons with considerable experience in astral projection can apparently enter the dreams of others and influence them. It is sometimes said that such dominance can be achieved through hypnosis, but this is denied by the best authorities.

A more obvious kind of expersonation is found in the dominance a strong personality exercises over a weaker, often to such an extent that the subject ceases to have a will of his own. Theosophists speak of 'overshadowing', an operation by means of which occult masters and mahatmas work through disciples who are fitted by proper conduct in a previous incarnation or by selfless devotion in this life, to act as vehicles for the supernatural message or work. This overshadowing comes in the form of an impression upon the pupil's mind, through a form of higher telepathy, of the thoughts and ideals, and more specifically of the plans and intentions of the adept. It can also be transmitted as a kind of sustained inspiration, but rather more forcefully than we find in the case of sages and poets, for this method involves the surrender of the physical vehicle of the chela for the almost exclusive use of the master's ideas.

The ability to take possession of another person's body is supposed to be within the competence of advanced adepts, who with the permission of their pupils sometimes assume their fleshly vesture in order to know wherein their weaknesses lie, so that they may be able to correct them with proper understanding. Black magicians are sometimes reputed to take over the bodies of their weak followers in order to make use of them for their own ends. Murder can thus be committed through another's body and the blame attached to the innocent person whose body was occupied.

H. G. Wells, in *The Story of the Late Mr Elvesham* (1927), tells a horrifying tale of a decrepit old man at the end of his physical powers, who exchanges his body for that of a healthy and vigorous youth and begins life anew in full possession of abounding vitality and with the added experience of his own years. The young man on the other hand finds himself in a nightmarish predicament, where although young in mind and experience he is trapped in the senile body of a doddering old man. But such possibilities belong to fantasy, and those who are knowledgeable on the subject affirm that it is virtually impossible for a living person to drive out completely the astral double of another living person from the body endowed to it by birth, and occupy it.

But a body vacated by its occupant at death is another matter. Rishis when they become old and feeble are said to transfer their astral forms to the body of a recently dead child or young man, remove the defect that caused the death, and thus continue the earthly pilgrimage without interruption or impediment. An apocryphal biography of the Hindu philosopher Shankara tells how he once took possession of the body of a recently deceased king in order to sleep with his wives and learn the mysteries of love.

The story goes that he once engaged in a public controversy with a formidable adversary named Mandana, and defeated him in a debate lasting three days and three nights. As the victor's wreath was about to be placed upon Shankara's brow, Mandana's wife, no mean philosopher in her own right, challenged him herself. Knowing that the celibate sage was ignorant of sexual matters she asked him some questions pertaining to the art of love. The philosopher was nonplussed, but asked for a month's respite and left the hall. Taking certain trusted disciples with him he retired to the banks of a stream and lay down. By yogic power he left his physical frame, and availed himself of the corpse of a recently deceased king, and in this body made use of the royal wives and concubines, but was soon so intoxicated with the pleasures of love that he forgot his original purpose. The disciples were not unmindful of such an eventuality, and when the stipulated time was drawing to a close one of them went about singing religious verses which finally caught the ears of the voluptuary and brought him to his senses. Shankara returned to his own body, resumed the adjourned controversy with the female challenger and won the contest.

A rather more gruesome type of possession of a dead body, allegedly known to the voodoo practitioners of the West Indies is found in the zombie. The term is applied to certain kinds of 'undead' men created by animating a corpse, and making a non-human spirit possess it, or less commonly through a kind of occult murder, by displacing the animating soul of a living person and immediately recharging the body with an alien entity subservient to the sorcerer's will. According to the folklore of Haiti, zombies are employed as free labour in orchards and plantations; they can subsist indefinitely on a diet of gruel made with cereals, but must never be given meat or salt.

Akin to the zombie is the vivi, a person whose soul has been magically transferred to an animal or bird, while the soul of the latter is transferred to him. In such an exchange of egos the man occupying the animal body knows what has happened to him although he continues to behave like an animal. The soulless person inhabited by the animal spirit carries on an automaton-like existence for a few weeks and then dies. When the government introduced stringent measures in Haiti to put a stop to the human sacrifices that still prevailed in parts of the country, the Petro priests were said to have devised magical ceremonies for creating a vivi substitute. Because of the transfer of the astral form from the man to the animal, the killing of the animal became tantamount to the sacrifice of a human victim.

In his book W. B. Seabrook (1935, p. 66) gives a vivid eyewitness's account of one such rite in which the souls of a child and goat were exchanged as they stood before the altar. Spells were intoned and a long monotonous chanting set up, while the two victims listened as though spellbound. 'I could have almost sworn', says Seabrook, 'that the eyes of the girl were gradually, mysteriously becoming those of a dumb beast, while the human soul was beginning to peer through the eyes of the goat.' The animal suddenly gave out a cry like a human child and at this signal its throat was cut, while the child gave an agonizing bleat and collapsed in a senseless heap.

An ambivalent relationship, both of attraction and fear, has always existed between men and animals. Domestic animals are

158

coterminous with civilization and have a special place in human history, but other animal species have also eternally and irresistibly fascinated men, who have drawn instructive lessons from their behaviour, from the humblest species like the ant and the bee, to the mighty leviathans of the deep. *Moby Dick* (1852), one of the world's literary masterpieces which some devotees regard as a cosmic allegory worthy to be ranked with inspired scripture, is about a man's dedicated and almost fanatical pursuit of a whale.

Biologists have found traces of our simian, reptilian and remoter animal past in various features of our anatomy, and moralists have not been slow to point out that the beast still dwells in us, and how easily the rage of the tiger and lust of the goat come to the surface when the restraints that society imposes upon us have been lifted. The work of Charles Darwin could be interpreted as an attempt to put in scientific terms the injunction that we should not be forgetful of our kinship with the animal kingdom.

Men have admired and envied animals for the gifts bestowed on them by nature: lions and bears that have the strength of ten men, birds that can transcend the confines of the ground, even fish that are at home in an alien element. And not least, they have envied their sexual prowess, and expressed their secret fantasies in fables: to be endowed like an ass, as the Roman writer Apuleius put it in his famous tale, or to be ravished by a bull like Pasiphaë of ancient Minos, who was able to satisfy her yearning by a cunning ruse.

In Greek myth ~~Jupiter~~ ZEUS took on the shape of various animals, the swan, ram, serpent, dove, eagle, satyr, bull, to have intercourse with mortal women. Norse mythology tells of the savage berserk warriors who were periodically afflicted with a violent blood-thirst and would rampage through the countryside tearing with their bare hands anyone who came their way, and mating in fierce intercourse with the wild beasts of the forest. Hindu legend relates that the gods and rishis of old transformed themselves into animals and came to their mates similarly metamorphosed, or to animals themselves, in order to enjoy the pleasures of intercourse in animal form.

Apart from such legends, shape-shifting has been attributed to ordinary mortals as well, the shape assumed usually being that

159

of an animal common to the region: tigers in Malaya, lions in Tanganyika, leopards in West Africa, foxes in China and Japan. In Europe a man takes on the likeness of a wolf and turns into a werewolf. According to popular belief, a person wounded while in his animal shape will bear the same wound on re-entering his own body. One story, which has several variations, relates how a posse of villagers search the forest for a ravening wolf and shoot it, but it runs off. Following the trail of blood they are led to a hut in which an old crone sits nursing a gaping wound and they soon dispatch her with an axe. Another story tells how a hunter kills a wolf, cuts off its paw as a trophy, wraps it in a piece of cloth and takes it to the village to show his friend. On producing the paw he is shocked to see that it is a woman's hand with a wedding ring on the finger. The friend identifies the ring as his wife's, rushes indoors and finds his wife with the end of her arm in a huge bandage which she pretends has been put on to cover a household wound. He tears off the bandage, and denounces her. She is tried and burned as a witch.

Totemic societies link themselves with certain animals that have mystically contributed something to the tribal psyche, and men of the tribe periodically take an atavistic journey into the primordial past to re-establish the ancestral links. They dress up in the skin of their totem animal and do a dance that imitates its behaviour. The verisimilitude of some of these dramatizations is so great that western observers have at times been drawn into the ambit of the 'glamour' cast by the performance. Frederick Kaigh, a doctor who witnessed such a tribal rite in central Africa, describes how a young man and woman completely naked danced the dance of the rutting jackals. The mimicry was so realistic that, he says, 'it brought the acid of vomit to the throat', and he avers the pair seemed to turn to jackals before his eyes and went through the act of mating. He concludes (1947, p. 32), 'I say with all the authority of long practice of my profession, no human beings, despite extensive and potent preparation, could have sustained the repeated sexuality of that horrid mating.'

Another observer, Dr H. B. Wright, describing the jackal dance of the Bapende tribe (1958, p. 144), of what was then the Belgian Congo, says that the men and women dance on all fours and in the middle of the dance jackals actually join the group and the dance ends with the mating of humans and animals. Geoffrey

Gorer says that in West Africa during an initiation into the panther fetish, first one and then a second and third panther appeared during the ceremony until there were fifteen panthers in all. After the rite he saw them slink back to the jungle. Gorer also describes the dance of Dahomey women of the convent of the chameleon goddess Lissa, and says that as they danced they changed colour quite noticeably. 'The effect', he comments (1949, p. 165), 'was extraordinary.'

The tiger is the common familiar of the Malay shaman, who when he performs his healing rites often takes on the character of that animal, growls and sniffs and licks the body of the patient, with what Skeat calls 'nauseating realism'. The shaman will not hold his seance near a town in case a real tiger which is often attracted to the scene, should appear and be shot. Skeat says that when the Malay monkey spirit is invoked and made to possess a girl, she achieves some extraordinary climbing feats, quite beyond her normal capacity. Sir James Frazer received a report about a man in the Fiji Islands possessed by spirits, whose body twitched and quivered in a most extraordinary manner, and his naked breast seemed to move as though snakes wriggled beneath the skin.

A somewhat different manifestation of the double from any of the pathological forms we have so far considered is seen in the vampire, another kind of 'undead' being which Montague Summers has described in his own picturesque way (1928, p. 6): 'It has a body and yet is without a body; it has a soul and yet is soulless; it is neither alive nor dead, but living in death. It is hated by the world of men and rejected by the world of spirits. It is a veritable pariah among the fiends.'

Vampirism is unique in that it represents the re-possession of one's own dead body by the double, which together survive in a symbiotic relationship. The victim of this form of living death is allegedly a person who during his lifetime was dedicated to the powers of darkness, and who through his own cruelty and lust for blood, through using blood during his sorcerous rites and drinking blood to replenish his strength, becomes an earth-bound entity after death and seeks to continue its existence on the earth-plane. This it can only do by keeping its own corpse alive and providing it with nourishment by seeking out living victims and drinking their blood. It shapes itself a body from the ectoplasmic

161

or quaisi-physical material of the corpse and achieves a kind of corporeality, but casts no shadow and cannot be killed by ordinary means.

Further reading Bardens (1970); Daudet (*Notes sur la vie*); Faraday (1970); Frazer (1911); Oesterreich (1930); Skeat (1900); Tymms (1949).

Chapter XI

The Metaphysics of the Double

Our experiences in the varying ranges of xenophrenic states raise interesting philosophical problems whose solution might provide practical answers to many important questions relating to the validity of sensory experience as a whole, and help in estimating the value of our knowledge of the material world, and in determining the nature of the fundamental reality that is believed to underlie it.

The branch of philosophy known as epistemology is devoted to examining the origins, extent and limitations of human knowledge. Two kinds of knowledge are distinguished, namely, knowledge of phenomena or the things we see in the world around us; and knowledge of noumena, the things as they are in themselves, or in reality.

The basis of all scientific method is observation and experiment. These are two faces of the same coin, since experiment consists in altering the condition of an object that is to be subjected to further observation. Ultimately then, science is dependent on observation, and we are confronted at the very threshold of our enquiry with a strange epistemological problem, namely, the validity of scientific method in forming general conclusions about the universe. It is now being increasingly realized that nothing can be observed in the pure state. Not only do the senses modify reality but the things we see are not the same for other creatures observing them.

A further interesting problem arises from an analysis of the nature of observation itself. The very act of observing an object alters it to an appreciable extent. We distort and are ourselves often distorted by the impact of what we see. The anthropologist studying the behaviour of a tribe produces an effect on them that alters his view, so that his mere presence and study interfere with true objectivity. In the same way, psychological situations are conditioned by the procedures of the psychologist. Jung writes that the analyst becomes involved in the psychic process of the treatment as much as the patient, and it is well established in analytical knowledge that the patient often behaves or misbehaves in order to produce a reaction of approval or condemnation in the analyst. Ouspensky who tried to probe his dreams gave up writing them down, studying and analysing them, because he found that these methods produced changes in the dreams themselves.

Similarly in a microphysical event the presence of the observer and his apparatus have to be taken into account since they deflect the agents being observed and interfere with the experiment. The physicist Werner Heisenberg once said that in natural science, 'the object of research is no longer nature itself, but nature subjected to man's questioning'. Moving into the macrophysical sphere we know that since the mutual relation and relative speeds of the heavenly bodies change with one's observation post, the astronomer observing the heavenly bodies is permanently limited by the fact that he himself is situated on one of them (Toynbee (1968), p. 180).

In Hinduism there is a science known as *kaka-shastra*, 'crow science', which studies the behaviour of crows, their number, the way they fly, the manner in which they perch on the branches of trees or housetops, the direction they face, the number of caws they give out and at what intervals. By this means it is possible to predict the weather, find hidden treasure, divine the future, and a great deal else besides. The only snag is that crows have a sixth sense that tells them that they are being observed for divination and deliberately mislead the watcher. This produces the unresolvable paradox: the inestimable science of crowology is known in full detail, but it is of no use because the moment we watch them the crows start playing tricks. Man's study of phenomena might well be likened to the science of these recalcitrant and uncooperative birds.

The only means at our disposal for observing the objects of our experience are the senses, and the data taken in by the senses are processed by the reason; and by means of these two agencies we take in the world around us. Our scientific instruments, no matter how sensitive, do not create new senses, but only amplify, often very meagrely, the range of our existing ones. However far we go in refining and extending our sense aids, we are still hampered by their limitations.

Any addition to the agencies by which perception of the physical world is carried out would add to our knowledge but would still fail to give us a true insight into what it is like 'out there', beyond the reach of our senses. Voltaire indeed conceived of beings with nearly a thousand senses, who were no nearer to an understanding of what reality was like than creatures like ourselves with only five. *or 6 !* *see "sense" in diction.*

Perhaps Sir Isaac Newton appreciated better than most scientists the poverty of human knowledge as compared with the vast expanse of what there is to be known. He wrote, 'I do not know what I may appear to the world; but to myself I seem to have been only like a boy playing on the seashore, and diverting myself in now and then finding a smoother pebble or prettier shell than ordinary, whilst the great ocean of truth lay all undiscovered before me.'

To understand reality we would have to observe with a total outsideness, a feat that is beyond human capability. We are like the legendary astronomer who made a telescope of infinite power and eagerly scanned the heavens to see what lay on the outer limits of space, and discovered a small round patch on the very edge of the universe. Puzzled he raised his hand to his head and found that he was looking at his fingers scratching the back of his own bald pate.

Undoubtedly the senses and reason do provide a wide synoptic view of phenomena, but it would be a mistake to believe that these modes of acquiring knowledge are final and unalterable, or that they are the exclusive means by which knowledge is to be acquired, or indeed that reality is to be known by these modes at all. There may exist other channels, admitting a kind of knowledge not in accord with conventional scientific attitudes, that lie outside the scope of orthodox disciplines, channels unobfuscated by the senses through which we perceive, and untrammelled by the bias of reasoning with which we sift and analyse the raw material brought in by the senses.

The picture we receive of the world through our senses does not have a universal validity, and is limited, distorted, untrue, and in a sense non-existent. We know that the sound of a dog-whistle does not exist for us, but has sound itself any real

165

existence? There is an old riddle about whether a large rock falling into some remote sea would make what we call a 'sound', if
there were no one there to hear it. One answer is that without a
hearer the sound of the mighty splash in the ocean would only
be a vibration in the air. Sound as we hear it, has no existence in
reality, and we only call it a sound when it is received by our
hearing apparatus and interpreted by our brain. Out there, beyond the senses, sound is an unrecognizable something else.

Time likewise is one of the supreme illusions of our conscious
state. It is determined by physical facts, and measured objectively
by the heavenly bodies and subjectively by our pulses or other
physiological rhythms. We exist in time in this world and are
aware of it in our conscious mind. When consciousness is in
abeyance, however, we can move forward or backward in time
with no trouble at all. Death puts a stop to time as we know
it, for then we have neither pulses nor the sun to guide us. 'Man
dies because his time ends', said Ouspensky, and he adds, 'There
is no tomorrow after death.' The study of time is more fruitful
for the metaphysics of the double, the area of its operation
and its essential non-materiality, than perhaps any other physical
factor. We all experience the illusoriness of time every night in our
dreams.

Related to time is the concept of space, which is the 'place'
where matter exists, providing room for its movement. According
to Aristotle it is the 'container' of all objects. It is a concept that
clothes an abstraction, and like time is confined to the physical
plane. Along with time, the three dimensions of space form the
co-ordinates by which we apprehend the physical world about
us. But again, in the realm of mind, space loses its reality, for
phenomena like ESP override the limitations imposed by space
on our physical surroundings. There are in fact many 'spaces', if
we conceive of space as an area where things occur, as they
do, not only in the material world of physical events, but in the
'areas' of our senses, of our emotions, and in the field of psychical
and mystical experiences, all of which it would seem occur Elsewhere. 'If it is possible that there are extensions with other
dimensions,' said Kant, 'such higher spaces would not belong to
our world, but must form separate worlds.'

Another basic factor in our understanding of the phenomenal
world is causality, which is the relationship between the cause of

166

something and its consequence. The subject, simple as it may appear, is extremely complex, and our solution to the problem set by the mathematics of causality depends on the kind of axioms we adopt in defining cause. In any case we can never go back far enough in tracing the cause of a cause, because we do not know about first causes. Some thinkers hold that ultimately the cause of things does not lie in what has happened before, but in what will happen in the end. This doctrine, known as teleology, concerns itself with the final purpose and destiny of things. The human being, according to this line of thinking, is actuated not so much by drives pushing him from behind, but by aims pulling him from the front, and this pull from the front lies outside his control. Cause is actually a purpose, directed to a cosmically designed goal. It has therefore been said that 'cause lies in the world of spirit, consequence in the world of the living'.

In their consideration of cause, both philosophers and scientists leave a liberal margin for the interplay of forces outside their calculations, which in popular language is called chance. The so-called natural laws which are based on causality are no more than statistical truths, working hypotheses, and probabilities. Perhaps the astronomer-philosopher Sir Arthur Eddington (d. 1944) was near the truth when he declared, 'There is no strict causal behaviour anywhere.'

Finally, we come to the most tangible characteristic of physical phenomena, materiality. What we observe as matter is a configuration imposed by our senses upon some unknown forces, and is therefore an illusion and not a fundamental reality. Science has resolved matter into a system of energies and events and reduced it to an abstraction, an 'emanation in a locality'. As Bertrand Russell put it, 'Matter is a convenient formula for describing what happens where it isn't.'

It has long been a favourite device of scientists who have tried to present their subject in simple language to point out that the very substantial chair, like the very substantial person seated upon it, is largely empty space, and consists of a pattern of vibrations or rays. It would seem that God's fiat, 'Let there be light', that brought the phenomenal world into existence, is as near as we can get to a precise formulation of the origin of the material universe. Substance is a form of specialized light or pulsation of energy. The scholastics of the middle ages, following Aristotle, spoke of matter, or prime matter as they called it, as pure potentiality, a radiant essence pervading the cosmos. Mme Blavatsky said the same thing in terms of nineteenth-century occultism: that solid matter and luminiferous ether were synonymous terms.

Matter sometimes becomes even more ghostly than vibrations, and fields rather than particles have been suggested to explain it. The whole panorama of the sky and its myriads of stars is as insubstantial as the lesser pageant of our own earth with its cloud-capp'd towers and gorgeous palaces. They are thoughts and not things any more. As Bishop Berkeley (1685–1753) expressed it, 'All the choir of heaven and furniture of earth which compose the mighty frame of the world, have not any substance without mind.' He only reaffirmed what had already been said long before his time, and has continued to be said down to our own day. 'The universe', said Sir James Jeans (1877–1946), 'begins to look more like a great thought than like a great machine' (1930, p. 137). 'The stuff of the world is mind-stuff', said Sir Arthur Eddington. More recent students have posited psychic elements and psychic particles as the basic stuff underlying the material world.

In large areas of human experience, as can be shown by the first-hand reports of those who have probed them, we find that the laws of space, time and causality, which are fundamental to the operations of the physical universe, have apparently been subverted. Prophecy, paracognition, mystical illumination, are only the higher peaks in a great range of xenophrenic insights that are beyond space, time and causal connection. Out-of-the-body experiences confirm that the material world is contingent on the material functioning of our lives and is not a permanent feature of every human experience. Science cannot take into account what does not fall within its purview. Like the fisherman in a parable of Eddington's, the scientist has hauled in a netful of fish, but he would hardly be justified in generalizing about all fish after surveying his catch, or in saying that what his net can't catch isn't fish. Human experience has caught a great many other creatures and these by other methods than those approved by science.

Belief in the supernatural and the occult has run a parallel trail with orthodox Christianity for twenty centuries, and will no doubt likewise continue to course with orthodox science to the end. Like two parallel lines, science and ultra-science do in fact appear to meet on the distant horizon. Scientists themselves are moving into a new mysticism, and finding paradoxical, almost magical formulas and modes of expression, reminiscent of old hermetic writings, for their new discoveries. The ultimate mysteries of science are enacted in a non-spatial, non-causal, non-temporal, non-material plane. Anyone attempting to define this elusive world will find himself in the dilemma of the Athenian priest Euthyphro, who gave up discussing with Socrates because, he complained, each time he put his words down, they got up and walked away.

For centuries the axioms of geometry, the postulates of mathematics, and what Aristotle called the laws of thought, were among the stout pillars upholding our concepts of the structure of the material world, but recently these pillars have been undermined. Today the scientist says that a proposition can be both true and not true; an entity can be at the same moment continuous and discontinuous; an object can be in more than one place at the same time; a particle can both be and not be; a statement and its opposite can both be true; a part can equal the whole; a straight line cannot be extended indefinitely. The distinction between physics and metaphysics has become blurred. Just as great mathematicians have had perforce to become metaphysicians, so great physicists have been drawn willy-nilly into philosophy.

There is a well-known metaphysical view, with a long and respectable ancestry, that maintains that reality, or true existence, does not belong to our world. There is another non-material or transcendental world where real things exist, and the phenomena of our world are reflections or copies of that reality. Men of religion find this idea in their scriptures, philosophers deduce it from their reflections.

In the Platonic view the world of reality consists of Ideas, permanent seminal essences that might be called the 'units' of that world. These exist in that other sphere, not as mere concepts but as actual existences and perfect archetypes or original forms. We appreciate beauty, goodness and truth in this world, because Beauty, Goodness, Truth and other virtues exist in that archetypal world. In the same world there also exist Ideas of man, dog, tree and all other natural creations. St Augustine (354–430)

M

spoke of the archetypes as existing in the mind of God and forming, like Plato's Ideas, the prototypal patterns on which the objects of the phenomenal world were modelled.

Medieval philosophers spoke of them as universals, and debated their precedence in the sequence of categories. An important scholastic school held the theory that universals existed *ante rem*, before the individual or particular things we know and which exemplified them, also a variation of Platonism.

From Plato onwards there have been mathematicians who have felt that apart from the variable geometries and changeable axioms of our mathematics, there exists an immutable mathematical reality outside ours, and that the whole scheme of numerical relations is discovered rather than invented, drawn down in fragments from that perfect system. Mathematical reality lies elsewhere, and in dealing with our particular mathematics, we are dealing with reflections of truths that have an eternal objectivity that no change in our viewpoint or other possible process can alter.

Similarly there are people so impressed with the inevitability of the musical world that they are convinced that there must be a kind of heaven where musical phrases and musical ideas exist in themselves, which comprehend within a larger frame all the musical modalities employed by men. The great composer 'overhears' snatches of these divine phrases and his music is an attempt to render them in his own idiom. Beethoven (d. 1827), who regarded great music as something that revealed a reality not normally perceived, said of his work, 'He who understands the meaning of my music shall be free from the miseries that afflict other men.'

All these notions presuppose the existence of an archetypal blueprint: the Idea, the Form, the Universal, which in their various facets comprise the original modes of Reality. Immanuel Kant spoke of the *Ding an sich*, the thing in itself, which like Plato's Idea, meant the transcendent reality behind the thing we perceive, the real Tree behind the trees we see. These things as they really exist, lie beyond normal human observation or experience.

For all we know to the contrary, our waking consciousness is the centre of our illusion, and the world around us, and time, space, materiality and causality, all form part of a pattern that holds us enmeshed within its structure. In a famous allegory Plato described how we are chained in a cave with our backs to the cave-mouth, beyond which a bustling procession is on the move, and our knowledge of it is no more than that of the shadows which play upon the walls of our cave. The procession of things that cast their shadows and the light beyond that is responsible for the shadow-play, these represent the Real.

Certain Hindu philosophers went even further. They denied that the phenomenal world had any reality whatsoever, even as shadows of more substantial things, and declared that the whole world we live in was *maya* or illusion, created by our conscious-ness. It was a play, or a deception perpetuated by God, whose imagination brought the whole pageantry into being, including our awareness of it. Schopenhauer, who was influenced by eastern philosophy, referred to our perceived world as a purely 'cerebral phantasmagoria'.

It was left to the aborigines of central Australia to come up with a concept of great psychological insight, that wrapped the notions of time, ritualism, and the protocosmic archetypes into a single coherent mythos which they called *alcheringa*, meaning past-presentness, usually translated Dream-Time or Great-Time. This extraordinary idea of the ago-now blends into a single metapsychical harmony the whole creative sequence. In the past there were, in the Biblical phrase, 'mighty men of old, men of renown', who were the cult heroes, like Platonic Ideas anthropo-morphized, whose words were scriptures and whose gestures were ceremonial deeds. And whatever they did left a deep groove in the collective psyche. In their days eternity entered time and they set a pattern whose fabric became interwoven with the tribal laws and customs.

Their deeds were enacted in the great calendar of Dream-Time, which cannot be dated, but as they roamed the earth they caused things to become creatively illumined, and the life with which they imbued things is what caused the world to flourish. It is meet that the mortals whom they taught should follow in their trail, re-enacting their deeds in due season and performing the gestures and saying the words with undeviating ritual. Then the object-souls residing in the rocks and trees will come forth and enter the body of the mother-to-be; and the witchetty grub, the honey-ant and the kangaroo will render service to the clans. This is proto-history, a record of events that have happened in a sacred, non-historical time. It has taken place not on our earth, but in Eden, in Arcadia, in Olympus, in another dimension, and, in accordance with the definition of the anthropologists, their myth becomes a 'reality lived'.

There are many eminent thinkers who feel that ours is fundamentally a spiritual world, that we are in essence spiritual beings, and that our best interests are therefore served by orienting ourselves to the spiritual order. An acceptance of another dimension is not a belief in fairy tales.

William James concluded his famous Gifford Lectures, which formed the subject matter of his classic work on the varieties of religious experience, by summing up the broad characteristics of the religious life. It included the belief (1902, p. 485) 'that the visible world is part of a more spiritual universe from which it draws its chief significance; that union or harmonious relation with that higher universe is our true end'. In 1927 in the course of his Gifford Lectures twenty-five years later, J. S. Haldane (d. 1936) concluded, after a life dedicated to natural science, that 'the universe as it is assumed to be in physical science is only an idealized world, while the real world is a spiritual universe in which spiritual values count for everything' (quoted by K. Walker (1942), p. 140).

Those who have some acquaintance with spiritual realities say that the 'world invisible' is not an empty phrase but a fact well established through the experience of wise men in all ages. The significance of life can only be discerned with the eyes of the spirit. St Paul declared that his citizenship was in heaven; and this is so of every person, according to the mystics. We can only flourish in the climate of our native land, and that is in a spiritual dimension.

Stephen Graham, the British traveller and writer said, 'This world affords no more adequate scope for our spirits than St Helena did for Napoleon.' 'Real life', said the poet Rimbaud, 'is elsewhere.' Dr C. E. M. Joad (d. 1953), for long an atheist, wrote in the last book he published (1952, p. 201), a year before his death, 'Spirit . . . is timeless. Its true home is not in this but in another order of reality.' Whatever is of significance or of supreme importance to us, says J. B. Priestley (1972, p. 67), 'takes place in the invisible and not the visible world.' Ludwig Wittgenstein (d. 1951), lecturer at the university of Cambridge, believed that 'the sense of the world must lie outside the world'. 'All that is passing is only a parable of the Permanent,' wrote Goethe. A volume could be filled with quotations from great men affirming that we are subject to a higher motivation from without, but perhaps all this weight of learning is best summarized in the words of an African bushman who said, 'We are being dreamed by a dream.'

The view of another reality beyond our mundane sphere is taken for granted by most religions. References to this other dimension abound in the Bible. The very first item in that catalogue of riddles and obscurities, the Book of Genesis, presents us with an anomaly. 'In the beginning God created the heaven and the earth.' This act took place even before the creation of light, which followed after. What 'earth' was this that was created in the beginning of time? Not ours, since our earth, we are told, was created on the third day. Some say it was the astral world; others that it was the archetypal world upon which our world was modelled. How else, it is contended, can we interpret the meaning of those other enigmatic verses in the same book as rendered in the authorized version, that speak of the generation or creation of plants and herbs *before* these grew on earth (Gen. 2: 5). Where did they exist? In some transcendental world along with Plato's Ideas, the mathematical Axioms, the metaphysical Postulates, Kant's *Ding an sich*, the Archetypes of St Augustine, and the Australian's Dream-Time?

The Garden of Eden, like that other world, is Elsewhere. In the Hebrew tradition it is situated in the third heaven called Shehaqim, a 'paradise' to which the righteous are admitted after death. In this transmaterial Eden, Adam and Eve sinned in a non-material body, for it was only after they had sinned that they were given—again that mysterious phrase—'coats of skins', before being driven out. In other words, man was clothed in flesh, given a physical body, and banished to a material world, only after the Fall.

But perhaps our habitation of a material environment does not totally exclude us from a knowledge of the real. Perhaps reality is one, but arranged in a hierarchy, and different creatures experience different ranges of it. All knowledge is related to consciousness, and the nature of the reality perceived depends on the qualities of the knower.

The consciousness arising from sense impressions and reason gives us a glimpse of one range of a vast totality. Certain xeno-phrenic intuitions, such as come by inspiration and visionary insight, enlarge our awareness and present another facet of truth. Some 'meaning' may suddenly be revealed to us at various times which in lesser or larger measure approaches the satori of Zen, the moksha of the Hindu, the nirvana of the Buddhist, the cosmic consciousness, peak experience and oceanic feeling of certain western writers.

Religious exaltation and mystical enlightenment perhaps pro-vide the clearest picture that the human being on the earthly plane can hope to have of the greater reality, and the history of religious mysticism has many instances of such illumination. We give here a single illustration, from the life of St Thomas Aquinas one of the greatest of the Church theologians (1966, p. 425).

As a young student Aquinas was not notably bright, but was known for his plodding industry and for his obstinacy in refus-ing to budge from a subject until he had understood it thoroughly. His colleagues referred to him as the 'dumb ox', a reproach that eventually came to the ears of his teacher Albertus Magnus. 'This ox', the perceptive Albertus remarked, 'will one day fill the earth with his bellowing.'

The result of Aquinas's labours was an immense cathedral of scholastic thought, the *Summa Theologica*, which has since re-mained the standard authority of the Catholic Church on most theological matters. This work systematized the whole philoso-phical heritage from antiquity to his own day, including the major writings of Jewish and Arab thinkers. There is hardly a question of religious interest on which Aquinas does not give a ruling or for which he does not provide an illuminating footnote. Among the many tributes bestowed on this prodigy of learning was the title of Universal Doctor.

But for a reason, which the chronicler makes clear, Aquinas left his vast undertaking incomplete. A curious story marks the final phase of St Thomas's enlightenment. He was saying Mass as usual one day in December 1273 in the chapel of St Nicholas at Naples when he suddenly had a vision. That other world whose delineations he had marked out so learnedly, that next dimen-sion that he knew only through books, was suddenly opened up to him in one brief and searing flash.

He returned to his chamber without saying a word and as one caught up in a dream. His friend and confidant Brother Reginald of Piperno, unaware that a spiritual upheaval had taken place, expected him to continue his work on the chapter on Penance on which he was currently engaged. But Thomas did not resume his writing, nor did he give any indication that he intended to go on. Pressed by his importunate friend to complete the great work which he had begun for the praise and glory of God and the enlightenment of the world, Thomas turned with the greatest earnestness to Brother Reginald and adjured him, 'By the living God Almighty, and by your duty to our Order, and by the love you have for me, never tell anyone what I am going to tell you, so long as I am alive.' In the solemnity of the moment Brother Reginald braced himself for what was coming. The few simple words he heard were probably one of the most extraordinary confessions ever made. Thomas continued, 'In comparison to the things I have seen and which have been revealed to me, everything I have written seems as worthless as straw' (1966, pp. 424–5).

One month later he was dead. He was not yet fifty years old at the time.

Further reading   Bradley (1893); Broad (1923); Buchan (1929); Dunne (1934); Eddington (1928); Smythies (1967); Stace (1960); Whitehead (1929).

Chapter XII

The Soul and its Destiny

The soul is the least known of all the components that are traditionally regarded as comprising the human being. While the workings of the body and brain can be sensed, and the existence of the astral body has been vouched for by the personal testimony of scores of people, the soul remains an unknown quantity, and information about it cannot be derived from any normal human experience, or field of practical knowledge. 'Men in all stages of ignorance and knowledge', says Sir James Frazer, 'commonly believe that when they die some part of them does not perish,' and that is as far as we can go with any certainty, for the belief is universal.

But slender as our resources are for obtaining direct information about the soul, men through the ages have considered the soul and its welfare of paramount importance to themselves, and have never ceased speculating about it. Eschatology, the branch of religious study that deals with such matters as death and the future state, is primarily concerned with the fate of the soul. Traditional beliefs concerning the soul and its destiny cover a very wide range of opinion, and we can do no more than make a cursory survey of the field.

The soul is distinct from the astral body. Whereas the astral body is an occult or psychical concept; the soul is essentially a religious one. The astral has qualities that remotely approach the material; the soul is wholly immaterial. The astral body occasionally becomes visible; the soul is never visible. Sometimes a distinction is made between the empirical ego, which thinks, acts and experiences, and the transcendental ego, a purely spiritual stratum which underlies these experiences, and these may be taken as defining the philosophical distinction between the two. The astral body survives the physical and continues to exist for some time after its death and perhaps even goes on to other fields of experience, but it perishes in time; the soul is imperishable and immortal, and not subject to death. The astral body has been called the garment of the soul in this world. In the usual religious view, animals have an astral body that survives the death of the physical body, but they have no immortal soul. There is no part of divinity in animals. As the Bible has it, God breathed into man the breath of life and man became a living soul, and the human being is unique in possessing the spirit of God.

Is this divine spirit the same as the self, or is the self also to be distinguished from the soul? Buddhist philosophers taught that what we call the self is an aggregate of five *skandas*, five discontinuous psycho-physical elements, namely, the physical body, the senses, reason, volition and consciousness, none of which has any permanence, and they therefore posited the doctrine of *anatta* or non-soulness, denying that the soul has any existence whatsoever. Among European thinkers, David Hume in his *Treatise on Human Nature* (1739) concluded that the self consists of 'nothing but a bundle or collection of different perceptions, which succeed each other with inconceivable rapidity and are in perpetual flux and movement'.

These and other philosophies identify the soul with the experiencing self which they separate into its constituent functions and then dismiss because they are evanescent. But if we conceive of man as a three-fold being, made up of physical, astral and spiritual elements, namely, body, psyche and soul, the essential self is the soul. The two remaining elements go to make up his personality. Medieval mystics drew a distinction between the what (*quid*) and the who (*quis*) of a man; the what being the underlying self, or soul; and the who being the personality.

The word personality is said to be derived from an Etruscan word meaning 'mask', and it still carries overtones of its origin. The show we put on before the world is not our real selves. Psychology has mercilessly stripped off the outer covering with which we adorn ourselves, and novelists and dramatists have not been slow to follow up with portrayals in brutal reality of the paltry element that hides within the defensive armour that men don. Deprived of his possessions and acquisitions the strutting figure on life's stage more often than not becomes a pathetic slug that one could puncture with a toothpick.

The greater part of our personality is made up of the impedimenta we carry about with us and which we shall have to shed. There is no place for it in the next world. In the end, the man with an IQ of 170 has no more reason to be proud than the weight-lifter with 17-inch biceps. When the plutocrat is warned about the moneybags that he cannot take with him, he is not the only one who needs to be reminded of what will have to be shuffled off along with the dead flesh. The beauty queen cannot take her charms with her, the athlete will have to leave his prowess behind, and the learned professor his weight of scholarship. Such admonitions are among the beloved platitudes of all religions.

But after everything else has been discarded, something permanent abides, and that, most people like to think, is the soul. The soul is a fragment of the universal Soul, and therefore imperishable. It has always existed, having come from God, and will always exist, being destined to return to Him. The Upanishads describe the soul as 'That which is everywhere, without a body, without a form, whole, wise, all-knowing, resplendent, self-sufficient, all-transcending. It is not born, does not die, is not the consequence of any cause, is everlasting, self-existent, imperishable, ancient.' 'Whatever road you may explore', said the Greek philosopher Heraclitus, 'you will not reach the limits of the soul, for the soul has no limits.'

A French philosopher referred to the soul as the *moi central*, the central or innermost me. One strange feature is said to characterize this interior self. It appears to be a totally passive agent, a silent recipient of the stresses placed upon it by the individual's thoughts and actions, like the picture of Dorian Gray hidden in the attic, in Oscar Wilde's story. The portrait, it will be remembered, bore all the marks of Dorian Gray's dissolute life that should in the natural course have been marked on his face. We are indeed much more than what we consciously know about ourselves.

Without interfering in any way, the soul records upon its own slate the good deeds and derelictions of the man, a concept which is commonly symbolized in the figure of the Recording Angel which attends each one of us. Being divine the soul has an intuitive knowledge of goodness, and this archetypal pattern ingrained within us is there to serve as a guide and prompter. It is like

178

'a deep-seated unchanging conscience, owing nothing to local and temporary moralities', which J. B. Priestley suggests is implanted in man (1972, p. 129). Immanuel Kant (d. 1804) gives a more rhapsodic statement concerning this indwelling monitor: 'Two things fill the mind with ever new and increasing wonder and awe; the starry heavens above me, and the moral law within me' (quoted by Jaspers (1967), p. 90).

The aloofness of the soul is illustrated in a parable in the *Mundaka Upanishad* about two birds who have made their home in the same tree. One bird, the experiencing or personal self, pecks at the fruit; while the other, the impersonal and transcendent self, which may be likened to the soul, just looks on impassively and does nothing. As the Hindu philosopher Shankara said, 'The atman [soul] is the Witness of the individual's mind, and its manifold operations.'

At death the soul is released from its confinement and, in the words of the neoplatonists, 'restored to life'. To use an old simile as the resplendent winged creature emerges from the chrysalis, so does the spiritual body emerge from the body of flesh, ready for a new life. But if the destiny of the soul is to return to God, do we immediately on death find ourselves in the divine presence? In the deepest mystical tradition this is not so, and this idea has probably never been better expressed than in the dying statement of a sufi saint, Mansur al-Hallaj (859–922), a native of Fars, in Persia, and one of the world's great mystics. He taught that man was God incarnate, although the divinity in man, in the form of his soul, was manifest in varying proportions, depending on the spiritual development of that individual. He regarded Christ as the supreme example of the divine man, in whom deification was perfectly realized. Hallaj announced his own status by declaring, 'I am the Truth.'

For this and similar heretical pronouncements he was arrested by order of the caliph of Bagdad, condemned to death by flogging, and placed in the custody of the chief of police to await execution. Before the execution the vizier called the police chief and warned him, 'If while he is being punished he tries to seduce you by saying that he will make the Tigris and Euphrates run gold and silver, do not believe him, but carry on with the punishment until the end.'

On the following day, in the presence of a great concourse of

179

people, which included his disciples as well as his revilers, Hallaj was dragged to a platform on which the executioner stood with his massive thonged whip, and tied to a post. At the first stroke the sage's breast was deeply lacerated so that his white robe was soaked with blood. His disciples raised a cry of pity to see their beloved master in this terrible plight. While the lashes were being inflicted Hallaj never uttered a sound, but after the sixteenth stroke he whispered to the executioner, 'Let the chief of police be brought near me.' When that official came to him Hallaj said, 'I want nothing except to reveal a secret which is worth more than the taking of Constantinople.' Remembering the vizier's warning, the chief of police drew away and gestured to the executioner to continue with the punishment, which was carried out till Hallaj expired.

What this secret was, no one knows, although according to an apocryphal tradition the chief of police did hear the message and communicated it direct to the caliph. It consisted of the following simple statement: 'We are two steps away from God. One step out of this world. *One step out of the next world.*' This extraordinary message summarizes much of our speculation concerning the soul and its final destiny. Death is not the end. Another life awaits us. In the next world we are just as 'mortal' as we are here. We have to exit from the next world, as we have to exit from this.

But first, what is death? Of one thing we can be sure. It is as personal as life itself. Just as hunger cannot be satisfied through a deputy, so death is a venture all one's own. However much a loving parent may watch over the bedside of a helpless child as it crosses the border, that child has to do its own dying. Death is a metaphysical event, both literally and figuratively. Although it occurs through the intermediary of the body, the experience transcends the physical plane. The primitive believes that death is supernatural in all its different guises, and due in every case to the intervention of gods, demons or sorcerers. Medieval Europeans depicted Death as a skeleton armed with a reaping-hook, who executes a grotesque caper before his victim, and then bears him off. Man, in times before our own, was always in close contact with death, and sought constant reminders of his mortality, like the ancient Egyptians, who during the height of their festivities brought a mummified body into the banqueting hall, to remind themselves that they too must die.

Today death is no more the Dread Reaper. It has become death with a small 'd', and joined life with a small 'l', in our biological vocabulary. We are being increasingly debarred from the offending spectacle. As far as we are able we push death out of sight and out of mind, and like to believe that death, that 'greatest of certainties' as Karl Jaspers called it (1967, p. 106), is for the other fellow and not for us.

Swedenborg held that death was one of the punishments of the Fall. If Adam had not sinned man would not have had to undergo the ordeal of dying in order to effect the release of his soul for its onward journey to the higher regions. Instead, he would have sloughed off his body like a snake-skin.

We are afraid of death because often it is painful and vicious. We avoid thinking about death because it is ugly and inconvenient. We hate death because it is hostile to life; it dispossesses us of our goods, and is an alien intruder into our affairs. We are humiliated by death because we believe it is responsible for our permanent extinction.

Yet there are people who take a different view, and prefer to believe that death is a natural doorway into a new and wonderful world, and that we should be ready to cross the threshold without trepidation when we reach it. According to the psychologists a death-wish is inborn in all of us, and as motion tends to inertia, so we have the instinct for quietude from the stresses of life. Deep down we crave for death.

Many people deplore the efforts of doctors, who with drugs and other artificial expedients keep alive the flickering ember of some unhappy nonagenarian, almost totally divorced from participation in his own existence, like chicken tissue that goes on living endlessly in a laboratory, as if the mere continuance of the physiological processes were the test of being alive. We speak of a man in mortal peril as being in danger of death, and here one feels inclined to agree with Maurice Maeterlinck (1862–1949) who wrote that if the dead could be heard speaking of these desperate efforts to keep back the dying from their natural end, they might be heard to say, 'He is in danger of life' (quoted by K. Walker (1942), p. 84).

The act of dying, the sensations that accompany death and after-death, have been described in a voluminous literature, no less copious now than in the past. Many first-hand accounts have been written by those who have actually straddled the border of the two worlds and returned from a state of near-death and even clinical death.

The transition is not always easy. The dying often need reassurance, and such reassurance is provided in various last rites. For example, the priests of the Tibetans and Mongolians used to instruct the dying as they moved out into the next world, but the necessity, or indeed utility of such interference is questionable.

Even those who do not believe in the after-life dread the processes that accompany the end. As the self takes its final departure from this world, the body may suffer death-throes, marked by the death rattle, convulsions, agonizing sighs and groans. Strangely enough, many of those who have actually been through these experiences say that however painful dying might appear, there is no pain in the final moments. When the end comes the body collapses, the head falls, the breathing ceases and all is still. In a moment something that was present is there no more. A summons has been answered that awaits us all. To the onlooker the experience is baffling, thought-provoking, even frightening. He has had a brush with eternity.

The dying process takes place in a kind of timeless way, and out of the spatial environment. A frequent concomitant is the phenomenon known as 'lightning before death', when the dying person has a flash of super-consciousness before the extinction of his bodily activities, which seems to give him a momentary clairvoyance and even a brief omniscience. People have told of the panorama of their lives presented to them, not in a time sequence but, as it were, in an instantaneous burst of eternity that brings past, present and future like a flash before the mind. In a moment of something approaching ecstasy the significance of life is made known, the hopes of the future revealed. More rarely, the spirit of the person who is at the point of death may appear to those it loves in distant places or give premonitory signs of its approaching end.

There are discrepant versions of what happens immediately after death, and here again only the very broad trends of belief can be summarized. In a normal case, the moment of death is accompanied by a blackout. According to the materialists and others who hold the opinion that the end of physical life is the end of existence, this is it. Death is annihilation. This sombre view had its advocate in the Roman philosopher Lucretius (95–51 B.C.) who put it into sublime poetic form. All phenomena, he said, have natural causes; belief in the supernatural or in the divine is folly; death is the natural end of man; immortality is an empty dream.

But the vast majority of mankind believe that something does survive. The orthodox religious view is that the surviving element is the soul or spirit, which is brought before a heavenly tribunal for judgment, and gets its due meed of reward or punishment according to its deserts. The occult view is that the astral cord is severed at death, and the astral body, along with the soul, passes into the next world, to a different life. As a group, spiritualists are unanimously optimistic about death and the hereafter. 'There is no death', is the predominant theme of hundreds of spiritualist books, articles and lectures. What we call death is merely another stage in a long pilgrimage.

The blackout that accompanies death slowly fades, and a new light gradually emerges. In some cases it seems as if one is crossing a dark river and stepping off on the other bank into a sunlit landscape; or entering a tunnel black as pitch and then slowly emerging into a bright country at the other end. Loved ones, relatives, and friends who have passed over are there to meet you. Those who have none are received by friendly helpers. These spiritual beings are entrusted with the task of guiding the bewildered newcomer in the new life that now faces him.

Many reports state that conditions in the immediate post-mortem world are very much like those on earth; indeed that that world is an exact replica of ours, and existence there is the same as here. When he first arrives the deceased may not even realize that he is dead, and may believe that he has awakened from a deep sleep. He finds no difference between the world he has left and the world he has entered.

Sylvan Muldoon stated that if the testimony of every person who has died could be taken, the majority would say that on awakening after death they thought they were still in the physical body. Swedenborg, who claimed to have paid many visits to the other planes, said that those whom he interviewed told him they had lost nothing in the transition and even had bodies and senses to prove it.

The dead on arrival can identify themselves in terms of their usual form and feature. They show no evidence of age or affliction. They are free from pain and the infirmities of sickness, and have no material anxieties. Children grow up and old people grow younger until an optimum age is reached, somewhere between 25 and 35. This has no relationship to chronological age as we understand it on earth, but signifies a capacity for understanding the experiences that the spirit will now have to undergo.

The dead can move 'objects' in their sphere, but are unable to move or even see objects in the earth-plane. Men and women in the earth-plane are as invisible to them as they are to us. In special circumstances they may get through to the earth-plane and then the earth's inhabitants appear to them as a glow. But the dead who for any reason are strongly earth-bound might continue to stay in the astral sphere of the earth and continue to see material things. They try to communicate in the normal way but find to their chagrin that no one listens to what they say. Their attempts to eat or drink, or move things are fruitless. Strange as it may seem, the natural conclusion that might be drawn from these anomalies, that they are not of this world any more, does not occur to them.

People can be powerfully fettered by their own preoccupation with the sensual side of life and this can lead to very distressing situations. Persistent habits uncontrolled on earth, create phantom senses and phantom desires that cannot be appeased. Sensitives have described the spirit of the dead drunkard haunting bars and drinking houses, avidly savouring the smell of the alcohol to which he is enslaved, but devoid of the physical means to quench his unquenchable thirst, and finding his craving only intensified by what can never be his. Sexual desire if uncontrolled can become the most nightmarish of obsessions. To be so utterly sense-bound in the next world is to be in a hell of one's own making.

It would seem, however, that all these conditions apply only to the lower ranges of the next world, and are confined to the early phases of post-mortem experience. On first arrival, as we have seen, and for some time thereafter, the newly dead continue to believe that they are mortal, with mortal needs that have to be met, and they are accordingly provided with a bodily form and an earth-like environment in order to render the transition less difficult, but they are slowly weaned away from their former associations. Subsequent life is graded for the progressive readjustment of the spirit to the unaccustomed life he will have to face.

A matter of some concern and even distress to many people is the thought that the ties of affection that bind them together on earth are not always maintained after death. This is the general view of many students of the subject. Oliver Fox, who was closely attached to his mother, received a communication from her through automatic writing. His heart sank when he read the message, for his mother, so warm-hearted when alive, seemed now so calm, so remote, and non-human, 'so utterly lost to the small boy who still exists in me'.

Spirits who are united on earth by ties of kinship, marriage or affection, do not necessarily continue their relationship in the next life. Husband and wife, parent and child, are relative terms, significant only on the earth-plane, and have no permanent validity. Selfish love, or the love that is confined to individuals or groups will vanish, and much more spiritualized affiliations will take its place. Where a strong love does exist on earth, for whatever reason, then the link remains for some time, but in the end every soul finds his or her own counterpart, and this elective affinity has nothing to do with sex, and may have no connection with ties on earth. In any event, no personal relationship, even of counterparts, continues for long, although every assistance is given to spirits through helpers and guides, for their own advancement. In that world, as in this, every one eventually has to work out his own salvation.

To a very considerable degree the emotional maturity that a man has acquired during his term on earth determines the well-being and happiness of his soul in the next world. Ripeness is all. Death does not change a person's character or his thinking; and in that world our thoughts are our emotions, only more so. A man can become blinded by his own passions, driven to morbid depths in a vicious circle of blazing emotions that are excrutiatingly increased in the next world. The sufi saints say that if we do not resolve discord within ourselves, paradise itself would not make us happy. Jonathan Swift (1667–1745), author of many biting satires, whose life was filled with bitterness and whose tormented mind drove him to the verge of madness, wrote his own epitaph in Latin, which he wanted cut on his gravestone, and which ex-

N

pressed his hope for the life eternal: that he would go to a place 'where savage indignation will gnaw at my heart no more'. Conan Doyle, who was deeply interested in psychical research and particularly in life after death, came to the conclusion that our condition in the next world is very much like the one we have left, but 'emotion is a thousand times stronger' (see Phillips (1972), p. 216). We sow the wind and reap the whirlwind.

If a person does not learn to acquire control over his emotions while alive, he is presented with situations in the next world where he has to face them repeatedly until he has overcome or outgrown them. He must learn or perish. According to the English mystic, William Law (1686–1761), the light of heaven flows unceasingly from God, and men are in hell and darkness not because God is angry with them, but because they have done to the light of heaven 'as that man does to the light of the sun who puts out his own eyes'. In a sense we are the sculptors of our own post-mortem bodies, and the architects of the dwellings we shall occupy. We stock up coal for the fires of our private hells, and the demons who will prod us are the thought-forms we ourselves have conjured up and brought into existence. Each one is responsible for his own fate. The gods, as Plato said, are guiltless.

Most religious traditions give support to the idea that there are many spheres in the hereafter. Some are designed for purification, others provide a testing ground, all offer scope for advancement. The Hebrew commentaries on the scriptures mention the seven houses comprising paradise, and the seven layers of hell. The Hindus speak of the seven realms of bliss and the seven abodes of punishment. The Greeks too recognized several celestial regions, from Olympus where the gods dwelt, to the Elysian Fields reserved for the virtuous dead. Hades had its divisions, separated one from the other by the Styx, Lethe, Cocytus, Phlegethon and Acheron. And Christ spoke of the 'many mansions' in the next world. In Greek the word *monē*, which is translated 'mansion', also signifies a stopping place or station, so that 'many mansions' could equally well be rendered 'many stages'.

The next world extends outwards on all sides in ascending and descending gradations, and the region to which a soul is assigned depends on a number of factors, such as the particular religion or deity to which one has given allegiance, or the extent to which the ethical and moral teachings have been followed or trans-

gressed. We do not escape our past, which catches up with us when
the allocation of our grade is first being determined. A person's
spiritual advancement on earth is set up against the advantages or
drawbacks of his inheritance, environment or natural abilities, to
see whether his achievements have been commensurate with his
opportunities and endowments. Wealth can be the needle's eye
and a great barrier, since much more is expected of the rich, as of
the talented.

There are several stages in the individual's evolution, and the
future holds out promise of existence in many ranges of experience,
but he has to earn the right to move upward. Many of the qualities
that make for success in this world are obstacles in the next. Vanity,
selfishness, anger, lust, greed, envy, and the other weaknesses
variously catalogued as 'deadly sins', are flaws that must be eradi-
cated. At each stage he learns his lessons, remedies his imper-
fections, and adds to his store of experience. Thus as he
matures and undergoes modification, he rises from sphere to
sphere.

The spirits of the dead in the post-mortem world are aware that
the passage has to be made to another realm which differs beyond
description from the plane they occupy. This has frequently been
reported in accounts of the other world. John Oxenham, a Metho-
dist minister, who had never been predisposed to supernaturalism
and had no interest in spiritualism, recorded an experience he had
some four months before his death. Feeling rather more exhausted
than usual one day, he lay down and fell into a deep sleep, regain-
ing consciousness in a non-physical environment of great beauty,
which filled him with a sense of great tranquillity. Before he reluctantly returned to what he calls 'the bondage of the flesh', he met
his deceased wife and friends and relations. He learned from them
that the psychical phase of life that they were experiencing at the
time was, like physical life on earth, a stage in human progress, and
there would be yet another phase which involved discarding the
psychical body and entering into conditions of True Heaven. *Ultimate*

From the accounts we have it is difficult to determine whether
the transition is easily achieved or not. F. W. H. Myers, after his
demise, explained in a communication through the famous medium
Geraldine Cummins how the spirit or soul-world was composed
of several spheres, each a little higher than its predecessor. As it
progressed the soul passed through these spheres until it gained

all the experience necessary to enable it to reach the Godhead. Myers then went on to say, 'Very few souls are able to attain this exalted position, but those who do, pass beyond the spheres and become united with God' (see Phillips (1972), p. 217).

Another message from a different source sounds a more promising note. It is mentioned in Dennis Bardens's book (1970, p. 128). Three years after his death C. S. Lewis (d. 1963) author of *The Screwtape Letters* and other popular theological works, appeared to his friend Canon J. B. Phillips, translator of the New Testament into modern English, and said to him with a smile, 'It's easier than you think.' A week later Lewis appeared once more and repeated, 'It's not so hard as you think, you know.' What he meant is not clear, but it was an encouraging voice from Beyond.

In whatever manner the transition is made, and religious beliefs differ in this respect, the promotion to paradise is the final stage in the soul's progress. Jakob Böhme, a shoemaker of practically no education but of great mystical insight, who influenced some of the greatest minds of his own and the following generations, including Sir Isaac Newton, said with a smile as he lay on his deathbed, 'Now I enter paradise', and for all we know his certitude was justified. But men of lesser calibre have perforce to move at a slower pace.

A rather different view is expressed by the school of thought that believes that the after-death planes do not provide significant opportunities for our advancement. The earth is the school for our education, and we have to return to the earth again and again for our prizes and punishments, until we have learned all the lessons that life has to teach. The belief that after death the soul is incarnated again on the earth-plane in a new body, was common to many primitive societies and a few advanced ones, although it has generally been abandoned by the latter. Today Hinduism is the most notable of the religious systems that still adhere to the belief. Reincarnation is linked with the idea of *karma*, which means that we are responsible for the consequences of all our deeds, which itself is based on the doctrine of causality and on the law of retributive justice. Our actions in a past life have determined our present existence; our present conduct will determine our next incarnation. Each soul has dwelt before in the bodies of successive men and women through the ages.

Proofs of reincarnation have allegedly been provided from a

number of sources. A strong feeling of *déjà vu*, of having been in a certain place before, even though we know we have never actually visited it, is regarded as a recollection of an experience in that place in a previous life. Precocity in a child is interpreted as signifying the recapitulation of an earlier endowment or gift, by means of which the child is enabled to carry on from the point where he left off in a former incarnation. Some people claim to remember their past lives, and offer proof of it by describing the houses where they lived, their parents, playmates or associates. Critics tend to ascribe all such retrocognitive phenomena to self-delusion, or, when they have some factual verisimilitude, to self-acquired information, or the telepathic picking of the minds of others.

The theory of reincarnation has been called the nightmare of Hinduism. It has tangled with the doctrine of time and causality and been confronted with the dogma of eternal return. The retributive justice of the cosmos unmitigated by divine clemency leaves little hope for erring mankind, for, in Biblical terms, 'all have come short of the glory of God'. Apollonius of Tyana (d. A.D. 98) a late follower of Pythagoras composed a prayer for silent meditation that was meant to bring out the full implication of human unworthiness. It was: 'O ye gods, give me what I deserve.' He warned his pupils never to utter the prayer aloud or with intent, in case the gods heard and answered it. God's justice can be even more terrible than His wrath. For His wrath chastises, but His justice is Judgment.

Whether karma or deeds have a transcendent validity is metaphysically doubtful. Theology emphasizes faith rather than works. Action was regarded by ancient Greek philosophers as one of the categories, along with time, space, substance, causality and the other principles we have considered in the previous chapter. All these are modes that appertain to material existence and together constitute descriptive co-ordinates or points of reference within a material framework. The categories taken together form the polar opposite of the Absolute, which has no relationship and is not subject to any categorization.

Opposites are built into the structure of the manifest universe; without them things would not come into existence or be able to function. The contrasting and complementary opposites of the universal duality are symbolized in the Chinese concept of Yang and Yin, equated with our earthly opposites of male and female, light and dark, active and passive. In Hinduism the two principles are the god Shiva and his consort Shakti, whose energies form the warp and woof of the fabric that composes the cosmos.

The tension of opposites is found all down the line in every aspect of life and activity. Every existent has an antisistent, and every ent an antent. Opposites are found in the pathemic relationship of sympathy and antipathy; in pairs and genders of all kinds as in sex; in laterality or the right and left sides of things; in symmetry or the identically balanced relationships between two parts of whole; in polarity or the dynamic opposition of potencies. There is an underlying antimorphism in the very constitution and structure of the universe, in atoms and anti-atoms, matter and anti-matter, in worlds and anti-worlds.

The attempt to translate this opposition into the religious sphere, in terms of a dualism between the powers of good and evil was first clearly made in Zoroastrianism, and the idea thereafter entered the theological field like an army with banners, and never more frightfully than in the teachings of Isaac Luria (1522–70), a Palestinian kabbalist who found the opposition interpolated between God and the world as it emanated from His creative breath. Luria claimed that during trance his soul would ascend to heaven and hold converse with Elias (Elijah) and other prophets of old who communicated to him the deepest mysteries of the universe. His chosen disciples were sworn never to publish these mysteries with their staggering implications.

According to Luria the world was created for some undisclosed reason, although it is known that its creation had become necessary. In order to make room for creation God withdrew a part of Himself, but during the retreat from the divine plenum a vacuum was also created, and as a result of a cosmic accident evil came into being. Part of the creative process was, to use the Lurian metaphor, the formation of certain vessels, which were made to receive the outpouring of God's light, but because of a defect in their structure they could not hold it and the vessels were shattered. The harmony of the universe was disrupted and, in the terrifying words of the Lurian kabbalah, 'damage was done to the Deity'. The broken vessels now emptied of the light became the habitation of the *klifoth*, an invading hierarchy of evil forces who filled the emptied shells. These forces are hostile to the divine plan, and represent all the disorganized and unbalanced energy of the universe. The process of 'mending' is possible, but can only be complete with the coming of the Messiah who alone can repair the fracture.

The dualism of Lurian cosmogony holds a permanent menace for mankind. The emergence of the klifoth represents the supremacy of time, space, matter, action and the other material conditions that make up the sphere of their operations. Like it or not, man, being immortal, is destined to tread the mill of existence for ever. Existence is a calamity, and to be alive is to be everlastingly exposed to the klifoth. Significantly, Luria believed in reincarnation; he was also greatly influenced by gnosticism. Fourteen centuries earlier the gnostic Marcion (d. 165) saw in creation the act of a malevolent being, and following his trail certain early Christian sects held that creation was the work of Satan, and birth an unmitigated evil, and felt that every man had cause to rue the day that he was brought into existence.

The idea of a transcendent God, permanently ostracized by a creative catastrophe from a world where He can gain no entrance into time and space, makes a vivid reality of the hells of the theologians. There is no more hideous prospect for mankind than that of a God who cannot intervene on our behalf, His angelic hosts helpless, the material world left to the klifoth, and we at their mercy. This concept is reflected in the medieval versions of an everlasting hell, and in the lurid recitals of revivalist preachers such as Jonathan Edwards (d. 1758), whose descriptions of the eternal torments have never been more gruesomely conveyed in all religious literature.

The congregation were invited to imagine themselves cast into a fiery oven for fifteen minutes, and, after a single minute had passed, to think how overpowering would be the realization that they would have to endure it for the remaining fourteen minutes. But what would be the effect on their souls, the preacher would continue in a rising crescendo, if they knew that they must endure the torment for twenty-four hours, and how much greater if it was for a whole year. But how their hearts would sink in utter desolation and hopelessness if they knew that they must bear it for ever, 'and that for millions and millions of ages your torments would be no nearer to an end, and that you would never, never be delivered' (see Davenport (1905), pp. 110 ff).

This apalling theology cannot be reconciled with reason, common sense or religion and has few adherents today. Sin is a human failure due to human ignorance, disbelief and weakness in a temporal sphere, and it is hardly reasonable to suppose that God would condemn for eternity a dereliction enacted in time. New Testament allusions to hell refer to it as *gehenna*, a name taken from the valley of Hinnom near Jerusalem, where the city refuse was dumped and which burned night and day, and in this sense was 'the fire that is not quenched', and not a hell in which transgressors were burned everlastingly.

The New Testament further suggests that man's immortality has to be earned and that the names of those who fail are blotted out from the book of life, and that they, along with Death and Hell, are cast into the lake of fire. They suffer total annihilation in what is known as the 'second death'. This view is modified by the belief, also supported by Biblical texts, that Christ descended to the lower planes to reclaim souls who were in hell, and made his proclamation to the imprisoned spirits there, a tradition that is preserved in the clause in the Apostles' Creed which says that Christ 'descended into hell'.

In the nature of monistic belief the existence of an everliving Satan and an everlasting hell are incompatible with the concept of divine unity. Those who believe that God is love are driven to conclude that His mercy is greater than His justice. Origen (A.D. 185–254), the most learned of the early Church Fathers, held that in the end all souls would be gathered back into the Infinite, and that even Satan and his hosts would be purified and redeemed. The agent for this universal redemption, Origen said, is the Son of God.

The gnostics, who salvaged much of the scrap from the wreckage of the pagan world around them, and added to it their own assortment from the Christianity that was being propagated in their midst, had a number of unusual theories that scholars are studying once more with renewed interest. Gnostic cosmology was based on geocentricity, an idea still current in their day, according to which the earth was the centre of the solar system. Encompassing the earth, like the coats of an onion, were a series of transparent hollow spheres, each successive one enclosing the others. Around the earth was the first sphere carrying the moon, then larger ones carrying the planets, the sun, the fixed stars, and finally the great firmament, which was known as the crystalline sphere The whole formed an immense globe which was symbolically represented by the lower bulge of a device that looked like the figure 8. The upper bulge was the globe of heaven.

Between these two cosmic globes, that is, above the crystalline sphere and below the heavenly sphere, was the boundary region, comprising the 'waist' of the 8-shaped figure, which formed the dividing line. This region was variously called the fiery empyrean, the great whirlpool, the great gulf, the divide, the bourn, the profundity, the depths, the vortices, the flaming walls, the ring-pass-not, the rope of the angels.

The 'waist' itself, having a cruciform figure, was known as the Stauros or Cross, which the English mystic Thomas Vaughan (1622–66) referred to as 'a thing appointed to a most secret and mysterious office'. This cross marked the boundary between two distinct and irreconcilable worlds. On this side lay our world, comprising the natural, physical, astral, etheric, klifothic, demonic spheres, essentially imperfect, empty and illusive, and on the other side the pleroma or fullness of the heavenly abode. According to Christian gnosticism the Stauros was manifested on earth as the Cross of Christ, and they held that the mystery of the Crucifixion provided the only means of exit from the material, and entry into the celestial realms.

Without the Cross men are held in thrall by time, hence such doctrines as eternal recurrence, reincarnation, the ages of Brahma, endless duration, cyclic time, everlasting hell, perpetual perdition. To use another gnostic symbol, the lower bulge of the figure 8 was the ourobouros, the serpent biting its own tail. There is no way out. Men are trapped in Time. Like the reincarnationists they step out of this world, only to step back again, never able to take Hallaj's second stride 'out of the next world'.

The Stauros is the axis of a mighty spiral, which reverses the whole cosmos and takes man from reincarnation to redemption, from the temporal to the eternal, from the empty shells of the klifoth to the pleroma or fulness; from the phenomenal to the noumenal world; from the world of illusion to the world of Reality.

What finally happens to the soul is the ultimate eschatological question, and the answer appears to be that the soul's destiny is to lose its identity in a larger unity, a paradox whose truth is endorsed by every great mystical system, irrespective of the religious background from which it emerged. Progressively, we lose the

o

body on earth; the personality, ego or self in the post-mortem planes; and in the celestial abodes, the sense of separateness and individuality.

In the religious view the purpose of our journey through the material and spiritual spheres, is to provide the soul with the opportunities to advance from merely personal survival to genuine immortality. It is the nature of the soul to return to its source, and we can truly find ourselves only in the fuller and higher existence that abides in the Godhead. We attain to our true destiny by participating in the eternal. 'I am the vine', said Christ, 'ye are the branches.'

In one form or another this idea is expressed in sacred and mystical writings the world over:

O Lord Mazda, grant that we may catch sight of thee, may approach thee, may be united with thee. *Zoroastrian Hymn* (*c.* 800 B.C.).

As the flowing rivers disappear into the ocean, quitting form and name, so the wise man goes into the Heavenly Being, higher than the high. *Mundaka Upanishad* (*c.* 650 B.C.).

I shall go soaring to the firmament of heaven, to be made one with Zeus. *Euripides* (480–406 B.C.).

The course of our progress, when our nature has been developed to the full, ends in our return to the source, in Not-Being. *Lieh Tzu* (450–375 B.C.) Taoist philosopher.

The enfranchised soul tends to God. He is her home, her Author and her end. No death is hers; when earthly eyes grow dark she soars, and godlike melts in Him. *Virgil* (70–19 B.C.).

When I have surrendered my soul I shall become what no mind ever conceived. O let me cease to exist, for Non-Existence only means that I shall return to Him. *Jalaluddin Rumi* (1207–73) Persian mystical poet.

Further reading   Austin (1931); Barratt (1926); Birrell (1930); Cornillier (1921); Ducasse (1961); Eddy (1950); Myers (1961); Osis (1961); Oxenham (1941).

Bibliography

ABRAMSON, H. (ed.) (1950), *Problems of Consciousness*, J. Macy Foundation, New York.

ADDISON, J. T. (1958), *Life Beyond Death in the Beliefs of Mankind*, Allen & Unwin, London.

ADRIAN, E., *et al.* (1954), *Brain Mechanisms and Consciousness*, Blackwell, Oxford.

ALLPORT, G. (1937), *Personality: A Psychological Interpretation*, Holt, New York.

ALVAREZ, A. (1971), *The Savage God: A Study of Suicide*, Weidenfeld & Nicolson, London.

ANDREAS, P., and ADAMS, G. (1967), *Between Heaven and Earth*, Harrap, London.

AQUINAS, ST THOMAS (1966), *Aurora Consurgens*, ed. Marie-Louise von Franz, Routledge & Kegan Paul, London.

ARNOLD-FORSTER, H. O. (1921), *Studies in Dreams*, Allen & Unwin, London.

ASSAGIOLI, R. (1965), *Psychosynthesis: A Manual of Principles and Techniques*, Hobbs & Dorman, New York.

AUSTIN, MARY (1931), *Experiences Facing Death*, Bobbs-Merrill, New York.

BACH, MARCUS (1966), *The Power of Perception*, Doubleday, New York.

BAGNALL, OSCAR (1957), *The Origin and Properties of the Human Aura*, Routledge & Kegan Paul, London.

BAILEY, ALICE (1944), *A Treatise on Cosmic Fire* (3rd ed.), Lucis, New York.

BAKAN, DAVID (1958), *Sigmund Freud and the Jewish Mystical Tradition*, Van Nostrand, New York.

BALDICK, ROBERT (1955), *The Life of J. K. Huysmans*, Clarendon Press, Oxford.

BANKS, FRANCES (1962), *Frontiers of Revelation*, Max Parrish, London.

BARDENS, DENNIS (1970), *Mysterious Worlds*, W. H. Allen, London.

BARNARD, G. C. (1953), *The Superphysical*, Rider, London.

BARRATT, WILLIAM (1926), *Deathbed Visions*, Methuen, London.

BATTERSBY, H. P., (n.d.), *Man Outside Himself*, Rider, London.

BAZETT, L. M. (1946), *Beyond the Five Senses*, Blackwell, Oxford.

Bibliography

BEATY, MABEL (1929), *Man Made Perfect*, Rider, London.
BEAUSOBRE, JULIA DE (1948), *The Woman Who Could Not Die*, Gollancz, London.
BELL, E.T. (1946), *The Magic of Numbers*, McGraw Hill, New York.
BENNETT, ALFRED GORDON (1953), *Focus on the Unknown*, Rider, London.
BENNETT, ARNOLD (1909), *The Glimpse* (2nd ed.), Chapman & Hall, London.
BESANT, ANNIE (1911), *Man and His Bodies*, Theosophical Publishing, London.
BESTERMAN, T. (1930), *In the Way of Heaven*, Methuen, London.
BIRD, MALCOLM (1923), *My Psychic Adventures*, Allen & Unwin, London.
BIRRELL, F. F. L. and LUCUS, F. L. (1930), *The Art of Dying; An Anthology*, Hogarth Press, London.
BLEIBTREU, JOHN N. (1968), *The Parable of the Beast*, Gollancz, London.
BOISEN, A., (1952), *The Exploration of the Inner World*, Harper-Row, New York.
BONHOEFFER, D. (1953), *Letters and Papers from Prison*, Macmillan, New York.
BOZZANO, E. (1938), *Discarnate Influence on Human Life*, Watkins, London.
BRADLEY, F. H. (1893), *Appearance and Reality*, Sonnenschein, London.
BRANDON, WILFRED (1935), *Open the Door*, Alfred A. Knopf, New York.
BRAZIER, M. (1960), *The Electrical Activity of the Nervous System* (2nd ed.), Pitman Medical, London.
BRENNAN, J. H. (1971), *Astral Doorways*, Aquarian Press, London.
BROAD, C. D. (1923), *The Mind and Its Place in Nature*, Kegan Paul, Trench, Trübner, London.
BROAD, C. D. (1953), *Religion, Philosophy and Psychical Research*, Routledge & Kegan Paul, London.
BRUNER, J. (ed.) (1957), *Contemporary Approaches to Cognition*, Harvard University Press, Cambridge, Mass.
BUCHAN, JOHN (1929), *The Causal and the Casual in History*, Cambridge University Press.
BUCKE, RICHARD, M. (1905), *Cosmic Consciousness*, Innes, Philadelphia, 1905; (1972) Olympia Press, London.
BUDGE, E. A. WALLIS (ed.) (1950), *The Book of the Dead*, Routledge & Kegan Paul, London.
BULFORD, STAVELEY (1941), *Man's Unknown Journey*, Rider, London.
BULTMANN, RUDOLF (1962), *History and Eschatology: the Presence of Eternity*, Harper, New York.
BURNEY, C. (1952), *Solitary Confinement*, Coward-McCann, New York.
BURT, CYRIL (1967), 'Psychology and parapsychology', in Smythies, J. R. (ed.) *Science and ESP*, Routledge & Kegan Paul, London.

196

BURT, CYRIL (1968), *Psychology and Psychical Research*, F. W. H. Myers Memorial Lecture, Society for Psychical Research, London.

BYRD, R. (1938), *Alone*, Putnam, New York.

CARRINGTON, HEREWARD (1919), *Modern Psychical Phenomena*, Kegan Paul, Trench, Trübner, London.

CARRINGTON, HEREWARD (1920), *Higher Psychical Development*, Kegan Paul, Trench, Trübner, London.

CARRINGTON, HEREWARD (1938), *The Psychic World*, Methuen, London.

CAVENDISH, RICHARD (1967), *The Black Arts*, Routledge & Kegan Paul, London.

CHANG, G. (1963), *Teachings of Tibetan Yoga*, University Books, New York.

CHAUDHURI, H. (1965), *Philosophy of Meditation*, Philosophical Library, New York.

CHRISTOPHER, MILBOURNE (1971), *Seers, Psychics and ESP*, Cassell, London.

CLARK, J. and SKINNER, J. (1958), *Treatises and Sermons of Meister Eckhart*, Harper, New York.

CLISSOLD, AUGUSTUS (1870), *The Prophetic Spirit in Relation to Wisdom and Madness*, Longmans, London.

COHEN, J. (1964), *Behaviour in Uncertainty*, Allen & Unwin, London.

COHEN, J. (1966), *Human Robots in Myth and Science*, Allen & Unwin, London.

COHEN, S. (1964), *The Beyond Within: The LSD Story*, Atheneum, New York.

COLLINGE, EDWARD (1952), *Life's Hidden Secrets*, Rider, London.

COOPER, L. and ERICKSON, M. (1954), *Time Distortion in Hypnosis*, Williams & Wilkins, Baltimore.

CORNILLIER, P. E. (1921), *The Survival of the Soul*, Kegan Paul, Trench, Trübner, London.

CRESPIGNY, P. C. DE (1934), *This World—And Beyond*, Cassell, London.

CRICHTON-BROWNE, JAMES (1895), 'Dreamy Mental States', *Lancet*, 2, pp. 1–5, 73–5.

CROOKALL, ROBERT (1961), *The Study and Practice of Astral Projection*, Aquarian Press, London.

CROOKALL, ROBERT (1964), *The Techniques of Astral Projection*, Aquarian Press, London.

CROOKALL, ROBERT (1969), *The Interpretation of Cosmic and Mystical Experiences*, James Clark, London.

CUMMINS, GERALDINE (1935), *The Road to Immortality*, Nicholson & Watson, London.

CUMMINS, GERALDINE (1948), *Travellers in Eternity*, Psychic Press, London.

197

Bibliography

CUSTANCE, J. (1951), *Wisdom, Madness and Folly*, Gollancz, London.

D'ASSIER, ADOLPH (1887), *Posthumous Humanity*, translated and annotated by H. S. Olcott, Redway, London.

DAVENPORT, F. M. (1905), *Primitive Traits in Religious Revivals*, Macmillan, New York.

DAVID-NEEL, ALEXANDRA (1936), *With Mystics and Magicians in Tibet*, Penguin, Harmondsworth.

DE LA MARE, WALTER (1939), *Behold This Dreamer*, Faber & Faber, London.

DE MARTINO, ERNEST (1972), *Magic: Primitive and Modern*, Tom Stacey, London.

DEMENT, W. (1960), 'The Effect of Sleep Deprivation', *Science*, 131, pp. 1705–7.

DERREY, FRANÇOIS (1938), *The Earth is Alive*, trans, by G. Roy, Arlington, London.

DE ROPP, R. (1875), *Drugs and the Mind*, Grove Press, New York.

DEUTSCH, FELIX (ed.) (1945), *On the Mysterious Leap from the Mind to the Body*, Grune & Stratton, New York.

DOBBS, A. (1965), Article in *Proceedings of the Society for Psychical Research*, August 57, Part 197.

DODDS, E. R. (ed.) (1963), *Proclus: The Elements of Theology* (2nd ed.), Clarendon Press, Oxford. (Appendix II, 'The Astral Body in Neoplatonism'.)

DOYLE, ARTHUR CONAN (1924), 'Early Psychic Experiences', *Pearson's Magazine*, March.

DUCASSE, C. J. (1961), *A Critical Examination of the Belief in a Life After Death*, Thomas, Springfield, Ill.

DUNNE, J. W. (1934), *An Experiment With Time*, Faber & Faber, London.

EASTMAN, M. (1962), 'Out of the Body Experiences', *Proceedings of the Society for Psychical Research*, London, 53, pp. 287–309.

ECCLES, J. C. (1953), *The Neurophysiological Basis of Mind*, Clarendon Press, Oxford.

ECCLES, J. C. (1963), *The Brain and the Unity of Conscious Experience*, Cambridge University Press.

ECCLES, J. C. (ed.) (1966), *The Brain and Conscious Experience*, Springer, Heidelberg.

ECKSTEIN, GUSTAV (1971), *The Body Has a Head*, Collins, London.

EDDINGTON, ARTHUR (1928), *The Nature of the Physical World*, Cambridge University Press.

EDDY, SHERWOOD (1950), *You Will Survive Death*, Rinehart, New York.

EISENBUD, JULE (1967), *The World of Ted Serios*, Morrow, New York.

ELIADE, MIRCEA (1965), *The Two and the One*, Harvill Press, London.

ELKIN, A. P. (1944), *Aboriginal Men of High Degree*, Angus Robertson, London.

ELLENBERGER, H. F. (1972), *The Discovery of the Unconscious*, Allen Lane, London.

ENGLISH, HORACE and AVA (1958), *A Comprehensive Dictionary of Psychological and Psychoanalytical Terms*, Macmillan, London.

EVANS-WENTZ, W. Y. (1912), *Fairy Faith in Celtic Countries*, Frowde, London.

EYSENCK, H. J. (1957), *Sense and Nonsense in Psychology*, Penguin, Harmondsworth.

FAIR, C. M. (1963), *The Physical Foundations of the Psyche*, Wesleyan University Press, Middletown, Conn.

FARADAY, ANNE (1970), 'Is Your Mind a Thief?' *Sunday Times*, 22 November, London.

FAWCETT, DOUGLAS (1939), *Oberland Dialogues*, Macmillan, London.

FINGARETTE, H. (1964), *The Self in Transformation: Psychoanalysis, Philosophy and the Life of the Spirit*, Basic Books, New York.

FIRSOFF, VALDEMAR AXEL (1967), *Life, Mind and Galaxies*, Oliver & Boyd, Edinburgh.

FITZSIMONS, F. W. (1933), *Opening the Psychic Door*, Hutchinson, London.

FLEW, A. (1953), *A New Approach to Psychical Research*, Watts, London.

FLOURNOY, THÉODORE (1900), *From India to the Planet Mars*, ET, London.

FODOR, NANDOR (1933), *Encyclopedia of Psychic Science*, Arthurs Press, London.

FODOR, NANDOR (1964), *Between Two Worlds*, Prentice-Hall, New York.

FORTUNE, DION (1935), *The Mystical Qabalah*, Williams & Norgate, London.

FORTUNE, DION (1952), *Psychic Self Defence*, Aquarian Press, London.

FOULKES, D. (1966), *The Psychology of Sleep*, Scribners, New York.

FOX, Oliver (1962), *Astral Projection*, University Books, New York.

FRAZER, JAMES (1911), *The Magic Art* (2 vols), Macmillan, London

FREELAND, NAT (1972), *The Occult Explosion*, Michael Joseph, London.

FREUD, SIGMUND (1925), 'Thoughts for the Times on War and Death', *Collected Papers*, Vol. 4, Hogarth Press, London.

FREUD, SIGMUND (1954), *The Interpretation of Dreams*, Allen & Unwin, London.

FULLER, JEAN (1965), *The Magical Dilemma of Victor Neuburg*, W. H. Allen, London.

FULTON, ROBERT (ed.) (1965), *Death and Identity*, Wiley, New York.

GARRETT, EILEEN J. (1939), *My Life as a Search for the Meaning of Mediumship*, Rider, London.

GARRETT, EILEEN J. (1949), *Adventures in the Supernormal*, Garrett, New York.

Bibliography

GASTAUT, HENRI (1954), *The Epilepsies*, Thomas, Springfield, Ill.

GEDDES, LORD (1937), 'A Voice from the Grandstand', *Edinburgh Medical Journal*, n.s. (IVth), **44**, p. 367.

GERHARDIE, WILLIAM (1934), *Resurrection*, Cassell, London.

GHALIOUNGUI, P. (1963), *Magic and Medical Science in Ancient Egypt*, Hodder & Stoughton, London.

GODWIN, JOHN (1972), *Occult America*, Doubleday, New York.

GOLDBRUNNER, J. (1955), *Individuation*, Hollis & Carter, London.

GORER, GEOFFREY (1949), *Africa Dances* (rev. ed.), John Lehmann, London.

GRANT, KENNETH (1972), *The Magical Revival*, Frederick Muller, London.

GRAVES, ROBERT (ed.) (1950), *The Golden Ass of Apuleius*, Penguin, Harmondsworth.

GRAVES, ROBERT and PATAI, RAPHAEL (1963), *Hebrew Myths: The Book of Genesis*, Cassell, London.

GREEN, CELIA (1968a), *Lucid Dreams*, Hamish Hamilton, London.

GREEN, CELIA (1968b), *Out-of-the-Body Experiences*, Hamish Hamilton, London.

GRODDECK, GEORGE W. (1951), *The Unknown Self*, Vision Press, London.

GRUBB, W. B. (1911), *An Unknown People in an Unknown Land*, Seely, London.

GUNTRIP, H. (1968), *Schizoid Phenomena, Object Relations and the Self*, Hogarth, London.

GURNEY, EDMUND, MYERS, F. W. H. and PODMORE, FRANK (1887), *Phantasms of the Living*, Trübner, London.

HALDANE, J. S. (1928), *The Sciences and Philosophy*, Hodder & Stoughton, London.

HALL, M. P. (1947), *Man: The Grand Symbol of the Mysteries* (5th ed). Philosophical Research Society, Los Angeles.

HANSEL, C. E. M. (1966), *ESP: A Scientific Evaluation*, Scribner, New York.

HARDING, ROSAMUND (1948), *An Anatomy of Inspiration* (3rd ed.), Heffer, Cambridge.

HARDY, ALISTER (1966), *The Divine Flame*, Collins, London.

HARLOW, S. RALPH (1961), *A Life After Death*, Gollancz, London.

HART, HORNELL (1959), *The Enigma of Survival: The Case For and Against an After Life*, Rider, London.

HEARD, GERALD (1932), *This Surprizing World*, Cobden-Sanderson, London.

HERZOG, EDGAR (1966), *Psyche and Death*, Hodder & Stoughton, London.

HEYWOOD, ROSALIND (1959), *The Sixth Sense*, Chatto & Windus, London.

HEYWOOD, ROSALIND (1968), 'Attitudes to death in the light of dreams and other out-of-the-body experience' and 'Death and psychical research' in Toynbee. Arnold, Heywood, Rosalind, Price, H. H. *et al.*, *Man's Concern with Death*, Hodder & Stoughton, London, pp. 185–250.

HILL, J. ARTHUR (1918), *Man is a Spirit*, Cassell, London.

HIVES, FRANK (1931), *Glimpses into Infinity*, Lane, London.

HOWE, ELLIC (1972), *The Magicians of the Golden Dawn*, Routledge & Kegan Paul, London.

HUXLEY, ALDOUS (1946), *The Perennial Philosophy*, Chatto & Windus, London.

HUXLEY, ALDOUS (1954), *The Doors of Perception*, Chatto & Windus, London.

JAFFÉ, ANIELA (ed.) (1963), *Memories, Dreams and Reflections by C. G. Jung*, Collins; Routledge & Kegan Paul, London.

JAMES, WILLIAM (1902), *The Varieties of Religious Experience*, Longmans Green, New York.

JASPERS, KARL (1967), *Philosophy is for Everyman*, trans. by R. F. C. Hull and G. Wels, Hutchinson, London.

JEANS, SIR JAMES (1930), *The Mysterious Universe*, Cambridge University Press.

JOAD, C. E. M. (1952), *The Recovery of Belief*, Faber & Faber, London.

JOHNSON, R. C. (1953), *The Imprisoned Splendour*, Hodder & Stoughton, London.

JOHNSON, R. C. (1957), *Nurslings of Immortality*, Hodder & Stoughton, London.

JOIRE, PAUL (1966), *Psychical and Supernormal Phenomena*, Rider, London.

JUNG, C. G. (1953), *Psychology and Alchemy*, Routledge & Kegan Paul, London.

JUNG, C. G. and PAULI, WOLFGANG (1955), *The Interpretation of Nature and the Psyche*, Routledge & Kegan Paul, London.

JUNG, C. G. (1967), 'The Visions of Zosimos', *Alchemical Studies*, Routledge & Kegan Paul, London.

KAIGH, FREDERICK (1947), *Witchcraft and Magic in Africa*, Lesley, London.

KILNER, WALTER J. (1911), *The Human Atmosphere*, Dutton, New York.

KING, C. (1963), *States of Human Consciousness*, University Books, New York.

KING, FRANCIS (1971), *Astral Projection, Magic and Alchemy*, Spearman, London.

Bibliography

KLEITMAN, N. (1963), *Sleep and Wakefulness as Alternating Phases in the Cycle of Existence*, Chicago University Press.

KOESTLER, ARTHUR (1972), *The Roots of Coincidence*, Hutchinson, London.

LAKHOVSKY, G. (1939), *The Secret of Life: Cosmic Rays and Radiations of Living Beings*, Heinemann, London.

LANGHAM, JAMES (1951), *More Than Meets the Eye*, Evans, London.

LARSEN, CAROLINE (1927), *My Travels in the Spirit World*, Tuttle, Rutland, Vt.

LASKI, MARGHANITA (1961), *Ecstasy: A Study of Some Secular and Religious Experiences*, Cresset Press, London.

LEADBEATER, C. W. (1957), *Man Visible and Invisible*, Theosophical Publishing, London.

LEADBEATER, C. W. (1968), *The Astral Plane: Its Scenery, Inhabitants and Phenomena* (rep.), Theosophical Publishing, London.

LEONARD, GLADYS OSBORN (1931), *My Life in Two Worlds*, Cassell, London.

LESTER, REGINALD M. (1952), *In Search of the Hereafter*, Harrap, London.

LÉVY-BRUHL, LUCIEN (1928), *The 'Soul' of the Primitive*, Allen & Unwin, London.

LEWIN, B (1950), *The Psychoanalysis of Elation*, Norton, New York.

LILAR, SUZANNE (1965), *Aspects of Love*, trans. by J. Griffiths, Thames & Hudson, London.

LODGE, SIR OLIVER (1919), *The Survival of Man*, Methuen, London.

LUCE, GAY GAER (1972), *Body Time*, Temple Smith, London.

LYTTLETON, EDITH (1931), *Our Superconscious Mind*, Philip Allan, London.

MAGOUN, H. (1958), *The Waking Brain*, Thomas, Springfield, Ill.

MAITLAND, EDWARD (1896), *Life of Anna Kingsford* (2 vols), Redway, London.

MALCOLM, N. (1959), *Dreaming*, Routledge & Kegan Paul, London.

MARAIS, EUGÈNE (1937), *The Soul of the White Ant*, Methuen, London.

MARECHAL, J. (1964), *Studies in the Psychology of the Mystics and Magi*, Albany, New York.

MARTIN, P. W. (1955), *Experiment in Depth*, Routledge & Kegan Paul, London.

MASLOW, A. (1962), *Towards a Psychology of Being*, Van Nostrand, Princeton.

MASLOW, A. (1964), *Religions, Values and Peak Experiences*, Ohio State University Press, Columbus.

MASTERS, R. and HOUSTON, J. (1967), *The Varieties of Psychedelic Experience*, Blond, London.

202

MAY, ROLLO (1970), *Love and Will*, Souvenir Press, London.

MEAD, G. R. S. (ed.) (1921), *Pistis Sophia*, Watkins, London.

MEAD, G. R. S. (1967), *The Doctrine of the Subtle Body in Western Tradition*, Stuart & Watkins, London.

MEDUNA, L. (1950), *Carbon Dioxide Therapy*, Thomas, Springfield, Ill.

MEYRINK, GUSTAV (1915), *Der Golem*, Kurt Wolff, Leipzig.

MOBERLY, A. and JOURDAIN, E. (1911), *An Adventure*, London (published under the pseudonyms Elizabeth Morison and Frances Lamont).

MONROE, ROBERT A. (1972), *Journeys Out of the Body*, Souvenir Press, London.

MONTEITH, MARY (1929), *A Book of True Dreams*, Heath Cranton, London.

MOSS, C. (1967), *The Hypnotic Investigation of Dreams*, Wiley, New York.

MOTTRAM, V. H. (1944), *The Physical Basis of Personality*, Penguin, Harmondsworth.

MULDOON, SYLVAN J. (1936), *The Case for Astral Projection*, Aries Press, Chicago.

MULDOON, SYLVAN J. and CARRINGTON, HEREWARD (1958), *The Projection of the Astral Body*, Rider, London.

MURPHY, GARDNER (1961), *Challenge of Psychical Research*, Harper, New York.

MURRAY, E. (1965), *Sleep, Dreams and Arousal*, Appleton-Century-Crofts, New York.

MURRAY, OSWALD (1924), *The Spiritual Universe*, Duckworth, London.

MYERS, F. W. H. (1961), *Human Personality and Its Survival of Bodily Death*, University Books, New York.

NEAL, J. H. (1966), *Ju-ju in My Life*, Harrap, London.

NEUMANN, E. (1954), *The Origins and History of Consciousness*, Routledge & Kegan Paul, London.

NICOLL, MAURICE (1964), *Psychological Commentaries on the Teachings of Gurdjieff and Ouspensky*, Vincent Stuart, London.

NOTT, S. C. (1961), *Teachings of Gurdjieff*, Routledge and Kegan Paul, London.

OESTERREICH, T. K. (1930), *Possession, Demoniacal and Other, among Primitive Races in Antiquity, Middle Ages and Modern Times*, Kegan Paul, Trench, Trübner, London.

OPHIEL (1961), *The Art and Practice of Astral Projection*, Peach, San Francisco.

OSIS, KARLIS (1961), *Deathbed Observations by Doctors and Nurses*, Parapsychology Foundation, New York.

OSTY, DR EUGÈNE (1923), *Supernormal Faculties in Man* (E. trans.), Methuen, London.

203

Bibliography

OSWALD, I. (1962), *Sleeping and Waking, Physiology and Psychology*, Elsevier, New York.

OTTO, RUDOLF (1923), *The Idea of the Holy*, Humphrey Milford, London.

OUSPENSKY, P. D. (1960), *A New Model of the Universe*, Routledge & Kegan Paul, London.

OXENHAM, JOHN (1941), *Out of the Body*, Longmans Green, London.

PAYNE, PHOEBE (1938), *Man's Latent Powers*, Faber & Faber, London.

PENFIELD, W. and ROBERTS L. (1959), *Speech and Brain Mechanisms*, Princeton University Press, New Jersey.

PHILLIPS, PHIL and SYBIL (1972), *Is Death the End?*, Corgi, London.

PIKE, JAMES A. (1969), *The Other Side*, W. H. Allen, London.

PLUTCHIK, R. (1962), *The Emotions: Facts, Theories and a New Model*, Random House, New York.

PODMORE, FRANK (1909), *Telepathic Hallucinations: The New View of Ghosts*, Milner, London.

POULAIN, A. (1950), *The Graces of Interior Prayer: A Treatise on Mystical Theology*, Herder, St Louis.

POWELL, A. E. (1925), *The Etheric Double*, Theosophical Publishing, London.

POWELL, A. E. (1927), *The Astral Body and Other Astral Phenomena*, Theosophical Publishing, London.

POWELL, A. E. (1941), *The Mental Body*, Theosophical Publishing, London.

PRICE, H. H. (1968), 'What kind of Next World?', in Toynbee, Arnold, Hayward, Rosalind, Price, H. H. et al., *Man's Concern with Death*, Hodder & Stoughton, London, pp. 250–6.

PRIESTLEY, J. B. (1972), *Over the Long High Wall*, Heinemann, London.

RANK, OTTO (1925), *Der Doppelgänger: eine psychoanalytische Studie*, Internationales Psychoanalytischen Verlag, Vienna.

READ, J. (1957), *Through Alchemy to Chemistry*, Bell, London.

REDFIELD, R. (1953), *The Primitive World and Its Transformations*, Cornell University Press, Ithaca.

REDLICH, F. C. and FREEDMAN, D. X. (1966), *The Theory and Practice of Psychiatry*, Basic Books, New York.

REICH, WILHELM (1948), *The Discovery of the Orgone: The Cancer Biopathy*, Orgone Institute Press, New York.

REICHENBACH, CARL VON (1926), *Letters on Od and Magnetism*, ed F. D. O'Byrne, Hutchinson, London.

RICHET, CHARLES (1923), *Thirty Years of Psychical Research*, Collins, London.

RITTER, C. (1954), *A Woman in the Polar Night*, Dutton, New York.

ROBBINS, ANN MANNING (1910), *Both Sides of the Veil*, Unwin, London.

RUSSELL, G. W. (1918), *Candle of Vision*, Macmillan, London.

204

SALTER, W. H. (1961), *Zoar, or The Evidence of Psychical Research Concerning Survival*, Sidgwick & Jackson, London.

SALTER, W. H. (1970), *The Society for Psychical Research: an Outline of Its History*, ed. Renée Haynes, Society for Psychical Research, London.

SARGANT, WILLIAM (1957), *Battle for the Mind*, Heinemann, London.

SCHOLEM, G. G. (1955), *Major Trends in Jewish Mysticism*, Thames & Hudson, London.

SCHROEDINGER, ERWIN (1951), *What is Life?* Cambridge University Press.

SCHULTZ, J. and LUTHE, W. (1959), *Autogenic Training*, Grune & Stratton, New York.

SEABROOK, W. B. (1935), *The Magic Island*, Harrap, London.

SEWALL, MAY WRIGHT (1921), *Neither Dead Nor Sleeping*, Watkins, London.

SHERWOOD, JANE (1945), *The Country Beyond*, Rider, London.

SHIRLEY, RALPH (1972), *The Mystery of the Human Double*, Rider, London.

SIDGWICK, ELEANOR (ed.) (1894), *The Census of Hallucinations*, London.

SIFFRE, MICHEL (1964), *Beyond Time*, McGraw Hill, New York.

SKEAT, W. W. (1900), *Malay Magic*, Macmillan, London.

SMITH, SUSY (1965), *The Enigma of Out of the Body Travel*, Helix Press, New York.

SMITH, W. WHATELY (1920), *A Theory of the Mechanisms of Survival*, Kegan Paul, Trench, Trübner, London.

SMYTHE, F. S. (1935), *The Spirit of the Hills*, Hodder & Stoughton, London.

SMYTHIES, J. R. (ed.) (1967), *Science and ESP*, Routledge & Kegan Paul, London.

SOLOMON, PHILIP, et al. (1961), *Sensory Deprivation*, Harvard University Press, Cambridge, Mass.

SPIEGELBERG, MR. et al. (1964), *The Concept of the Subtle Body*, Esalen Institute, Big Sur, California.

STACE, W. (1960), *Mysticism and Philosophy*, Lippincott, New York.

STAFFORD, P. G., and GOLIGHTLY, B. H. (1967), *LSD—The Problem-Solving Psychedelic*, Award Books, New York.

STEVENS, WILLIAM OLIVER (1950), *The Mystery of Dreams*, Allen & Unwin, London.

STEWART, KILTON (1969), 'Dream Theory in Malaya', in Tart, Charles T. (ed.), *Altered States of Consciousness: A Book of Readings*, Wiley, New York.

STUART, GRACE (1956), *Narcissism: A Psychological Study of Self-Love*, Allen & Unwin, London.

Bibliography

SULLIVAN, HARRY STACK (1962), *Schizophrenia as a Human Process*, Norton, New York.

SULLY, J. (1905), *Illusions: A Psychological Study*, Kegan Paul, Trench, Trübner, London.

SUMMERS, MONTAGUE (ed.) (1927), *Demonality, or Incubi and Succubi* by Sinistrari, Fortune Press, London.

SUMMERS, MONTAGUE (1928), *The Vampire: His Kith and Kin*, Kegan Paul, Trench and Trübner, London.

SWEDENBORG, EMANUEL (1850), *Heaven and Hell*, ed. J. W. Hancock, London.

SWEDENBORG, EMANUEL (1883–1902), *The Spiritual Diary* (Vols. I–V), eds. G. Bush and J. H. Smithson, Speirs, London.

SZASZ, THOMAS (1961), *The Myth of Mental Illness*, Harper, New York.

TAPPAN, CORA L. V. (1878), *Discourses*, J. Burns.

TART, CHARLES T. (1968), 'A psychophysiological study of out-of-the-body experiences in a selected subject', *Journal of the American Society for Psychical Research*, 62, pp. 3–27

TART, CHARLES T. (ed.) (1969), *Altered States of Consciousness: A Book of Readings*, Wiley, New York.

TEMKIN, O. (1945), *The Falling Sickness: A History of Epilepsy from the Greeks to the Beginning of Modern Neurology*, Johns Hopkins Press, Baltimore.

THOMAS, C. DRAYTON (1928), *The Life Beyond Death, With Evidence*, Collins, London.

THORWALD, J. (1962), *Science and Secrets of Early Medicine*, Thames & Hudson, London.

TOYNBEE, ARNOLD, HEYWOOD, ROSALIND, PRICE, H. H. *et al.* (1968), *Man's Concern with Death*, Hodder & Stoughton, London.

TROMP, S. W. (1949), *Psychical Physics*, Elsevier, New York.

TYLOR, E. B. (1903), *Primitive Culture* (4th ed.), Murray, London.

TYMMS, RALPH (1949), *Doubles in Literary Psychology*, Bowes & Bowes, Cambridge.

TYRRELL, G. N. M. (1938), *Science and Psychical Phenomena*, Methuen, London.

TYRRELL, G. N. M. (1946), *The Personality of Man*, Penguin, Harmonds-worth.

ULLMAN, M. and KRIPPNER, S. (1970), *Dream Studies and Telepathy*, Parapsychology Foundation, New York.

VAN EEDEN, FREDERIK (1913), 'A Study of Dreams', *Proceedings of the Society for Psychical Research*, 26, pp. 431–61.

VESME, CAESAR DE (1931), *Peoples of Antiquity*, trans. by F. Rothwell, Rider, London.

VINACKE, W. (1952), *The Psychology of Thinking*, McGraw-Hill, New York.

WALKER, BENJAMIN (1968), *Hindu World* (2 vols), Allen & Unwin, London.

WALKER, BENJAMIN (1970), *Sex and the Supernatural*, Macdonald, London.

WALKER, D. P. (1958), 'The Astral Body in Renaissance Medicine', *Journal of the Warburg and Courtauld Institute*, 21, pp. 119ff.

WALKER, KENNETH (1942), *The Circle of Life*, Cape, London.

WALKER, KENNETH (1962), *The Diagnosis of Man* (rev. ed.), Penguin, Harmondsworth.

WALLACE, ALFRED RUSSEL (1910), *The World of Life*, Chapman & Hall, London.

WALLACE, MARY BRUCE (1919), *The Thinning of the Veil*, Watkins, London.

WALLIS, G. (1926), *The Art of Thought*, Harcourt, New York.

WALTON, A. H. (1969), *The Open Grave*, Spearman, London.

WATTS, ALAN W. (1962), *The Joyous Cosmology: Adventures in the Chemistry of Consciousness*, Pantheon, New York.

WERNER, H. (1957), *Comparative Psychology of Mental Development*, International Universities Press, New York.

WEST, D. J. (1954), *Psychical Research Today*, Duckworth, London.

WHITEHEAD, A. N. (1929), *Process and Reality*, Cambridge University Press.

WHITEMAN, J. H. M. (1965), *The Mystical Life*, Faber & Faber, London.

WILBERFORCE, BASIL (1913), *Spiritual Consciousness*, Stock, London.

WILKINSON, DENYS H. (1960), 'Matter and Sub-Matter', *Listener*, 31 July.

WILLS, ARTHUR J. (1942), *Life Now and Forever*, Rider, London.

WILSON, COLIN (1971), *The Occult*, Hodder & Stoughton, London.

WOOD, FREDERIC H. (1954), *Through the Psychic Door*, Spiritualist Press, London.

WOODROFFE, J. (1953), *The Serpent Power* (5th ed.), Ganesh, Madras.

WRIGHT, H. B. (1958), *Witness to Witchcraft*, Souvenir Press, London.

WYLDE, GEORGE, *Christo-Theosophy*, Kegan Paul, Trench, Trübner, London.

YOUNGHUSBAND, SIR FRANCIS (1933), *The Living Universe*, Murray, London.

'YRAM' (n.d.), *Practical Astral Projection*, Rider, London.

ZAEHNER, R. (1972), *Drugs, Mysticism and Make-Believe*, Collins, London.

Index

Name of Famous People

P

Index

210

211

Index

212

Index

Index